THE PROFESSIONAL SERVER

THE PROFESSIONAL SERVER

THIRD EDITION

Edward E. Sanders
New York City College of Technology

Marcella Giannasio
Johnson & Wales University

330 Hudson Street, NY, NY 10013

Vice President, Portfolio Management: Andrew Gilfillan
Portfolio Manager: Pamela Chirls
Editorial Assistant: Lara Dimmick
Development Editor: Pamela Chirls
Senior Vice President, Marketing: David Gesell
Field Marketing Manager: Thomas Hayward
Marketing Coordinator: Elizabeth MacKenzie-Lamb
Director, Digital Studio and Content Production:
  Brian Hyland
Managing Producer: Cynthia Zonneveld
Managing Producer: Jennifer Sargunar

Content Producer: Rinki Kaur
Manager, Rights Management: Johanna Burke
Manufacturing Buyer: Deidra Smith
Full-Service Management and Composition:
  iEnergizer Aptara®, Ltd.
Full-Service Project Manager: Megha Bhardwaj
Cover Design: Studio Montage
Cover Photo: Courtesy of Steelite International
Printer/Binder: LSC Communications, Inc.
Cover Printer: LSC Communications, Inc.
Text Font: Sabon LT Pro, 10.75/12

Library of Congress Cataloging-in-Publication Data

Sanders, Edward E., author. | Giannasio, Marcella, author.
The professional server: a training manual / Edward E. Sanders, New York City College of Technology;
  Marcella Giannasio, Johnson & Wales University
Third edition. | Hoboken: Pearson, 2018. | Includes index.
LCCN 2016043184 | ISBN 9780134552750 (alk. paper) | ISBN 013455275X (alk. paper)
LCSH: Table service. | Waiters. | Waitresses.
LCC TX925 .S26 2016 | DDC 642/.6—dc23 LC record available at https://lccn.loc.gov/2016043184

3   17

ISBN 10:   0-13-455275-X
ISBN 13: 978-0-13-455275-0

To the past, present, and future great servers—
the ones who make our dining experiences more enjoyable and memorable.
We always look forward to returning to the restaurants where they greet us with smiles
and an at-home welcoming feeling.

BRIEF CONTENTS

CONTENTS

FOREWORD

More than ever before, today's dining-out guests are seeking a total dining experience and receiving professional service is a major part of that overall dining experience. Dining out is overall a tactile experience at all price and quality levels. Good restaurateurs understand that professional service is a true differentiator in an extremely competitive industry.

In this third edition of *The Professional Server*, authors Sanders and Giannasio have continued to address all the basics of professional restaurant service in a straightforward, easy-to-understand manner. Equally important, this new edition has kept pace with an incredibly dynamic restaurant industry, updating relevant evolving trends in areas such as technology, changing food and beverage trends, and what today's dining-out guest expectations are and their definitions of what constitutes great service.

Knowledge, experience, and confidence provide the foundation for a professional server. In this book, the beginning student of service will gain the knowledge and information to get them started on the road to being a professional restaurant server. For the veteran server, this new edition is organized in such a way as to provide an easy update to make their skills relevant to delivering an elevated guest experience in any restaurant concept type of today—from fast casual to white tablecloth.

While quality food and beverage remain important, professional service provides the backbone to the exceptional guest experience. I couldn't think of a better educational resource than *The Professional Server, Third Edition*.

Dave Turner
Tabletop Journal

From the foreword *Service at Its Best, First Edition, 2002*

"Exceptional service doesn't simply happen. It is the result of careful initial training and constant attention to ongoing training. *Service At Its Best* is a comprehensive and informative training and reference manual. The book has brought together all of the basic elements that can effectively inform and train the new waiter or waitress in all aspects of professional table service. It presents the material in an easy-to-read and understandable format."

Herman Cain
CEO, T.H.E., Inc. (The Hermanator Experience)
Former CEO and President of the National Restaurant Association
Former CEO and President of Godfather's Pizza

A review quote from *The Professional Server, Second Edition*, 2012

"I'm a chef first and foremost and all I think about is food, food, food! That said—SERVICE IS INFINITELY MORE IMPORTANT THAN CUISINE. This extraordinary book delivers that message superbly!"

Charlie Trotter

PREFACE

Successful restaurateurs understand that guests will return to the restaurants that consistently provide excellent service. The competitive nature of the restaurant business demands more than just great food creatively prepared and presented. Guests return to the restaurants that create that welcoming home feeling with every visit that is conveyed by sincere smiles accompanied by professional service. This occurs when servers enjoy pleasing people and make an emotional connection with guests that result in creating guests' loyalty.

Servers, by nature, enjoy working at a quick, steady, and methodical pace. They are able to anticipate guest needs and adjust timing and service according to the expectations and needs of multiple guest situations. Furthermore, they have the ability to be flexible, diplomatic, patient, understanding, and cooperative in the fast-paced work environment that supports a common goal of providing the highest quality of guest service.

The Professional Server: A Training Manual, Third Edition, introduces the student to the many aspects of being a professional server. The experienced server will also find the book to be an excellent reference to consult for various techniques and service situations. The basics for becoming a successful server have not changed, but the methods and procedures continue to be refined in many areas, including technology.

New to this Edition

The revised and updated third edition further addresses the following:

- Rules of good service.
- Typical experiences for which the server needs to be prepared.
- How the server can effectively deal with and solve problems.
- The value of good communication skills.
- Advancements in POS systems, server tablets and tabletop tablets.
- Restaurant Reality Stories that follow each chapter bring the added dimension of what often occurs in the restaurant business.

This book is written in such a way that the chapters flow in a logical sequence, establishing a step-by-step procedure for understanding and learning appropriate server skills. The chapters are also self-contained, so that the student can go directly to any chapter for specific information. Therefore, the book can be used as a training guide or a reference manual for specific service questions.

Chapter 1—The Professional Server—introduces the student to the economic importance of the restaurant industry along with income and advancement opportunities for servers. The tipping standard, tip credit, and tip income reporting to the Internal Revenue Service are explained. Also, the advantages and disadvantages of non-tipping restaurants are presented with a non-tipping menu example. Occupational advantages and disadvantages are identified along with the basic job qualifications.

Chapter 2—Professional Appearance—discusses the importance of server health and the many aspects of grooming standards and guidelines. Correct body language, poise, and posture are presented along with the types of uniforms and aprons that may be used and the value of safe shoes.

Chapter 3—Table Service, Table Settings, and Napkin Presentations—begins with detailed explanations for the specific types of table service, which includes the following: American service (individual plate service), butler service, English service, modified English service, Russian service, and French service. The other types of service are also explained, such as family service, counter service, banquet service, and room service; and in addition the effective use of salad bars and dessert tables and trays is presented. Setting a table and the basic table settings for breakfast, lunch, dinner, and formal dinner along with the appropriate wine and beverage settings are explained. The use of place mats and the correct placement of salt and pepper shakers, sugar and creamers, rolls and butter, and side dishes are discussed. Napkin presentations and various folding procedures are clearly illustrated.

Chapter 4—Service Readiness—presents the responsibilities of a server that support good service, which include opening and closing side-work as well as closing procedures. The chapter further discusses breakfast, lunch, brunch, dinner, and dessert menus, along with tablet menus and wine lists. The importance of gaining menu knowledge by the server is emphasized along with the role of the server in helping the guest understand the menu and menu terms.

Chapter 5—Serving Food and Beverages—explains proper table service and service etiquette that include the technique of carrying multiple plates, carrying glasses, and also the correct procedures for loading and carrying trays. The role of the bartender/server is also discussed. Service priorities and timing, along with effectively handling difficult situations, are identified and supported with positive responses. Table bussing is detailed with procedures for using a cart or tray, as well as the procedure for setting up with the use of a tray, along with identifying additional server's assistant/busser responsibilities.

Chapter 6—Beverages and Beverage Service—begins with responsible alcohol service being reviewed and emphasized. The proper temperatures for serving wines are identified along with the correct procedures for using an ice bucket. The presentation and service of wine is illustrated step by step, beginning with presenting a bottle of wine to a guest, properly opening it, and the appropriate method of pouring the wine. The reasons and the procedure for decanting wine are also discussed. The various shapes of wine glasses are shown, identifying their appropriate use for the type of wine being served. Wine varietals are introduced and explained so that the student gains a basic understanding of wine, along with food and wine pairing. Spirits and cocktails are discussed, along with popular spirit brands, cocktail choices, and related terms the server should know. Beers, lagers, and ales are defined, and the correct procedure for serving beer is explained. The correct procedure for serving bottled waters is discussed. Coffee drinks that include espresso, café lattes, cappuccino, mochas, and the application of coffee with a spirit beverage are explained, along with the use of the French Press for coffee service. Tea varieties and service are also presented.

Chapter 7—Guest Communication—begins with the server personally connecting with the guest through an individual sense of enthusiasm. Varieties of possible guest types are discussed, along with tips for anticipating the guest's needs and how to look for nonverbal cues and prompts. Suggestive selling is detailed, with techniques for upselling to the guest, suggesting related menu items, new menu items or the chef's specialties, items for special occasions, and take-home items. The guidelines for suggestive selling are presented and illustrated. The correct procedure for taking the guest's order is discussed, as is the guest check and the importance of service timing. Correct reaction in a professional manner to emergency situations is also addressed.

Chapter 8—The Technology of Service—identifies the basic benefits of technology and technology applications. Handheld touch-screen tablets, product management applications, and tabletop tablets are illustrated and explained, along with an example of a kitchen production screen. Handheld pay-at-the-table devices as well as an alert manager application and CRM (Customer Relationship Management) application are discussed; and the convenience of employee scheduling and communication including training with technology. Table management applications, guest paging, and online table reservations and restaurant websites are further reviewed.

Chapter 9—Dining Room Management—begins with discussing the responsibilities of the maître d' or host, followed by managing reservations, effectively greeting guests, and table selection. Menu meetings, professional courtesies, responding to complaints, taking telephone reservations and "take-out" orders, server supervision, and server training are all detailed in the discussion of the important functions of dining room management.

Chapter 10—Banquet, Catering, and Buffet Management—defines the three distinct types of service. The importance and value of an Event Plan Details work sheet is clearly explained in a manner that covers all of the essential details for any planned banquet, catered, or buffet service event. Such details as knowing the difference between "approximate, guaranteed, and confirmed" number of guests; knowing the differences between an open bar, cash bar, and open–cash combination bar; understanding how to calculate a room's capacity for comfortable seating; and a knowledge of the various accessory details that can be added to an event are presented and discussed.

The Glossaries have been designed to provide the student with a quick reference source for common menu terms; and wine, beer, spirits, and beverage terms.

Welcome to *The Professional Server: A Training Manual, Third Edition*, an indispensable guide to becoming a successful server.

Instructor's Resources

To access supplementary materials online, request an instructor access code. Go to www.pearsonhighered.com/irc, where you can register for an instructor access code. Within 48 hours after registering, you will receive a confirming e-mail, including an instructor access code. Once you have received your code, go to the site and log on for full instructions on downloading the materials you wish to use.

NOTE: This book is designed to provide accurate and authoritative information with regard to the subject matter covered. It is provided with the understanding that the authors are not engaged in rendering legal, accounting, or other professional services. If legal advice or other expert assistance is required, the services of a competent professional should be sought. The authors have made every effort to provide accurate Internet addresses, and other contact information at the time of publication—neither the authors nor the publisher assumes any responsibility for errors, or changes that occur after publication.

ACKNOWLEDGMENTS

We would like to acknowledge the following people:

Ron Wilkinson and Paul Paz, coauthors to the first and second editions of this book. Their contributions were appreciated and further expanded with revised material and up-to-date information.

Our Portfolio Manager, Pamela Chirls, for the great suggestions and comments that have indeed enhanced the quality and presentation for every chapter of this edition.

Lara Dimmick, Editorial Assistant, who was always quick to respond with helpful information whenever needed.

Arvind Sharma, Copy Editor, for the thoroughness and accuracy to every detail.

Megha Bhardwaj, Project Manager, for keeping the editorial and production schedule on time.

Again, thank you from the authors.

My sincere gratitude to:

Sophitmanee Sukalakamala, Assistant Professor at Johnson & Wales University, Charlotte campus, for sharing her expertise on tea with a smile and words of encouragement.

Kristen Depaul, for her input on coffee. She was ready, willing, and able to help as soon as she was asked. Kristen is a graduate of Johnson & Wales University, Charleston campus.

Martin Lovelace, who was always available to help with any technical questions, a former student and dear friend.

My love to my parents, Hilda and Joseph A. Giannasio, who always told me I could do whatever I put my mind to. That encouragement pushed me forward during challenging times. They appreciate good food and service and exposed all four of their children to the pleasures of both.

A special thank you to Alain Sailey, Franz Meyer, and Karl Guggenmos, restaurateurs and mentors, who gave me an opportunity to work and learn from them for over twenty-five years. Their generosity of spirit inspired me to become a teacher.

In memory of Alva W. Alsbrooks, Shane Pearson, and John Kacala, who looked after me every day and were always ready to offer a kind and loving word when things got hard. Their support is greatly missed.

Marcella Giannasio

I would like to acknowledge the following people:

Professors from the Hospitality Management Program, New York City College of Technology: Rosa Abreu, for providing critical input when reviewing every chapter and for helping to direct and be part of the photo presentation in the photos taken by Dwayne Philibert; and James Reid, for being involved with the wine service photo presentation and for the many discussions on the subject of exceptional service, along with his comments on the bartender/server in Chapter 5—Serving Food and Beverages.

A heartfelt gratitude to my children, who continue to give great service in their own careers: Mark Sanders, who encouraged his father to begin the process that initiated the first edition; Jay Sanders, who worked as a server's assistant (busser) and server during his college years shared many experiences that brought additional focus to several topics; and Katherine Sanders, who continually provided great suggestions during the writing process.

A special thanks to my wife, Linda, for her suggestions, ideas, and constructive comments for all three editions, and who is an example of great service in everything she does.

In memory of Nick and Dorothy Drossos, lifetime restaurateurs, mentors, and dear friends, who introduced me to formal dining room service in 1971, and were still able to point out a few more tips in 2001.

Edward Sanders

ABOUT THE AUTHORS

Edward E. Sanders is an adjunct professor of Hospitality Management at New York City College of Technology. He is a Certified Food Executive and Certified Purchasing Manager and has a Master of Science in International Management from Thunderbird School of Global Management and a Doctor of Business Administration degree in Management and Organization. Through his career in business and education, he has been associated with Xerox, Sky Chefs-American Airlines, Marriott, Delaware North, Brigham Young University, Oregon State University, and Southern Oregon University. Ed owned a restaurant, operated a chain of restaurants, founded and operated *Hospitality News* (1988–2006), has been an associate professor of business, and cofounded and directed a hospitality and tourism management university program. He is also the author of *Food, Labor, and Beverage Cost Control © 2016 (Waveland Press)* and the lead coauthor of *Catering Solutions: For the Culinary Student, Foodservice Operator, and Caterer © 2000 (Prentice-Hall)*.

Marcella Giannasio is an Associate Professor at Johnson & Wales University, Charlotte, North Carolina, and teaches in the culinary department. She has also taught and supervised students in Koblenz, Germany, at the Deutsche Wein und Sommelierschule, and At-Sunrice GlobalChef Academy in Singapore, and participated in the Banfi scholastic tour in Italy. Marcella is a graduate of the College of Charleston and earned a master's degree in management from Southern Wesleyan University. Her certifications include Certified Hospitality Educator through the American Hotel & Lodging Educational Institute, Foodservice Management Professional through the National Restaurant Association, and a Court of Master Sommelier Level 1. She is a Bordeaux wine ambassador and holds an advanced wine & spirits certification from the Wine & Spirit Education Trust Limited based in London, and is a Hospitality Grand Master through the Federation of Dining Room Professionals. She joined the Johnson & Wales University faculty in 1997, with many years of management experience within the hospitality industry.

CHAPTER 1

The Professional Server

INTRODUCTION

The culinary and service aspects of the food and beverage industry continue to experience significant advancements with changes that keep pace with the increased sophistication of restaurant customers and the accessibility to new food sources.

There are a growing number of college-educated passionate food and beverage enthusiasts, who are trained professional servers enjoying the flexibility of a server's schedule in a fun and exciting career with a good income.

CHAPTER 1 LEARNING OBJECTIVES

As a result of successfully completing this chapter, readers will be able to:

1. Understand the economic importance of the restaurant industry.
2. Recognize the advancement opportunities within a restaurant and related career tracks.
3. Analyze income opportunities.
4. Know the range for a tipping standard.
5. Understand what "Getting Stiffed" means.
6. Understand how tip credit is applied.
7. Identify the factors associated with non-tipping restaurants.
8. Understand the occupational advantages for professional servers.
9. Understand the occupational disadvantages for professional servers.
10. Recognize the challenges for the restaurant industry.
11. Identify professional server job qualifications.
12. Recognize the value of not making an incorrect judgment based upon a guest's appearance.

CHAPTER 1 OUTLINE

The Economic Importance of the Restaurant Industry
Advancement Opportunities
Income Opportunities
Tipping Standard
Getting Stiffed (Left with No Tip)
Tip Credit
Non-Tipping Restaurants
Occupational Advantages for Professional Servers
Occupational Disadvantages for Professional Servers
Challenges for the Restaurant Industry
Job Qualifications
    Education

Intelligence
Product Knowledge
Service Knowledge
Timing and Attention to Details
Personality
Initiative
Positive Attitude
Teamwork Ability
Good Manners
Professional Appearance
Honesty
Sense of Humor
Reliability
Summary
Discussion Questions and Exercises

The Economic Importance of the Restaurant Industry

Learning Objective 1

Understand the economic importance of the restaurant industry.

According to the National Restaurant Association, the restaurant industry is the second largest private sector industry in the United States and is responsible for generating over $780 billion in annual sales, employing over 14 million people in 1 million restaurant locations and outpacing the national average in job growth. The industry is expected to create 1.7 million new jobs by 2026. The restaurant industry, in general, offers boundless advancement opportunities in all segments of hospitality service. This offers a positive outlook for the many people who are interested in a career in the hospitality industry.

Advancement Opportunities

Learning Objective 2

Recognize the advancement opportunities within a restaurant and related career tracks.

There are advancement opportunities in most restaurant operations depending upon the size of the operation and other services offered, such as banquets, on- and off-premise catering, and a bar. Table 1.1 reflects the available advancement positions in a typical full-service restaurant. Besides the positions listed in Table 1.1, there are a number of other lucrative career tracks that server skills can transfer to, such as those identified in Table 1.2. It is not uncommon for a server to discover additional career interests while working in the restaurant industry. Servers often have occasion to interact with some of the companies doing business with the restaurant, which in turn may create an interest to explore other career options with those businesses. Servers also find career paths that can combine their skills with personal interests, such as travel and tourism, sports and entertainment, nutrition and healthcare, and so forth.

Income Opportunities

Learning Objective 3

Analyze income opportunities.

Professional servers have income and advancement opportunities available at many levels within the hospitality industry. According to the National Restaurant Association, servers on average earn over $16 per hour. Serving tables of customers should be viewed as an entrepreneurial business opportunity because each table has the potential to provide a minimum or maximum income through an earned tip.

A server's income is usually derived from two sources: wages and tips. There are few other businesses that the employee has so much control over their own income. A server's income is typically based on tips, which are directly linked

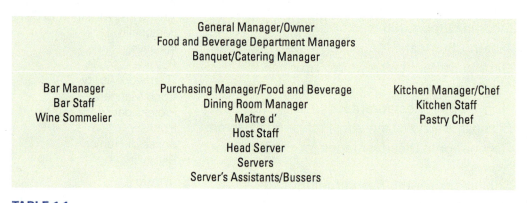

TABLE 1.1

Available Advancement Positions

Private Catering

Hotel/Lodging Management

Tourism

Corporate/Government Foodservice

College/School Foodservice

Resorts/Spas Management

Nutrition/Healthcare

Food & Beverage Brokerage/Suppliers

Sports/Entertainment/Event Management

Winery–Brewery–Spirits

Hospitality Equipment & Technology

Hospitality Internet Services

Hospitality Consulting

Customer Service Training

Hospitality Journalism

Senior Living Facilities Management

Chef/Culinary

TABLE 1.2
Restaurant-Related Career Tracks

to sales. There are many types of servers in many different areas of a hotel or restaurant. They include room service attendants, banquet servers, and any tipped associate of a large hotel, such as a bell person or a parking attendant for valet parking. Some of these positions, such as banquet servers and room service attendants, receive their tips on a paycheck. Banquet servers pool their tips, which are divided among the number of servers who worked for a particular banquet function. Professional servers are more than order takers; they are instead salespeople who can increase their income as well as the income of the restaurant by increasing the food and beverage sales at each of their tables. Listed below are a number of sales techniques that are commonly used in the restaurant industry to increase guest checks, thereby increasing the potential revenue for the restaurant owner and wages for the servers.

1. Suggestive selling—suggesting additional items for a guest's order.
2. Upselling—increasing the value of the items a guest orders.
3. Highlighting—pointing out the special of the day to a guest, including favorite or popular menu items to encourage the guest to order them and highlighting gluten-free, organic, locally sourced items, or farm/estate brand menu items.
4. Open-ended questions—a question the guest cannot answer with a yes or no, such as, "Would you like to make a selection from our fresh fruit and artisanal cheese offerings or from our chocolatier chef's creations?" A question that allows the guest to think about ordering an item that they were not considering until they were asked this question.

These sales techniques, which are further discussed in Chapter 7, Guest Communication, are used to encourage guests to have the most enjoyable meal possible and to increase the guest check total, as well as the server's potential tip. Table 1.3 is an example of the results when sales techniques are effectively applied.

So, how does a career professional server in a tipping restaurant get a raise? The answer is that guests provide the raises with *tips*. Furthermore, the level of the

Guest Check #1 Low Salesmanship		Guest Check #2 High Salesmanship	
1 Crabcake Appetizer	$10.00	2 Crabcake Appetizer	$20.00
1 Chowder	$7.00	1 Chowder	$7.00
		1 Caesar Salad	$8.00
2 Trout	$36.00	1 Trout	$18.00
2 Chicken	$32.00	2 Chicken	$32.00
		1 Lobster Special	$25.00
1 Dessert	$7.00	2 Desserts	$14.00
2 Coffee	$6.00	1 Coffee	$3.00
		1 Cappuccino	$5.00
TOTAL	$98.00	TOTAL	$132.00
15% TIP	$14.70	15% TIP	$19.80

TABLE 1.3

Comparison of Two Guest Checks Representing Four Guests

server's competence determines the size of the raise. The average dollar amount in guest check sales varies and is correlated to the style of restaurant. Typically, a fast-paced casual restaurant may average $9–$15 per person, a casual-dining table service restaurant may average $15–$25 per person, and a fine-dining table service restaurant may average $25–$70 and higher per person, not including wine or other alcohol beverages. Guest check sales also vary at breakfast, lunch, and dinner, as the dollar amounts are smaller for breakfast, increase with lunch, and are greater for dinner.

There are technical skills needed to be a successful server, such as serving with the correct hand from the correct side, carrying a beverage tray, and working in a timely and efficient manner. Guests do not like to wait for long periods of time to eat. A server must understand the sequence of service, which should have a steady flow that is natural and unrushed.

Service skills are trainable; a server can learn the technical skills and can become proficient in them. In addition to the technical skills, a server's success is greatly linked to the innate desire to serve and the ability to make a guest feel valued. The desire to serve is difficult to teach and is something that the server must naturally possess, and it can be further enhanced with good training. Below are examples of variables that directly impact a server's success. The combinations of the three variables are the foundation for excellent guest service and satisfaction.

The three critical variables within the server's control that directly impact their earnings are as follows and will be further discussed in Chapter 7, Guest Communication:

The desire to serve Genuinely and sincerely wanting to create a pleasant dining experience for all your guests. Reading what your guest needs from you, through observation and timeliness.

Personalized service Consistently creating and delivering a distinctively personalized service that increases tip percentages through perceived value. A guest needs to be cared for in a manner that best fits their expectations. This is accomplished by rendering the highest possible quality of service. A server can achieve this by using basic technical service skills as well as being attentive without being intrusive.

Marketing skills Suggestively selling items such as appetizers, beverages, and desserts to increase the dollar amount of guest checks. Guiding guest through the offerings of the restaurant and exceeding expectations.

Service has become so important to the dining-out public that it is not unusual for neighbors, friends, and colleagues to discuss and critique a restaurant experience. Servers have the most direct contact with guests and therefore have the biggest impact on the success of a restaurant business. Guests will not return to a restaurant with unsatisfactory service but will often return to a restaurant with service that made them feel valued and welcomed. As a general rule, people dining out want to feel cared for, engaged, and valued; therefore, good service is the key attribute for choosing a table service restaurant.

A server must understand their guests' needs and fill them in a professional, polite, engaging, and timely manner in order to earn their repeat business. Each guest's needs and wants are different, so a server has the responsibility of interacting with each guest in a professional but personal manner. Servers have the responsibility to ensure the continued growth and success of the restaurant by providing service that makes the guest want to come back time and time again. This is not a simple task, but requires a server to incorporate many skills in treating guests with care and respect. A server needs to listen, suggest, and be engaging so that their guests look forward to returning for the experience. Along with expecting good service, there is an increase in demand for healthy eating options ranging from items like gluten-free, whole grain, low-calorie, and fresh produce choices. The interest in where food comes from and in the desire for fresh, organic, and local ingredients sourced close to the restaurant or even grown on the premises has become important to guests. There is also an opportunity to tap into locally produced beer, wine, and spirits, and nonalcohol beverages in order to create signature cocktails, house-made soft drinks, and specialty teas and coffees as discussed in Chapter 6, Beverages and Beverage Service.

In addition, there are a growing number of restaurants focusing on in-house preparation methods such as pickling, fermenting, smoking, sous vide, and fire roasting. Servers must be knowledgeable about menu item ingredients and cooking techniques so that they match the restaurant's unique products to the individual guest needs while nurturing the guest's experience. This is a challenging but rewarding task successfully delivered by embracing the true meaning of hospitality and caring for each guest with great pleasure.

New technology such as tabletop tablets, electronic pay-at-table, and mobile payments offer many benefits and will be further discussed in Chapter 8, The Technology of Service, but the personal touch element when serving guests will always remain a key component for successful restaurant operators.

Tipping Standard

Learning Objective 4

Know the range for a tipping standard.

The current national tipping standard for table service is 15–20 percent of the meal's cost, excluding taxes. Tipping over 15 percent is quite acceptable and in certain establishments can average 20–30 percent. Who made up this rule of thumb? It evolved as a customary standard established by the hospitality industry and its consumers. There are numerous stories of servers being "stiffed" (left with no tip) or given outrageous tips. There are news-making stories of the Chicago cocktail server who got a $10,000 tip from an English doctor who truly appreciated the careful attention given to his special request drink order and the pleasant manner in which the drinks were served to him and his associates. There is also the Boston bartender who shared the idea for her restaurant concept with a regular guest who turned out to be an investment banker. He liked her idea and her business plan, and as a result, made her a partner and invested over $1,000,000 to launch her dream restaurant. A server can never know in advance whether the person who they may be serving could in some way reward personalized service with an extraordinary benefit.

Tips are not mandatory. Some servers think that they are, and they are routinely outraged when a guest leaves a tip that is less than they think appropriate. Some establishments set automatic gratuities or a service charge of 15 percent or more for certain circumstances such as special events, banquets, and groups of diners over a certain size. In these cases the guest is notified either on the menu, during the process of making reservations, or by the server.

Getting Stiffed (Left with No Tip)

Learning Objective 5

Understand what "Getting Stiffed" means.

Many servers have experienced the penalty of a short tip or no tip as the result of a guest's dissatisfaction. There are occasions where indeed the server did not deliver the service expected and should be tipped (or not tipped) accordingly. Some conditions are beyond the server's control, such as being short staffed, being out of certain food items, and a kitchen equipment failure. As a result, the tip is reduced or lost. For the most part, guests are forgiving of momentary glitches if they are informed of the circumstances and the restaurant makes a sincere attempt to reconcile the inconvenience. What guests will not excuse is a bad attitude on the part of the server or a projected sense of entitlement when it comes to tipping. Sometimes the best tip is no tip at all.

There are certain guests who do not believe in tipping. That is their choice; and it is one of the occupational hazards of the profession. Most people prefer having the option on tips and rebel at being told that they owe tips.

The rule to remember when getting stiffed is: Get over it! Reset the table for the next party and work toward a 15 percent tip or more.

Tip Credit

Learning Objective 6

Understand how tip credit is applied.

Many states have mandated the legal authority to apply what is known as a tip credit. Section 3(m) of the FLSA [Federal Labor Standards Act] permits an employer to take a tip credit toward its minimum wage obligation for tipped employees equal to the difference between the required cash wage (which must be at least $2.13) and the federal minimum wage. Thus, the maximum tip credit that an employer can currently claim under the FLSA is $5.12 per hour (the minimum wage of $7.25 minus the minimum required cash wage of $2.13). Refer to U.S. Department of Labor, Wage and Hour Division, Fact Sheet #15: Tipped Employees under the Fair Labor Standards Act (FLSA) (http://www.dol.gov/whd/regs/compliance/whdfs15.pdf).

The formula is simple: The more a server earns in tips the less the employer is required to pay in wages. If $2.13 plus tips received equals at least the federal minimum wage, the employee retains all the tips. If an employee's tips combined with the employer's direct wage of $2.13 an hour do not equal the federal minimum hourly wage, the employer must make up the difference.

Minimum wages are increasingly different from state to state, which complicates the concept of the tip credit and puts more responsibility on the restaurant owner. The concept remains the same; however, tipped employees must make at least the state minimum wage per hour or employers must make up the difference in the hourly wage. For example, the 2016 state minimum wage in New Jersey is $8.38 that equates as follows: $6.25 maximum tip credit against minimum wage per hour combined with $2.13 minimum cash wage per hour equals $8.38. The formulas for allowing tip credit vary from state to state and some states such as California, Oregon, and Washington do not allow tip credit to be applied, and have a state minimum wage higher than the federal minimum wage. A list of how states apply or do not apply tip credits is available on the U.S. Department of Labor website (http://www.dol.gov/whd/state/tipped.htm).

Annual sales of $276,250 (Amount taken from customer guest checks) $1,105 per day in customer sales × 5 days a week = $5,525 × 50 weeks = $276,250 (A total of $1,105 per day in customer sales based upon serving 65 people with a $17.00 per person average guest check) Working 30 hours per week × 50 weeks = 1,500 annual work hours			
Annual Sales	Tip (%)	Annual Tip Income	Hourly + Federal Minimum = Hourly Wage
$276,250	0.10	= $27,625 ÷ 1,500 hours =	$18.42 + $2.13 = $20.55
$276,250	0.15	= $41,437.50 ÷ 1,500 hours =	$27.63 + $2.13 = $29.76
$276,250	0.20	= $55,250 ÷ 1,500 hours =	$36.83 + $2.13 = $38.96

TABLE 1.4

Potential Server Earnings

Reporting tip income so that the restaurant complies with the Tax Equity and Fiscal Responsibility Act (TEFRA) is the responsibility of the restaurant owner. The amount of tips that are placed on customer credit cards is totaled for each server by the POS system at the end of each day. At the end of each shift servers should enter the total amount of their cash tips along with entering the time their shift ends.

Table 1.4 demonstrates potential server earnings with the tip credit application.

There are additional factors that can increase or decrease a server's income, such as the following:

1. Working more or fewer hours.
2. Shifts worked: breakfast, lunch, or dinner.
3. Weekday or weekend shifts that are typically busier.
4. Banquet or special functions.
5. Weather conditions that slow business.
6. Holidays such as Mother's Day or Valentine's Day.
7. Seasonal fluctuations in customer counts.
8. Tip pooling. This (where legally allowed) occurs when all tips go into one pot and are divided equally among the servers and server's assistants/bussers. Usually the employer establishes a house policy and then determines who will share the tips and applies the percentage formula. A policy may state that all servers receive 70 percent of the tip pool and all server's assistants/bussers receive the remaining 30 percent.
9. Tipping out other positions. Under this system, a percentage or specific amount goes to any one or a mix of the following positions: host, bartender, cocktail servers, or server's assistants/bussers. Again, the employer usually sets the house policy on distribution.

Non-Tipping Restaurants

Learning Objective 7

Identify the factors associated with non-tipping restaurants.

Some restaurants are choosing to do away with server tipping and have created house policies to increase menu prices or include an administrative fee on the guest check; an example of a "No Tipping" policy with an administrative fee added to the guest check is as shown in Figure 1.1. The objective is to be able to financially compensate both kitchen and dining room employees in a more equitable manner and to further support and advance the restaurant's concept of teamwork. If properly implemented, all restaurant employees would receive a higher and more

SNACKS & SIDES

Jalapeño *Hush Puppies*

MAPLE BUTTER

$7

SHANGHAI SHOOTS

WITH FERMENTED BLACK BEANS

$6

Lilac Spinach Salad

GRAPEFRUIT, PISTACHIOS, LION'S MANE MUSHROOMS

$9

Korean Fried Broccoli

GARLIC SESAME SAUCE

$8

GRILLED & *Creamed* Chard

$7

WHATEVER PICKLES

$2

CURRY FRIES

WITH HOMEMADE PANEER

$8

GRILLED Onion Salad

$7

VEGETABLES

Mushroom

PORTOBELLO MOUSSE WITH SAUTEED ASIAN PEARS, CHERRIES AND TRUFFLE TOAST

$14

Fennel

RAW AND PICKLED FENNEL WITH CARAMELIZED YOGURT ON A CARTA DI MUSICA
(WHICH JUST MEANS "FANCY CRACKER" IN ITALIAN)

$11

KALE

KALE MATZOH BALL SOUP WITH POACHED EGG AND OKRA

$13

POTATO

WARM POTATO SALAD WITH OLIVES, BITTER GREENS AND CRISPY JAPANESE YAMS

$11

Carrot

CARROT SLIDERS WITH SPECIAL SAUCE ON AN ALL-CARROT SESAME SEED BUN

$13

RUTABAGA

GINGER & SAGE CAKE WITH MUSTARD TUILE AND SMOKED CREAM CHEESE

$14

RADISH

BLACK RADISH SPAGHETTI, HORSERADISH, MINT & LEMON LABNEH, RADISH NOODLES

$18

Broccoli

GRILLED & SMOKED BROCCOLI DOGS WITH BROCCOLI KRAUT AND MUSTARD BARBECUE SAUCE

$16

Cauliflower

CAULIFLOWER AND CURRY WITH GREEN PEA PANEER, PAPAYA CHUTNEY AND PAPPADAM

$18

Eggplant

MAPO EGGPLANT WITH BABY BOK CHOI, BABY PEA SHOOTS AND EGGPLANT SFORMATA
(A PRETENTIOUS ITALIAN WORD FOR EGGPLANT MOUSSE)

$18

TO SHARE

Cabbage HOT POT

ACCOMPANIED BY LOTUS ROOT, KIMCHI, RADISHES, GINGER, FRESH HERBS, SESAME FU, CABBAGE NOODLES, GRILLED CABBAGE

 $28 FOR 2 $32 FOR 4

Brussels Sprout TACOS

ACCOMPANIED BY SMOKED AVOCADO, PICKLED RED ONION, SALSA VERDE, CRISPY BRUSSELS SPROUT LEAVES, TORTILLA STRIPS, JALAPENOS, CREMA.

$28

Tip Policy

We pay our employees a fair wage, and they share in Dirt Candy's profits, so no tipping, please.
A 20% administrative fee is added to every bill to offset our costs. It is not a tip.

Amanda Cohen, Chef & Owner

FIGURE 1.1

No Tipping Tip Policy (at the Bottom of the Menu) that Defines a 20 Percent Administrative Fee Added to Every Bill. Courtesy of Dirt Candy, New York, NY.

predictable hourly wage and yearly income. There are many concerns with these policies beginning with motivation. A serious concern is that servers will not be motivated to give their best service. This may be an issue or it can be a way to set specific standards of service and hold servers to those standards. Servers will be expected to do a good job and paid according to their work performance. This can in fact make overall service better. A server's job may look more conventional in the future, with higher hourly wages, benefits, and seniority based pay. Guests may welcome the increased menu prices because it will eliminate having to calculate the tip at the end of the meal.

There are arguments for tipping establishments and non-tipping establishments. Guests will have to communicate their service dissatisfaction through verbal or written communication instead of immediate monetary compensation such as a tip. It may become difficult for employers in non-tipping restaurants to staff on holidays and weekends, whereas tipped restaurant servers find these shifts most desirable because of the high sales and high business demands. Unmotivated servers in non-tipping restaurants may want to work the slower nights, therefore having an uneven distribution of the work load for the same pay. Training all employees at a high level with measurable standards of service will be important to a restaurant's success. Creating various methods for guests to effectively communicate their satisfaction will assist non-tipping restaurants with maintaining service standards.

Non-Tipping Advantages

1. Servers will have a higher hourly wage.
2. Servers will be able to budget more accurately because of a consistent wage.
3. Eliminates IRS Tip Reporting.
4. Rewards senior staff, who can earn promotions and wage increases.
5. Compensates all restaurant employees equitably for their work.

Non-Tipping Disadvantages

1. Servers do not have as much control of their income.
2. Servers will be paid the same regardless of sales and work load (busy or slow days/shifts).
3. Standards of service must be maintained through measurable standards and ongoing training.
4. Servers are not immediately rewarded for their hard work.

Occupational Advantages for Professional Servers

Learning Objective 8

Understand the occupational advantages for professional servers.

The following advantages are motivating to many professional servers:

1. *Time flexibility* The nature of the business allows for the server's time to be flexible to schedule work hours and days off. It can also accommodate other things such as family activities, continuing education, a second job, leisure time, and other professional endeavors.
2. *High hourly wages* The potential to earn a high hourly wage (wage plus tips) is substantially greater than in many other occupations and can be achieved faster.

3. *Job mobility* When the server has mastered the basic skills of the craft, those skills are then transferable to any restaurant in the world.

4. *Minimal clothing expense* The investment in work clothing can be minimal, as most employers provide uniforms.

5. *Meal benefit* The server is typically provided a meal during a work shift.

6. *Physical fitness* The nature of the work provides a high level of physical activity.

7. *Opportunity to meet interesting people* The server has the opportunity to meet a wide spectrum of people during every shift. Friendships and lasting customer relationships often develop.

8. *Entrepreneurial experience* The server learns how to be an entrepreneur by being exposed to selling and the rewards of providing personalized service.

9. *Work unity* There can be a unique sense of family and camaraderie among restaurant employees that is not often found in other occupations.

10. *Sales training* The server has the opportunity to learn the art of sales and merchandising. This training to increase sales will result in increased income and greater guest satisfaction.

Occupational Disadvantages for Professional Servers

Learning Objective 9

Understand the occupational disadvantages for professional servers.

The following disadvantages can be discouraging for some servers:

1. *Working weekends, nights, and holidays* The nature of the restaurant industry often requires working weekends, nights, and holidays. These are typically the busiest times in most establishments.

2. *Work stress* The work can be physically, mentally, and psychologically intense, and can be emotionally demanding. The burnout possibilities are high for those who do not take the time to relax physically and mentally after work.

3. *Limited employee benefits* Some employers only offer limited benefits, although recent competition for labor has motivated many employers to offer expanded medical insurance, paid sick days, paid vacations, pension plans, and disability insurance.

4. *Lost income* Events beyond the server's control, such as shutdowns because of weather or equipment failure, mean the server will not be working.

Challenges for the Restaurant Industry

Learning Objective 10

Recognize the challenges for the restaurant industry.

Even though becoming a professional server has many advantages, the turnover rate in the restaurant industry remains quite high, topping over 70 percent for hourly wage and salary positions according to the National Restaurant Association. This continues to be one of the biggest challenges facing the restaurant industry today. As replacing the former stereotype of a server being a transient job filled by college students and temporary part-time employees is slowly changing, many restaurant operators offer various incentives to keep servers interested in their job and create healthy competition among the staff. It is not uncommon for a restaurant to offer its servers a chance to win a gift certificate to another restaurant or a gift card for high sales, perfect attendance, or loyalty to the restaurant. These incentives are becoming more and more popular and can be an excellent way of maintaining a positive work environment.

Job Qualifications

Learning Objective 11

Identify professional server job qualifications.

To be successful as a restaurant employee, an individual should review the following personal competencies:

Education

There are very few training schools for professional servers. Formal education is important but not necessary. The aspiring server should possess the ability to learn quickly on the job. Having the desire to serve and being willing to do your best is an asset to becoming a professional server.

Intelligence

A successful server should be alert and mentally sharp at all times. The job requires quick, organized thinking under stress, with the ability to adjust timing and service according to the expectations and needs of multiple guest situations.

Product Knowledge

The server must understand the menu descriptions of the food and beverage items in order to guide the guests through meal selections. Given the wide selection of products available, and new ones continually being introduced, the individual must take the initiative to stay informed about the latest food and beverage items.

Service Knowledge

A number of service methods, techniques, and standards require training (usually on the job) and experience to gain practice at understanding and executing basic tasks. The seasoned server will develop a personal style by drawing from what they learn of the basics. With a little imagination and creativity, the server will become increasingly more effective and profitable.

Timing and Attention to Details

There is nothing more important than timing and attention to detail when serving tables. It begins with getting ready on time. There needs to be a sense of urgency the minute a service employee walks in the door. Every detail must be finished and double-checked prior to opening for a shift. All work should be completed fully and accurately to ensure a successful meal period. If corners are cut or duties neglected, a shift can be chaotic and service will suffer. Every detail, regardless of how small, contributes to a positive guest experience. Table service itself should flow in a natural sequence and feel effortless. It takes training and practice to acquire the proper skills of timing during the dining experience. Also, the conscious ability to always be observing the table with a mental checklist of items that a guest may need is extremely important while servicing a meal. It allows the server to accommodate a guest needs without verbal interaction.

Personality

A server must have a pleasant manner and enjoy people. A server must be able to sustain a friendly demeanor with poise and self-confidence while under pressure.

Initiative

A server must take charge of the station (tables) and recognize when and what kind of service customers need and perform that service with a sense of urgency in every detail.

Positive Attitude

A positive or negative attitude affects performance. If one shows up for a shift in a bad mood, it is going to be a bad shift with bad guests and bad coworkers making bad tips. A positive "professional attitude" can generate positive, wonderful results.

Teamwork Ability

The server should be willing to work cooperatively with others in a fast-paced work environment that supports a common goal of providing the highest quality of guest service.

Good Manners

A server should have the understanding and ability to demonstrate the social skills of being polite, courteous, and respectful to coworkers and guests.

Professional Appearance

A server should maintain a professional appearance. Uniform should be clean, pressed, and fit properly. A server should practice good personal hygiene and pay attention to cleanliness of hair, fingernails, breath, and body odor. Men should be clean shaven or maintain a neat beard and women should use minimal makeup. Both men and women should not wear any fragrance.

Honesty

A server must have a strong sense of honesty when handling guest payment transactions, when sharing tips, and when equally sharing work responsibilities. Guests and fellow coworker must feel that they can trust and rely on a server. Many guests may feel uncomfortable turning over their credit cards to an unfamiliar server.

Sense of Humor

Learning Objective 12

Recognize the value of not making an incorrect judgment based upon a guest's appearance.

A good sense of humor is essential in order to survive the daily stresses of the job. When things seem to be getting a bit out of control, it is one's ability to step back and find humor in it all that helps to minimize the stress and tension.

Reliability

The server must always be on time for work, provide prompt service to guests, and complete all tasks, including opening, shift change, closing cleanup, and restocking service areas.

RESTAURANT REALITY: NEVER JUDGE A BOOK BY ITS COVER

All too often, a server can look at a guest in a restaurant and make an incorrect judgment based upon the guest's appearance. This can be a big mistake and a valuable lesson can be learned from the following true story.

A young mom, named Kristen, was a part-time server in a small, popular French restaurant. The restaurant had a reputation for excellent food and wine at reasonable prices. The restaurant was always busy and the servers had a heavy workload, being responsible for serving and clearing their own tables.

On a busy weeknight, a gentleman entered the restaurant and stood near the door. He had a disheveled appearance and was dressed very causally. The head server who seated guests walked by him. Kristen was extremely busy; she had several tables that needed to be bussed. The head server and another server had one available table each in their stations, but were not interested in serving the guest. Kristen asked the head server why the guest was allowed to stand at the front door. The head server told her that she could serve the guest. Kristen was disappointed with the servers. She politely acknowledged the guest and quickly bussed one of her two dirty tables, and then seated the guest who explained that he would be joined by two more guests. He asked that she present him with the bill at the end of the meal, and proceeded to order the most expensive bottle of wine on the wine list and waited for his guests to arrive. The two gentlemen who joined him were neatly dressed in classic business suits. Kristen waited on the three gentlemen who ordered several meal courses along with two additional bottles of high-end wines. The guest check was quite substantial, and as the meal came to an end it was time to present the bill to the guest. It was one of the highest bills Kristen had ever generated since her employment at the restaurant. She presented the bill, and the guest looked at it and placed a credit card in the leather check presenter.

He expressed his appreciation for her excellent and professional service. When she returned with the credit card and authorization slip, the guest signed the credit card slip and wrote the word "CASH" in the space for the tip. He then reached for his wallet and gave her a 40 percent cash tip. She was shocked and told him that it was too much. He disagreed and further complimented her on her professionalism, and he commented about the other servers passing him by as he patiently stood at the door. He felt that the other severs judged him by his appearance, but that she was respectful and professional in every way making him feel valued and welcomed. He told her that he was new in town and involved with a successful business, and enjoyed his meal immensely. He planned to frequent the restaurant, and he wanted her to be his server whenever he returned. He came in often and always gave Kristen a 40 percent tip.

Summary

The restaurant industry is an integral and growing part of American life, as shown by the impressive facts and figures that describe the industry, such as over $780 billion in annual sales and employing over 14 million people in 1 million restaurant locations. As a result, the number of opportunities for the professional server continues to grow. A wide selection of advancement opportunities exists within the restaurant industry, ranging from entry-level positions to actual ownership. For individuals with the interest, talents, and enthusiasm, along with the willingness to make a commitment to the industry, the income and professional development can be excellent.

The level of income that a professional server can earn will be increased or decreased by the number of hours they are willing to work, and by the type of restaurant operation (ranging from the fast-paced casual, casual table service to fine-dining table service).

The nature of the work allows the server to develop and exercise entrepreneurial skills by offering a personalized service to customers. In addition, it advances one's marketing talents through the merchandising and upselling of food and beverage items. Servers may also have the opportunity to be employed by a non-tipping restaurant that provides an equitable compensation for all employees.

The advantages of being a server are many and include the following: time flexibility to accommodate one's lifestyle; flexible income; high potential hourly earnings; career and job mobility; a meal provided during a work shift; physical exercise to keep fit; and the opportunity to meet interesting people. The disadvantages often discourage people from entering the occupation, and include the following: working weekends, nights, and holidays; physical, mental, and psychological stress associated with the work; and in some cases the absence of good employee benefits.

The qualifications of a successful server include competencies in the following areas: product knowledge with a sound understanding of food and beverage items; service knowledge in being able to provide each guest with a personalized service; a good sense of timing in serving the ordered items; a pleasant personality with a likable manner and positive attitude; the ability to support coworkers; a sense of humor coupled with the ability to handle the stress of the work; and an honest and reliable work ethic.

Discussion Questions and Exercises

1. Discuss the economic importance of the restaurant industry by identifying some statistics that were compiled by the National Restaurant Association.

2. Discuss potential career advancement opportunities within a typical restaurant operation.

3. Identify 10 different restaurant-related career track options.

4. Name the two sources of income for a professional server.

5. What are the three critical variables that the server controls that directly impact their earnings?

6. If the average daily total guest check sales for a server in a fine-dining table service restaurant is $2,400 and a server worked 5 days, 40 hours per week at minimum wage with tip credit applied and earned a 15 percent tip average, what would be her annual income? Refer to Table 1.4, Potential Server Earnings.

7. Identify three factors that can affect a server's income.

8. What is the current national tipping standard range for table service?

9. Explain what happens when a server experiences the "penalty" of getting stiffed.

10. What is the minimum cash wage per hour when the federal minimum wage is applied for employee tip credit?

11. Who is responsible for IRS tip income reporting?

12. List three advantages of non-tipping restaurants.

13. List three disadvantages of non-tipping restaurants.

14. Identify seven occupational advantages for professional servers.

15. List three occupational disadvantages of professional servers.

16. What remains the biggest challenge for the restaurant industry?

17. Describe 10 qualities within the list of job qualifications that an individual should have in order to be a successful server.

18. Among the job qualification for a professional server is timing and attention to details. Explain exactly what is required to be effective with appropriate timing and identify several of the details that a professional must attend to.

19. What are the consequences when a server inappropriately judges a guest's appearance?

20. Think about an unpleasant experience from a server that you may have encountered, and then describe how you had reacted to that experience.

21. Visit the National Restaurant Association website (www.restaurant.org) and report the statistics that support the restaurant industry in being a champion of diversity.

22. Discuss an example of personalized service that you have experienced or observed from a professional server.

23. Interview a professional server and ask what they like and dislike about the occupation. Write down the responses and report to the class.

24. Has your opinion of the professional server occupation changed after having read this chapter? If so, describe the change.

CHAPTER 2

Professional Appearance

INTRODUCTION

Public health is essential to all restaurant operations and every employee who prepares and/or serves food must meet the highest standards of neatness, cleanliness, personal hygiene, and good grooming. In order to prevent the contamination of food and food-contact surfaces, and the resulting potential transmission of food-borne illness, it is essential that servers follow strict, safe food-handling procedures as set forth in the ServSafe training certification program offered through the National Restaurant Association. This is important at all times—before starting work, during their shifts, or returning to work after breaks.

CHAPTER 2 LEARNING OBJECTIVES

As a result of successfully completing this chapter, readers will be able to:

1. Learn guidelines for maintaining good professional server health.

2. Learn good personal grooming standards for improving on-the-job professional server appearance.

3. Identify the personal grooming guidelines that are basic for servers.

4. Understand the value and importance of good body language, poise, and posture.

5. Know the importance of always wearing a clean, fresh uniform and apron each day.

6. Know the characteristics of a quality pair of work shoes.

CHAPTER 2 OUTLINE

Server Health

Grooming Standards

Grooming Guidelines

Body Language, Poise, and Posture

Uniforms and Aprons

Shoes

Summary

Discussion Questions and Exercises

Server Health

Learning Objective 1

Learn guidelines for maintaining good professional server health.

The health of servers is critical. Poor health in the restaurant industry can create a food-borne illness outbreak that may require a hospital stay or even be fatal. To avoid the possibility of an occurrence, no server, while infected with a disease in a communicable form that can be transmitted by foods or who is a carrier of organisms that cause such a disease, or while afflicted with a boil, an infected wound, or an acute respiratory infection, a cold or flu, should work in a restaurant establishment in any capacity in which there is a likelihood of contaminating food or food-contact surfaces with pathogenic organisms or of transmitting disease to other persons.

Disease transmitted through food frequently originates from an infected restaurant employee, even though the employee shows little outward appearance of being ill. A wide range of communicable diseases and infections may be transmitted by infected restaurant employees to other employees, and to the customer, through the contamination of food and through careless food-handling practices. It is the responsibility of both management and staff to see to it that no person who is affected with any disease that can be transmitted by food works in any area of a restaurant establishment where there is a possibility of disease transmission.

If a server suffers during an allergy season, the coughing and sneezing must be controlled with the proper allergy medication. "A server cannot successfully work with a coughing and sneezing problem in view of guests."

Servers should use gloves or tongs when handling any ready-to-eat food, which includes bread, lemons, salads, butter, or any other food that will not be cooked before the guest will eat it. The server should also be aware of the placement of their hands when carrying flatware, glassware, and china, which will be discussed in Chapter 3, Table Service, Table Settings, and Napkin Presentations.

Grooming Standards

Learning Objective 2

Learn good personal grooming standards for improving on-the-job professional server appearance.

Your personal appearance will reveal important characteristics of your personality and attitude, because while you are in contact with your guests, they will be judging you. Remember, as a server, you are on stage at all times.

Good grooming and posture has many benefits, and you, the server, benefit from all of them. The way to ensure good grooming and posture is to check yourself in the mirror while mentally asking the following questions:

- Does your posture consist of your head held high with your chin parallel to the floor?
- Are your shoulders held up, back, and relaxed, and your rib cage held high with the elbows slightly bent, and the hips tucked under?
- Are your knees relaxed? Do you look confident and professional? Would you make a good first impression?

The principles for good appearance are the same for men and women. Taking proper care of oneself is essential, and devoting time to your appearance will add to your confidence, peace of mind, and success. Guests expect to see well-groomed servers just as much as they expect to see a clean restaurant. The well-groomed server conveys a professional image that supports an overall dining experience. A well-groomed appearance is absolutely essential to project the image of good service, quality food, and a pleasant atmosphere. The individual server has a significant role in the restaurant and the most contact with the guests. Therefore, the restaurant operator is challenged in setting forth and maintaining server standards that will help to ensure that guests feel comfortable and confident in returning to the restaurant.

Most restaurants are somewhat conservative and expect their servers to reflect that image. Even though body art (tattoos) and piercings are popular and a form of self-expression, they do not project a conservative image. Body art (tattoos) should be covered up unless it supports the restaurant's image.

There are some nonconservative restaurants in today's eclectic market that offer a form of entertainment in addition to a guest's meal. Some of these concepts may impact dress standards by providing uniquely designed uniforms that may serve as costumes. Servers may be allowed to have bold hairstyles and colors, and to wear excessive jewelry. However, these concepts are the exception, unusual, and limited to a defined customer base.

FIGURE 2.1
Personal Hygiene Begins in the Bathroom. Graphic image by Dwayne Philibert.

Grooming Guidelines

Learning Objective 3

Identify the personal grooming guidelines that are basic for servers.

A server should practice good personal hygiene and pay attention to full-body cleanliness as depicted in Figure 2.1. It includes the following grooming guidelines.

Bathing and deodorants Good personal hygiene begins with daily bathing and the use of unscented deodorants or antiperspirants. Offensive body odors caused by poor personal hygiene can cause coworkers and guests to complain to the management. Offended guests may choose never to return.

Hair care The server should always have clean and fresh-smelling hair that is controlled in order to prevent hair from contacting or falling into food or onto food-contact surfaces. When hair is uncontrolled, it can be difficult to manage and distracting when serving food. The professional server will have her hair styled and the hairstylist can recommend a hairstyle that is attractive and easy to take care of. The hair should not be too long and preferably not go below the shirt collar. However, long hair should be restrained in a ponytail, twist, or hairnet. Servers should avoid fixing or touching their hair while in view of guests, and should wash their hands after coming in direct contact with their hair.

Skin care When experiencing problems with skin—acne, or dry or oily skin—the server should take appropriate measures to control them. Servers should never scratch dry or itchy areas of the body while in view of guests. Proper care of the skin requires cleanliness and protection.

Cosmetics The proper use of cosmetics can enhance one's appearance and overuse can detract from it. If the appropriate selection and application of cosmetics becomes a concern, the server should consult a cosmetics specialist. A restaurant may have certain standards regarding the use of cosmetics (facial makeup).

Fragrances The use of any fragrances may be offensive to some coworkers and guests, and make those who suffer from severe allergies sick. Fragrances can also distract from the natural aromas of the food being served and should not be used while at work.

Beards and moustaches A well-shaped clean beard or moustache can be very attractive and can enhance a man's appearance, but it needs to be washed and trimmed daily.

Teeth and breath Good oral hygiene is maintained by frequent tooth-brushing and flossing. A smile is always complemented by clean teeth and fresh breath. Breath fresheners should be used as needed. The chewing of gum should be avoided in order to maintain a professional image. Smoking should not be permitted during working hours. The smell of smoke in clothes and on one's breath can be offensive to guests.

Hands and fingernails The hands and fingernails of a server should always be immaculately clean and properly maintained. Servers must thoroughly wash their hands and the exposed portions of their arms with soap and warm water for at least 20 seconds before starting work, during work as often as necessary to keep them clean, and after handling dirty dishes and utensils, eating, drinking, using the toilet, or after performing a nonfoodservice activity. During busy periods when a hand washing sink may not be available, an alternative may be the use of a health department–approved hand sanitizer.

Foot care The correct type of shoes will minimize foot fatigue. The server walks many miles during the course of each shift. Therefore, it is essential to have well-fitting and comfortable shoes. Rubber heels and soles are best for reducing slips and skids on wet floors. Shoes should always be cleaned or polished and have clean laces. Clean socks for the men and clean hose or tights for the women should be worn daily, free of runs, and in a color that complements the uniform. The server may also find comfort in wearing support hose designed to help relieve leg stress. Support stockings or hose are available in basic black, brown, and navy blue for men and in a variety of shades for women.

Jewelry The jewelry worn by a server should be simple and should not interfere with the server's performance of job functions. A plain watch, smooth ring, or small earrings are acceptable and reflect a conservative image that does not bring attention to the server wearing it. When jewelry is large, ornate, or dangling, it becomes awkward and can be potentially hazardous if coming into contact with food or restaurant equipment. Such jewelry may be displeasing to some restaurant guests.

Body Language, Poise, and Posture

Learning Objective 4

Understand the value and importance of good body language, poise, and posture.

Body language can convey positive or negative impressions to the guest. A server should always be aware of their nonverbal communication. It is very easy for a guest to read a server's willingness and enthusiasm to serve them, through their body language. A server should smile, establish good eye contact, and be ready to respond to the needs of a guest. A frown, eye rolling, and crossed arms are signs of unwilling, insincere, and forced service. The guest's perception of a server is critical to a pleasant dining experience and repeat business; therefore, it is important to be aware of body language.

The professional server is always on display and should stand and walk with poise and self-confidence. By moving more gracefully, confidently, and efficiently, the server will not only make a better impression, but also conserve energy for a hardworking day ahead.

Uniforms and Aprons

Learning Objective 5

Know the importance of always wearing a clean, fresh uniform and apron each day.

Most restaurants require that the server wear a special uniform and apron or vest as shown in Figure 2.2a–d. Some uniforms are as formal as a tuxedo or can be as casual as a pair of khaki pants, a collared shirt, and white sneakers. If the restaurant does not require a specific uniform or apron, the server should select a type of clothing that projects a professional image.

The server should have enough uniforms and aprons to allow for daily changes. If a server is scheduled to work five days each week, the restaurant typically

(a)

(b)

(c)

(d)

FIGURE 2.2
(a) Bistro Apron; (b) V-Neck Bib Apron; (c) Cobbler Apron; (d) Server Vests. Courtesy of WaitStuff Uniforms/ Uncommon Threads Authorized Distributor.

provides three uniforms and aprons, allowing the server to wear a clean uniform and apron each day. The server should never wear a uniform that is obviously soiled or stained, because food may be repeatedly contaminated by food debris or other soil from the uniform of the server. The uniforms and aprons should always be cleaned carefully. They should never be wrinkled, torn, or frayed. Having a clean, fresh uniform and apron is, of course, essential to good sanitation. If the server lacks the ability to keep the uniform and apron looking professional, they need to find a good launderer. Uniforms should fit properly and allow for comfortable movement. Also, the restaurant operator may have a policy regarding the hem length of uniforms or shorts.

Uniforms help the customer identify who the employees are when they need assistance. They also add to the customer's perception of the cleanliness and organization of the server and the dining establishment overall.

Shoes

Learning Objective 6

Know the characteristics of a quality pair of work shoes.

Shoes are a significant part of the server uniform and should be selected for style, appearance, safety, and most of all total comfort. Shoes that have ergonomically designed shock-absorbent cushioned insoles, slip-resistant outsoles to prevent slips and falls, and full-grain leather uppers are readily available and competitively priced, as shown in Figure 2.3a and b. An investment in a pair of good-quality shoes pays for itself in a very short period of time. Sore feet can make a shift difficult and eventually lead to other physical problems.

(a)

(b)

FIGURE 2.3

(a) Slip-Resistant Shoe for Men and Women; (b) Nonslip Bottom. Courtesy of Warson Brands, Official Licensee of Reebok International Ltd.

RESTAURANT REALITY: WHEN HOW YOU LOOK AND PERFORM YOUR DUTIES IS NOTICED

Catherine, Kimberly, and Nicole all work the dinner shift as servers at a popular restaurant in a typical, mid-sized American city and have worked together for many years. Each employee has her own personality and has regular customers, who request a particular server.

Nicole arrived to work 15 minutes early as she always does. She has adapted this routine from her very first day of work at the restaurant. Nicole likes to have a few minutes before her shift begins to greet her coworkers, neatly hang up her coat, and stop in the ladies' room to check her appearance. She inspects herself before leaving the ladies room and feels good about her appearance. Catherine typically arrives on time, checks her appearance just before the shift begins, while Kimberly often has a tendency to be a bit rushed in starting the shift. The three confidently are ready to begin their shifts. On this ordinary Wednesday night, with all three servers working, a customer who looks familiar enters the restaurant, but none of them are able to identify that he is the president of the city's Chamber of Commerce, which regularly meets in the banquet room of the restaurant for their Tuesday lunch meetings.

He is seated at Catherine's table, which is next to Nicole's station. Catherine pleasantly greets him with a smile, makes suggestions from the menu and wine list, takes his order accurately, brings his food served hot, offers coffee and dessert, and then leaves his check in a timely manner. Catherine interacts with her guest appropriately and professionally. Her guest, however, is observing Nicole in the next station. She moves with grace and confidence throughout her station, smiles sincerely, presents a polished image, and is gracious and engaging to the guests seated in her station. Her makeup complements her uniform, her hair is neat, her white shirt is crisply ironed with a sharp pleat down the back, and her apron is immaculate. Nicole makes a positive first impression.

As the guest is finishing dinner, the manager recognizes and greets him by name. The guest expressed that his dinner was fine, and his service experience was among the city's best. He goes on to say that next Wednesday night the Chamber of Commerce will be hosting dinner for a group of businesspeople arriving from Japan, and that they will be accompanied by several Chamber of Commerce members. He made a request for a reservation for 12 people at 7:30 p.m. The Chamber of Commerce president mentioned that this would be the first dining out experience in the city for the Japanese visitors. He inquired if Nicole could greet the table and be their server for next Wednesday evening. The manager was happy to accommodate his request and shared the good news with Nicole. She was indeed honored and pleased that her attention to details and her appearance was noticed.

Summary

Servers must always be in good health. No server, while infected with a communicable disease, should be allowed to work in a restaurant establishment in any capacity. The potential to contaminate food and food-contact surfaces, and to transmit the disease to other persons, is too great.

The server is in contact with customers at all times; therefore, their personal appearance is important. A good appearance is necessary to project the image of good service, quality food, and a pleasant atmosphere, which begins with taking proper care of oneself. The following personal grooming standards are basic for servers: bathing and deodorants, hair care, skin care, cosmetics, beards and moustaches, teeth and breath, hands and fingernails, and foot care.

The server should always convey positive body language, and stand and walk with poise and self-confidence. Poor posture detracts from the server's appearance. The way that a server walks and carries themselves is almost as important as the way they speak and look.

Most restaurants require servers to wear a special uniform and/or apron. If the restaurant does not require a specific uniform or apron, the server should select the type of clothing that projects a professional image. The server should have enough uniforms to allow for daily changes. A clean, fresh uniform is essential for good sanitation.

Shoes are a significant part of the server uniform and should be selected for style, appearance, safety, and most of all total comfort. Slip-resistant footwear is increasingly popular, as the number of slips and falls has been reduced with these types of shoes. An investment in a pair of good-quality shoes pays for itself in a very short period of time.

Discussion Questions and Exercises

1. Why is server health so important for the restaurant industry?
2. What does a server's personal appearance reveal to guests?
3. How does a server ensure good grooming?
4. List 10 basic grooming guidelines that should be followed by servers.
5. What are some of the proper procedures a server should follow for maintaining their hair?
6. Discuss the importance of good body language, poise, and posture.
7. What is an adequate number of uniforms and aprons for a server working five days a week?
8. What should the server look for when purchasing a quality pair of work shoes?
9. If a server comes to work with a cough and occasional sneeze, how should management respond?
10. Discuss a positive or negative grooming issue that as a restaurant guest affected your dining experience.
11. Name three restaurants within your community that are noted for a professional server staff and impressive server uniforms and aprons.
12. Visit a restaurant of your choice and observe the servers in relation to what you have learned in this chapter. Write a one-page summary of your observations.

Table Service, Table Settings, and Napkin Presentations

INTRODUCTION

Server training begins with an understanding of correct table settings, and the correct way in which to handle linen, flatware, glassware, and chinaware. The server must have the knowledge and ability to correctly arrange table settings in a fast and efficient manner in order to keep pace with the demands of a busy restaurant. In time, the server will be able to immediately identify the most-used flatware and different serving pieces, such as a pasta spoon, cocktail fork, or escargot tong. The server will also know how many salt and pepper shakers, sugar bowls, and creamers to bring to the table, as well as the restaurant's method of serving bread and butter.

Napkin presentations are elegant and impressive, and a professional server will have the opportunity to perform a number of different napkin folds. Most restaurants will have identified one fold that they use consis-

tently, but in response to customer's requests may choose different folds for banquets or special events.

The professional server should also be acquainted with the five technically different methods of serving food: American Service, Butler Service, English Service, Russian Service, and French Service. Many restaurants have developed a contemporary style of foodservice that borrows from various aspects from all five methods. In addition to table service, a server may have the opportunity to work in counter service, banquet service, or room service, and they should be knowledgeable in these types of services.

Salad bars and dessert tables can be incorporated into service for buffets and catered events. The successful server understands each of their functions and setup, and how they have become part of the restaurant's service.

CHAPTER 3 LEARNING OBJECTIVES

As a result of successfully completing this chapter, readers will be able to:

1. Understand and explain the five distinctive methods of service styles.

2. Explain how "service teams" function in fine-dining restaurants.

3. Describe the functions of family service, counter service, banquet service, and room service.

4. Know the range of foods that can be offered on salad bars.

5. Explain how dessert tables and trays function.

6. Explain the proper placement of a tablecloth on a table being prepared to serve guests.

7. Understand when place mats are used.

8. Determine how many salt and pepper shakers to place at each table and when they should be

removed, along with how many sugar and creamer sets to place on the table and when to place them, whenever coffee or tea is served.

9. Explain the different ways that bread and butter can be served.

10. Understand how to place side dishes and condiments on a table.

11. Explain and demonstrate correct flatware placement.

12. Describe and demonstrate correct glassware placement.

13. Explain traditional breakfast, lunch, dinner, and formal dinner table settings.

14. Demonstrate a range of napkin folds.

Table Service

Learning Objective 1

Understand and explain the five distinctive methods of service styles.

The service style that a restaurant develops is one that will accommodate the menu, atmosphere, image of the restaurant, and nature of the clientele. The five technically distinct methods of serving food, often referred to as service styles, are American Service, Butler Service, English Service, Russian Service, and French Service. Historical references for the English, Russian, and French styles of service will correctly define these styles of service as they were originally set forth. Contemporary references are more focused on specific techniques that adapt the original definitions to what has transpired over the years, as shown in Table 3.1, Comparison of Services. These contemporary methods are a blend of one or more of the traditional methods that fall into the following generally accepted definitions, combining some historical reference with a modern application.

American Service (Individual Plate Service)

Learning Objective 2

Explain how "service teams" function in fine-dining restaurants.

This is the most popular type of service among today's restaurants. It has been widely accepted because it is simple and quick, uses a minimum amount of serving equipment, and meets a wide variety of service needs, and a server can serve a station of many tables. The food is plated in the kitchen and individually served to guests at the guest's right with the right hand. Although in fine-dining restaurants where food is plated in the kitchen and brought to the table on a serving tray (further discussed in Chapter 5, Serving Food and Beverages), all food items are served to the left of the guest with the left hand and all liquids (soups and beverages) to the right of the guest with the right hand. The guest's plate should be presented with the protein in front of the guest in the 6 o'clock position. Typically, a server in a casual-style restaurant would be responsible for four to six tables and, in an up-scale restaurant the server should have no more than four tables so that the attention to all service details can be obtained.

There is also a type of American plate service that is used in fine-dining restaurants, referred to as "team service." When applying this type of service, servers have specifically defined jobs to give broad coverage to the dining room. A service team can consist of three or more servers. There is commonly a front and a back server and a server's assistant; there may be a Sommelier who would be responsible for wine or a Barista responsible for specialty coffees, espresso, and spirited coffee drinks.

Simply stated, the front server is assigned all the tasks that require full guest contact, including taking an order, suggesting menu items, and interacting with the guest

Type of Service	Who Serves	From What Side of the Guest	Food Presentation
American Service	An individual server is responsible for a set number of tables.	The right side with the right hand. Fine dining: the left side with the left hand; liquids and beverages, the right side with the right hand.	The food is plated in the kitchen on individual plates for the server to pick up, then serve the guest. Place the protein in the 6 o'clock position when applicable.
Butler Service	A server presents a platter to the guests, and the guests serve themselves.	The food is placed before the guest.	The food is served on a platter.
English Service	The host carves and passes the plate to the co-host or closest guest.		The food is served on platters or in soup tureens.
Modified English Service	A server carves protein for the guest, and the guest then serves himself the sides.	The food is placed by the server to the guest's left.	The food is served on a plate.
Russian Service	A server serves guests from platters.	The plate is placed in front of the guest by the server from the right with the right hand.	The food is placed first on a platter, and then on a plate.
French Service	A server prepares food tableside using a guéridon and serves it to the guests.	The server serves the food from the right side.	The food comes out on a guéridon or flambé cart and is cooked and transferred to plates.

TABLE 3.1

Comparison of Services

so that all their expectations are met. The back server will pick up drinks from the bar, deliver food from the kitchen, and place any flatware that is necessary prior to each course being served. The server's assistant, often referred to as the SA, pours water, brings or serves bread, and removes plates from the table as guests finish eating.

The advantage of this type of service includes constant attention to guests in the dining room. There is always at least one service person in the dining room who assists the guest and upholds the established service standards. It is also the most sanitary way to serve guests—one service person handles clean plates and other service person handles dirty plates. When service teams are used, tips are usually divided among the team.

Butler Service

This type of service is provided during a cocktail party or during the cocktail portion of a banquet or catered event. Hors d'oeuvres and/or light refreshments are placed on handheld trays and offered to guests by servers. The guest will serve themselves off of the handheld platter, using a cocktail napkin. This may also be referred to as "flying service" or "flying platters."

English Service

Formal English service is taken from the traditional service in English country homes in which the head of the household acts as the carver and serves portions to family and guests with the assistance of servants. This type of service is often used in homes during holidays such as Thanksgiving and Christmas. The head of the household (host) carves the turkey, ham, or roast and places an individual portion on each plate. The plate is then passed on to another person (the co-host) who adds potatoes, vegetables, and other food items. Once the plate is complete, it is either served to a guest or given to the closest guests to be passed along to other guests. When soup is part of the menu, it would be served in the same manner. That is, the host ladles soup from a tureen and either serves the guest or gives it to the closest guests to be passed along to other guests.

Modified English Service

The professional (modified) application in the catering and restaurant environment adapts the above technique to a less formal presentation. The server would carve a protein such as Prime Rib or Beef Tenderloin for the guest and place it on their plate. The guests would then choose their other food items from a buffet or platters set on their table by the server.

Russian Service

Russian service is sometimes referred to as silver service because there is an extensive use of platters and serving bowls that create a dramatic table. Servers will serve guests from the platters. Russian monarchy favored this type of service and introduced it to France. This service is not often used because of the sizable investment in silver service and the additional service space required to accommodate the platters.

French Service

French service is reserved for very formal serving. Over time, it has been modified and has come in and out of fashion. It is a service that requires special equipment such as a guéridon or flambé (see Figure 3.1). The guéridon is used so that a server can cook and plate food in front of the guest. This requires servers to have additional

FIGURE 3.1

Guéridon (Flambé) Cart in Use.
Photo by Gerald Lanuzza.

culinary skills such as sautéing and flambéing. This type of service takes a longer period of time to prepare and is associated with high-end dining where there are a limited number of tables, creating an intimate dining room atmosphere. The tableside service adds an element of showmanship that can be very dramatic. Guests enjoy this element of French service and are willing to pay higher prices to experience it. Some fine-dining restaurants serve certain menu items from a cart, such as a Caesar salad or flamed desserts such as cherries jubilee.

Each type of service has its own application, style of restaurant, and advantages and disadvantages (see Table 3.1).

Other Types of Service

Learning Objective 3

Describe the functions of family service, counter service, banquet service, and room service.

Several other types of service can be offered in conjunction with the restaurant's table service. They are family service, counter service, banquet service, and room service.

Family Service

This type of service is when the guests place their order and the food is served on platters, in bowls, or in tureens that are placed on the table. Guests make their selection and serve themselves using service utensils provided. This type of service can be used in a causal setting such as a Chinese restaurant or when there is a large, wooden salad bowl and there are platters of pasta placed on the table for the guests to share. Bread is typically served in a basket. It can also be applied to a more formal setting such as Classic Afternoon Tea or elegant Tapas with the use of a tiered three-plate stand. For classical tea, each of the three courses—finger sandwiches, sweets, and scones—is placed on a plate in the tiered three-plate stand, as shown in Figure 3.2, and the guests serve themselves each course from the plates using small tongs and individual plates. For tapas, the guests would order and then in a similar manner serve themselves on their individual plate. The server would be responsible for clearing soiled plates.

FIGURE 3.2

Afternoon Tea Stand. Courtesy of Steelite International.

Counter Service

This is a quick service and is generally found in diners, cafes (coffee shops), or old-fashioned soda fountain shops. The service is informal. The counter server will typically be assigned 12–18 seats depending upon the menu and how quickly the seats turn over. The table settings will vary from no setting at all until the customer arrives or orders to a paper napkin with a fork, knife (blade turned toward fork), and teaspoon placed on top of the napkin and to the right of the counter seat as the customer would be seated. Or the table setting could include a place mat with the knife (blade turned inward), teaspoon to the right, and a fork and napkin to the left. Water is placed above and slightly to the right of the tip of the knife and if coffee or tea is served, the cup and saucer or mug is placed to the right of the teaspoon with the handle angled at 4 o'clock. Condiments are usually within easy reach for the server, as are napkins, flatware, water glasses, ice, coffee cups or mugs, and tote boxes (buss tubs) for placing dirty dishes, flatware, glasses, and coffee cups or mugs. The buss tubs are usually placed under the counters. The service pace is typically fast and the server is required to be conscious of keeping the condiments full and wiped clean, and maintaining an adequate supply of napkins, flatware, water glasses, and coffee cups or mugs. The tote boxes (buss tubs) need to be removed quickly to the dishwashing area and replaced with clean tote boxes. This may be either the server's responsibility or that of an assigned buss person. The guest check is given to the customer face down once the meal is served. Due to the nature of the service, customer tipping usually ranges from 10 to 15 percent and in some cases 20 percent or higher.

Banquet Service

This type of service can accommodate any size group ranging from one dozen to an unlimited number of guests. Banquet service is most commonly used for large groups of people celebrating an event together. The capacity of the banquet room will dictate the maximum number of people who can be served. A banquet menu can be limited and served quickly, or it may consist of several courses, elaborately presented and served. It may be a traditional breakfast, lunch, or dinner menu. The nature of the event typically influences the menu, such as a wedding reception, birthday party, anniversary party, bar or bat mitzvah, Christmas or New Year's Eve party, business awards luncheon, retirement dinner, or any other special occasion. Chapter 10, Banquet, Catering, and Buffet Management, presents the details.

Room Service

Many hotels and motels offer room service. The guests select from a room service menu and place their order through the hotel's website or over the telephone. The order is delivered to the room typically within 10–30 minutes from the time the order is placed. Delivery times can also be scheduled with advance ordering, such as for breakfast that could be ordered the night before. The food is placed on a service tray or rolling table cart as shown in Figure 3.3 and brought to the room from the kitchen by a server. Hot food plates are always covered to keep the food warm. The server has the added responsibility to double-check the order for its appearance and completeness along with bringing the appropriate condiments. When the server arrives at the room, they knock on the door and announce, "Room Service." The server, once having been admitted to the room, will typically set the table and serve the food. The cost of the meal is usually charged to the room, with the guest signing the guest check and either writing in a tip amount or giving a cash tip to the server. The tip will generally be 20 percent or higher. There are some operations that identify an automatic gratuity (service charge) on the room service menu. It is also common for the house to retain a portion of this charge, thereby sharing the gratuity (service charge) with the room service server.

FIGURE 3.3

Room Service Table Cart. Courtesy of Lakeside Manufacturing.

Salad Bars

Learning Objective 4

Know the range of foods that can be offered on salad bars.

The server, once having taken the guests' food and beverage orders, invites them to visit the self-serve salad bar. On occasion, a guest may request the server to prepare and serve their salad with choice of salad dressing. Salad bars can be limited to lettuce and a few fresh vegetables, or have extensive offerings that include fresh fruits, sliced and grated cheeses, a variety of prepared salads, anchovies, pickled herring, seasoned croutons, bacon bits, assorted crackers, and bread sticks. The server keeps the water glasses full and serves the guests' beverages while the guests are eating their salads. When the meal is ready to be served, the server removes the salad plates and forks if the guests are finished.

Dessert Tables and Trays

Learning Objective 5

Explain how dessert tables and trays function.

Desserts can be attractively presented and displayed in several ways. Dessert tables are typically set up for guests to serve themselves at a buffet or catered event. Desserts may be plated or dessert plates may be at the dessert table for guests to plate the dessert item they select. When a handheld dessert tray is used, a variety of dessert offerings may be shown to the guests on the tray. As a server walks the tray through the dining room, guests who are eating their meals may be enticed with the possibility of ordering dessert.

Setting a Table

Learning Objective 6

Explain the proper placement of a tablecloth on a table being prepared to serve guests.

A table can be set with a tablecloth or place mats along with presetting salt and pepper shakers, and sugar and creamers.

Tablecloths should always properly fit tables and drape approximately 1 inch above the chairs where guests will be seated. Before table settings are placed, the tablecloths must be clean and free of any spots or stains. The seam should face in. There are standard-size tables that require standard linen sizes. Most restaurants choose white linens for their tables because it adds a classical elegance to a dining room as shown in Figure 3.4. Many other types of colored linen can be used for special occasions and for catering as shown in Figure 3.5a–d. Figure 3.14 shows Tablecloth Sizes.

Place mats may be used for breakfast to clear and reset tables quickly or in casual dining rooms. When place mats are used on rectangular tables, they should

FIGURE 3.4
Classic White Tablecloth. Courtesy of SDI Brands.

(a)

(b)

(c)

(d)

FIGURE 3.5
(a) Checkered Square Tablecloth with Pointing-Up Napkins. (b) Tablecloth Topper and Border. Theme Tablecloths: (c) Concord Valence and (d) Fiesta. Courtesy of SDI Brands.

FIGURE 3.6
Place Mat—Table Setting. Courtesy of SDI Brands.

**Learning
Objective 7**

Understand
when place mats
are used.

**Learning
Objective 8**

Determine how
many salt and
pepper shakers
to place at each
table and when
they should
be removed,
along with how
many sugar and
creamer sets
to place on the
table and when
to place them,
whenever coffee
or tea is served.

be placed approximately one-half inch from the edge of the table. For round tables, rectangular place mats should be placed so that the corners of the place mat are one-half inch from the edge of the table. Place mats of varying shapes and sizes, such as oblong, oval, round, and so forth should be placed accordingly. Figure 3.6 is an example of a place mat setting for casual dining.

Salt and pepper shakers should be preset according to the number of guests at each table, typically one set per four to six persons, depending upon the menu. It is important to recognize also that some restaurants may choose not to preset salt and pepper shakers, but to bring them to the table as needed. As a general rule, they are removed after the main course. *Sugar bowls and creamers* are placed just prior to coffee or tea being served, although some fast casual restaurants preset sugar bowls and non-dairy creamers during peak serving times.

Bread and Butter

**Learning
Objective 9**

Explain the dif-
ferent ways that
bread and butter
can be served.

The *bread plate* is placed about 1 inch above the tines of the fork, but may also be placed to the left of the salad fork in order to accommodate another plate or bowl. For example, a restaurant serving shellfish may use a waste plate or small bowl located above the tines of the fork for guests' convenience in placing seafood shells.

Bread and butter may be served in several different ways, according to the policy of the restaurant. For example:

- A roll and slice of butter placed on a bread and butter plate for each guest prior to their arrival.
- Rolls in a basket and butter slices or balls in a dish for guests to serve themselves. The rolls may be served warm.

- Rolls and butter served to each guest by the server. This is typically done so that the rolls can be served hot. A server would use tongs or use the pincing method to serve bread in this manner. The pincing method requires a server to have a high skill level. If the server chooses the pincing method, they would hold a service set in one hand with the spoon on the bottom and the fork on the top.
- A small loaf of bread served on a cutting board with a bread knife, accompanied by a dish with butter slices.

Bread baskets and butter plates should be placed in a convenient location on the table when served.

Side Dishes and Condiments

Learning Objective 10

Understand how to place side dishes and condiments on a table.

Side dishes, such as a side order of mushrooms or creamed spinach, **and condiments**, such as Worcestershire sauce or Dijon mustard, may be placed in a convenient location on the table when served. It is best to place any jarred or bottled condiment on a small plate topped with a paper doily. This will allow the guests to easily pass the condiments to each other. The use of a doilied plate should also be applied to any items that more than one guest at the table will use—an example would be cream for coffee.

Flatware Placement

Learning Objective 11

Explain and demonstrate correct flatware placement.

It is important that a server understand the correct placement of flatware on a table. First and foremost, flatware is placed on a table so that the guest will use the flatware from the outside in. The first piece of flatware used is the flatware on the outside of the place setting. The forks, knives, and teaspoons are set approximately 1 inch from the edge of the table.

Forks are placed on the left of the place setting.

Knives and spoons are placed on the right of the place setting; the blade of the knife faces in.

Specialty knives for steak or fish are placed to the right of the knife, followed by the spoons; the blade of the knife faces in.

Butter knife is placed in the vertical position (parallel to the fork) on the right half of the bread plate; the blade of the butter knife faces left (outward) from the place setting. The butter knife may also be placed in a horizontal position across and on the upper half of the bread plate; the blade of the butter knife faces the tines of the fork.

Dessert Flatware is placed on the top of the place setting with the fork on the bottom and the spoon on the top. The handles face in the direction in which the flatware would be placed in the setting. Dessert flatware is used for a formal dinner, a banquet setting, or prix fixe (fixed price) menu. The small dessert spoon (or demitasse spoon) may be used for dessert or an intermezzo course that would be served during an upscale dinner. The intermezzo is often served between salad and the entrée. The intermezzo typically consists of a small portion of citrus-flavored sorbet. The purpose of the sorbet is to cleanse the palate of strong flavors.

Cocktail or seafood (lobster) fork is placed to the right of the teaspoon or may be conveniently placed when the item is served. The fork is used to remove seafood such as lobster, clams, mussels, and oysters from the shell. Some elegant classic restaurants may also have specialty flatware that is made for fish. This fork and knife has a unique design to help guests eat the delicate flaky flesh of the fish. This type of restaurant may also serve escargot in the shell that would require an *escargot tong*, specially designed for this use.

Pasta spoon is placed on the right. This may vary according to the policy of the restaurant.

To be able to identify the most commonly used flatware pieces, refer to Figure 3.7.

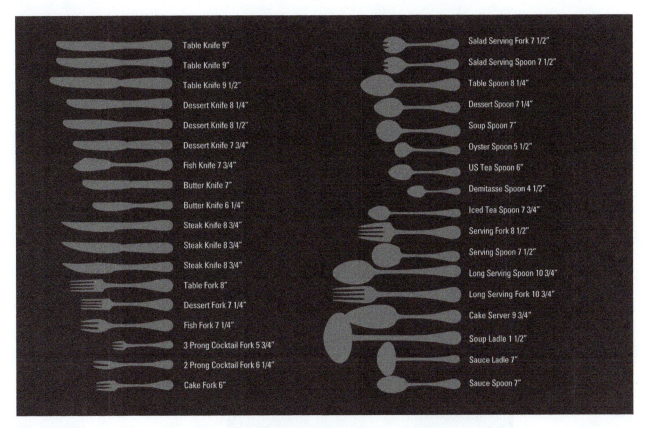

FIGURE 3.7

Commonly Used Flatware Pieces. Courtesy of Steelite International.

Glassware Placement

Learning Objective 12

Describe and demonstrate correct glassware placement.

The *water glass* is placed approximately 1 to 2 inches to the right of the tip of the knife. Glassware should be held by the stem for stemmed glasses or by the sides for glasses without stems and never by the rim of the glass, and should always be spotless when placed on the table.

Wine glasses When wine is served, the water glass is moved above and slightly to the left of the knife. The wine glass is placed above and slightly to the right of the knife. A wine would accompany one course of the meal and a second wine another course. There are fine-dining occasions when different wines are served with corresponding courses of the meal. Thus, a five-course meal could have five different wines. At the completion of each course, that glass would be removed. Figure 3.8 shows different glass shapes.

The wine glasses are set in order of use. Therefore, if a white wine was served first, the glass would be positioned to the right of the knife. White wine glasses are normally taller and narrower by design. If the second wine were a red wine, the glass would be positioned above the tip of the knife. Red wine glasses have a balloon-like shape that helps the wine to "breathe" by exposing more of its surface area. The balloon-like shape allows the guest to swirl the wine in the glass as it reacts with air.

When champagne is served, it would be positioned above and slightly to the right of the knife. If served with wine, the glass would be placed above the wine and slightly to the right of the water glass. Champagne glasses have a slim, flute-shape design that keeps the champagne from losing its bubbles too quickly.

When a before-dinner cocktail or after-dinner liqueur is ordered, it would be served centered between the fork and knife, about 3 inches from the edge of the table.

FIGURE 3.8
Glass Shapes. Courtesy of Steelite International.

Cup and Saucer

The *cup and saucer* are placed to the right of the teaspoons, approximately 1 to 3 inches from the edge of the table (depending upon the policy of the restaurant) with the handle angled at 4 o'clock (some prefer the handle angled at 3 or 5 o'clock). Cups should be spotless and held by the handle and never by the rim of the cup.

When a mug is used in place of a cup and saucer, the mug is often placed approximately 2 inches to the right of the teaspoon and 3 inches from the edge of the table.

Table Settings

Learning Objective 13

Explain traditional breakfast, lunch, dinner, and formal dinner table settings.

The following table setting diagrams represent the traditional settings for breakfast, lunch, dinner, and formal dinner. However, there are restaurant operations that may have a more casual or formal table setting variation that accommodates their menu and pleases their guests.

Breakfast and Lunch Table Setting

Refer to Breakfast Table Setting diagram, Figure 3.9, and to Lunch Table Setting diagram, Figure 3.10.

There should always be approximately 12 inches between the fork and the knife, depending upon the size of the plate that will be placed between them.

Napkin placement may be to the left of the fork or between the fork and the knife.

BREAKFAST

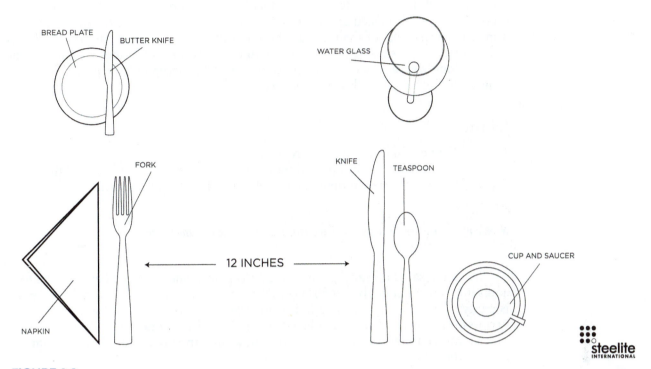

FIGURE 3.9
Breakfast Table Setting. Courtesy of Steelite International (DIAGRAM).

LUNCH

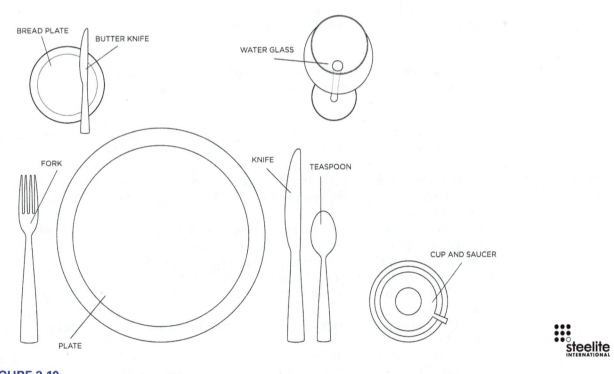

FIGURE 3.10
Lunch Table Setting Courtesy of Steelite International (DIAGRAM).

If breakfast toast is served, the plate is placed to the left of the fork and approximately 1 inch from the edge of the table. When the breakfast plate is ready to be served, the plate is placed and centered between the fork and knife, approximately 1 inch from the edge of the table as shown in the lunch table setting. If side dishes are ordered, such as a side of pancakes with breakfast or onion rings with lunch, the dishes, along with any accompanying condiments can acceptably be placed in a convenient location on the table when served.

Dinner Table Setting

Refer to Dinner Table Setting, Figure 3.11.

There should always be approximately 12 inches between the fork and the knife, depending upon the size of the plate that will be placed between them.

Napkin placement *may be to the left of the fork or between the fork and the knife.*

When the salad is ready to be served, it is placed and centered between the fork and knife, approximately 1 inch from the edge of the table. When the dinner plate is ready to be served, and the guest is not finished with the salad, with the guest's permission, the salad plate is placed to the left of the forks. The dinner plate is placed and centered between the fork and knife, approximately 1 inch from the edge of the table.

Formal Dinner Table Setting

Refer to Formal Dinner Table Setting, Figure 3.12.

Formal dinner settings often include a decorative service plate that will be removed and replaced with the actual plated entrée. At times, depending upon the menu, a salad plate or soup bowl may be set on top of the service plate, which is later removed with the salad plate or soup bowl.

Napkin placement *is centered between the fork and the knife or the napkin is placed at the center of a decorative service plate and removed by the guest or server when the guest is seated.*

When the salad is ready to be served, it is placed and centered between the fork and knife, approximately 1 inch from the edge of the table. When the dinner plate is ready to be served, and the guest is not finished with the salad, with the guest's permission, the salad plate is placed to the left of the forks. The dinner plate is placed and centered between the fork and knife, approximately 1 inch from the edge of the table.

When an appetizer such as shrimp cocktail or soup such as consommé royale is served, it is placed and centered between the fork and knife, approximately 1 inch from the edge of the table. The appropriate flatware, such as a cocktail fork or soupspoon, is conveniently placed when the item is served, or the cocktail fork may be placed to the left of the salad fork and the soupspoon may be placed to the right of the teaspoon.

The number of courses in a given formal dinner menu determines the number of forks, knives, and spoons that are selected for a preset table. Therefore, a seven-course meal may require five forks, four knives, a soupspoon, and three teaspoons. The rule to follow is that flatware is placed in order of usage from the outside inward.

DINNER

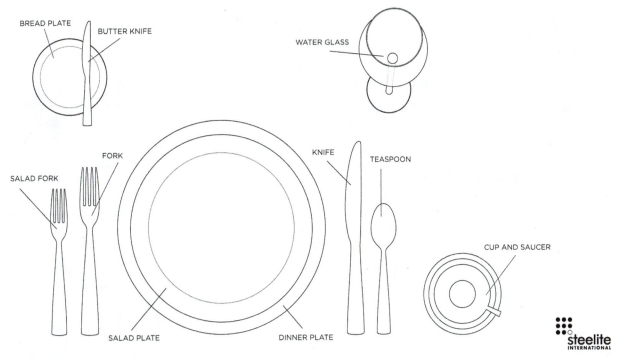

FIGURE 3.11
Dinner Table Setting. Courtesy of Steelite International (DIAGRAM).

FORMAL DINNER

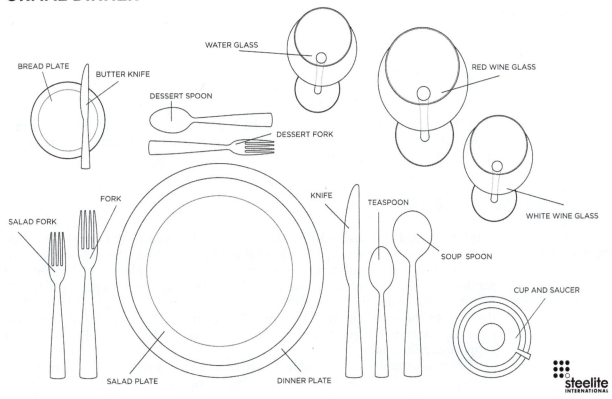

FIGURE 3.12
Formal Dinner Table Setting. Courtesy of Steelite International (DIAGRAM).

(a) Breakfast Table Setting.

(b) Lunch Table Setting.

(c) Dinner Table Setting.

(d) Formal Dinner Table Setting.

Photos by Dwayne Philibert.

Plates should be held by placing the hand at the bottom of a plate with the thumb at the rim for balance, but never on the plate. This is further explained and illustrated in Chapter 5, Serving Food and Beverages.

Napkin Presentations

Learning Objective14

Demonstrate a range of napkin folds.

Napkins folded in a distinctive pattern can further add to the professional look of the tabletop place setting. Napkin folds can range from the simple flat fold to any one of the more elaborate folds. The napkin can be placed in the center of a service plate, or if a service plate is not used, the napkin can take its place. The server should be acquainted with the most popular folds and develop the ability to do them as shown in Figure 3.13. For short, instructional videos that explain and demonstrate many different napkin folds, go to www.millikentablelines.com/en-us/support/napkin-folding.

Restaurant tables are available is different sizes and each table size requires an appropriate sized tablecloth, as shown in Figure Figure 3.14.

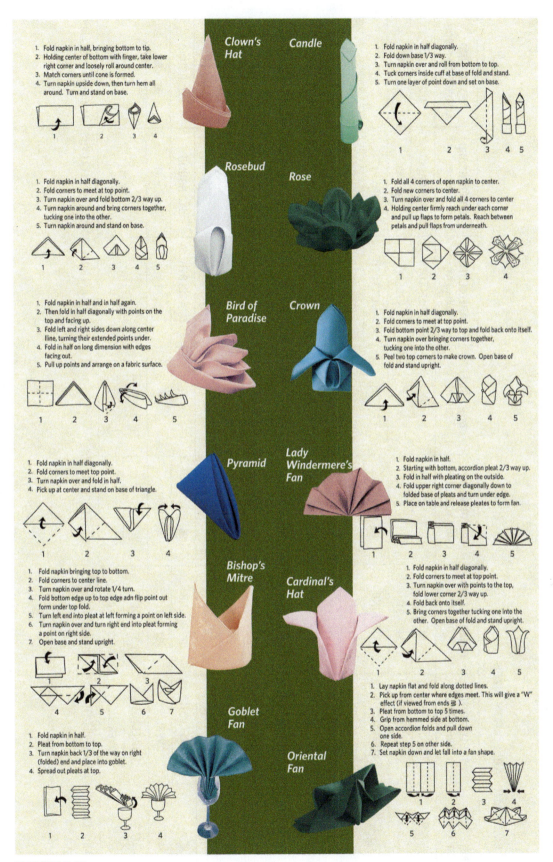

Clown's Hat

1. Fold napkin in half, bringing bottom to tip.
2. Holding center of bottom with finger, take lower right corner and loosely roll around center.
3. Match corners until cone is formed.
4. Turn napkin upside down, then turn hem all around. Turn and stand on base.

Candle

1. Fold napkin in half diagonally.
2. Fold down base 1/3 way.
3. Turn napkin over and roll from bottom to top.
4. Tuck corners inside cuff at base of fold and stand.
5. Turn one layer of point down and set on base.

Rosebud

1. Fold napkin in half diagonally.
2. Fold corners to meet at top point.
3. Turn napkin over and fold bottom 2/3 way up.
4. Turn napkin around and bring corners together, tucking one into the other.
5. Turn napkin around and stand on base.

Rose

1. Fold all 4 corners of open napkin to center.
2. Fold new corners to center.
3. Turn napkin over and fold all 4 corners to center.
4. Holding center firmly reach under each corner and pull up flaps to form petals. Reach between petals and pull flaps from underneath.

Bird of Paradise

1. Fold napkin in half and in half again.
2. Then fold in half diagonally with points on the top and facing up.
3. Fold left and right sides down along center lline, turning their extended points under.
4. Fold in half on long dimension with edges facing out.
5. Pull up points and arrange on a fabric surface.

Crown

1. Fold napkin in half diagonally.
2. Fold corners to meet at top point.
3. Fold bottom point 2/3 way to top and fold back onto itself.
4. Turn napkin over bringing corners together, tucking one into the other.
5. Peel two top corners to make crown. Open base of fold and stand upright.

Pyramid

1. Fold napkin in half diagonally.
2. Fold corners to meet top point.
3. Turn napkin over and fold in half.
4. Pick up at center and stand on base of triangle.

Lady Windermere's Fan

1. Fold napkin in half.
2. Starting with bottom, accordion pleat 2/3 way up.
3. Fold in half with pleating on the outside.
4. Fold upper right corner diagonally down to folded base of pleats and turn under edge.
5. Place on table and release pleats to form fan.

Bishop's Mitre

1. Fold napkin bringing top to bottom.
2. Fold corners to center line.
3. Turn napkin over and rotate 1/4 turn.
4. Fold bottom edge up to top edge adn flip point out form under top fold.
5. Turn left end into pleat at left forming a point on left side.
6. Turn napkin over and turn right end into pleat forming a point on right side.
7. Open base and stand upright.

Cardinal's Hat

1. Fold napkin in half diagonally.
2. Fold corners to meet at top point.
3. Turn napkin over with points to the top, fold lower corner 2/3 way up.
4. Fold back onto itself.
5. Bring corners together tucking one into the other. Open base of fold and stand upright.

Goblet Fan

1. Fold napkin in half.
2. Pleat from bottom to top.
3. Turn napkin back 1/3 of the way on right (folded) end and place into goblet.
4. Spread out pleats at top.

Oriental Fan

1. Lay napkin flat and fold along dotted lines.
2. Pick up from center where edges meet. This will give a "W" effect (if viewed from ends ⧢).
3. Pleat from bottom to top 5 times.
4. Grip from hemmed side at bottom.
5. Open accordion folds and pull down one side.
6. Repeat step 5 on other side.
7. Set napkin down and let fall into a fan shape.

FIGURE 3.13

Napkin Folds. Courtesy of Milliken & Company.

TABLE SIZES AND TABLECLOTH SIZES

TABLE SIZE/SHAPE	TABLECLOTH/OVERLAY	FOR STANDARD DROP	FOR ROUND 30" DROP TO FLOOR
24" (square)	TABLECLOTH	44" x 44"	
	OVERLAY	31" x 31"	
24" (round)	TABLECLOTH	44" ROUND	84" ROUND
	OVERLAY	31" x 31"	60" x 60"
30" (square)	TABLECLOTH	52" x 52"	
	OVERLAY	37" x 37"	
30" (round)	TABLECLOTH	52" ROUND	90" ROUND
	OVERLAY	37" x 37"	64" x 64"
36" (square)	TABLECLOTH	52" x 52"	
	OVERLAY	37" x 37"	
36" (round)	TABLECLOTH	52" ROUND	96" ROUND
	OVERLAY	37" x 37"	68" x 68"
42" (square)	TABLECLOTH	61" x 61"	
	OVERLAY	43" x 43"	

TABLE SIZE/SHAPE	TABLECLOTH/OVERLAY	FOR STANDARD DROP	FOR ROUND 30" DROP TO FLOOR
42" (round)	TABLECLOTH	61" ROUND	102" ROUND
	OVERLAY	43" x 43"	71" x 71"
48" (square)	TABLECLOTH	71" x 71"	
	OVERLAY	50" x 50"	
48" (round)	TABLECLOTH	71" ROUND	108" ROUND
	OVERLAY	51" x 51"	76" x 76"
30" x 72" (rectangle)	TABLECLOTH	52" x 92"	
60" (round)	TABLECLOTH	80" ROUND	120" ROUND
	OVERLAY	56" x 56"	84" x 84"
72" (round)	TABLECLOTH	90" ROUND	132" ROUND
	OVERLAY	64" x 64"	90" x 90"
30" x 96" (rectangle)	TABLECLOTH	52" X 114"	

NOTE: SOME ROUND CLOTHS MAY CONTAIN SEAMS

ACCEPTABLE DROP ON A TABLECLOTH IS 6" TO 12"; ROUND TABLE DROP TO FLOOR IS 30"

FIGURE 3.14

Table Sizes and Tablecloth Sizes. Courtesy of SDI Brands.

RESTAURANT REALITY: WHAT IS HAPPENING WITH TABLETOP PLACE SETTINGS?

A popular restaurant in a northeast American city will soon be celebrating its 75th anniversary of continuous operation under the same family ownership. Brian is the third-generation owner of the restaurant and has been successfully managing it for the past 9 years. The executive chef of many years recently retired and was replaced by Chef Andre, an award-winning chef who further adds to the reputation of this well-known restaurant.

The menu has always included several meat and seafood signature items, although Brian feels that the menu could be updated while still keeping those signature items. He asked Chef Andre for suggestions and was surprised when Chef Andre responded by saying, "Along with updating the menu, it might also be time to update the restaurant's tabletop place settings." This peaked Brian's interest and he wanted to know how the restaurant would go about making this change. Chef Andre was ready to explain how this could be done.

Chef Andre began by sharing the fact that he had been thinking of new menu items from the time he began working at the restaurant and was excited about the possibility of introducing those items to Brian and the restaurant staff. He complemented the existing menu and its traditional tabletop place settings, but further added that an updated menu with new items could be better served with tabletop place settings that framed the new menu. The new presentation would become part of the restaurant's identity and match the guests' expectations in reflecting the look and feel of the restaurant operation. In addition to being functional, the place setting would also meet service expectations.

The new menu items that Chef Andre presented included tapas plant-to-plate, small-plate signature menu items, and vegetable and pasta items in single serving shallow bowls. Brian and the restaurant staff were impressed with the new items and anxious to begin the process of selecting the new place setting service.

A budget for the new serviceware was established and an appointment made for Brian and Chef Andre to visit the showroom of a quality tabletop ser-viceware manufacturer. The manufacturer's representative inquired about the restaurant's menu, ware-washing system, and durability of its existing serviceware. Then the representative invited both Brian and Chef Andre to select from any of the items on display and begin by placing those items on the large table in the showroom. The various shapes of the glassware, plates, bowls, and flatware that would be unique to the restaurant and match guest expectations are selected by Brian and Chef Andre.

Brian and Chef Andre selected square and rectangular plates along with three sizes of shallow bowls all in gray-white. The different shapes and sizes framed the new menu items while the color complemented the restaurant's red tablecloths. They also selected stemmed water glasses and tasting spoons for appetizer plates. The new tabletop place settings were enthusiastically welcomed by the servers and earned the praise of the restaurant's loyal customers.

This is what's happening with restaurant tabletop place settings!

Summary

There are five distinctly different methods of serving food. These methods are often referred to as service styles, and are as follows: American Service, Butler Service, English Service, Russian Service, and French Service. It is important to recognize that many restaurants have developed their own service style that includes various features from the different methods. This is typically done in order to accommodate the menu, atmosphere, image of the restaurant, and the nature of the clientele. Therefore, many contemporary service styles have evolved in today's restaurant environment. Other types of service include family service, counter service, banquet service, and room service.

The knowledge of the various items that could be included in salad bars along with how desserts could be presented on dessert tables and trays is essential for the server. To correctly place and position a tablecloth, and when place mats are used (along with the correct number of salt and pepper shakers and sugar and creamers to bring to a table) are all the details a server must know. The different ways of serving bread and butter should also be understood.

Server training begins with an understanding and demonstrated ability of how to prepare correct table settings for breakfast, lunch, dinner, and a formal dinner prior to and as a meal is served. Also, the correct sanitary handling of flatware, glassware, and cups must be understood and adhered to.

Napkin folding is an integral part of a server's functions; therefore, the server should be acquainted with the most commonly used napkin folds and have a demonstrated ability to perform the folds.

Discussion Questions and Exercises

1. Contrast the similarities and differences between the five distinct methods of serving food, often referred to as service styles.
2. How many tables would a server usually be responsible for in a casual-style restaurant with American Service?
3. Explain the typical functions of a service team in a fine-dining restaurant.
4. When is Butler Service used?
5. Explain the difference between English Service and Modified English Service.
6. When is a guéridon cart used by a server?
7. Explain how counter service functions.
8. Describe the service procedure for room service.
9. When would Family Service typically be used?
10. List 10 different items that may be included on a salad bar.
11. Explain two different ways that desserts can be presented on a dessert table.
12. How is a tablecloth placed on a table that is ready to be set for serving guests?
13. When would place mats be used?
14. How many salt and pepper shakers would be placed on a table set for eight people? Explain the general rule regarding the number of salt and pepper shakers to be set on a table and when they should be removed.
15. When would sugar and creamers be placed on a table? How many would normally be set?
16. Describe three different ways that rolls and butter could be served to guests.
17. How would the side dishes and condiments typically be placed on a table?
18. Describe the flatware placement for a formal dinner.
19. Describe the two different positions that a butter knife could be placed on a bread plate.
20. Explain the glassware placement for a formal dinner when red wine is served first followed by white wine.
21. When champagne is served with wine, what is the proper placement for the champagne glass?
22. Explain the proper placement for a before-dinner cocktail.
23. Describe the correct placement of a cup and saucer.
24. When a mug is used in place of a cup and saucer, where is the mug placed?
25. What is the procedure to follow when the entrée is ready to be served and the guest has not finished the salad?
26. What determines the number of forks, knives, and spoons for a formal dinner setting?
27. Name eight different napkin folds and demonstrate how each one is presented.
28. Visit a restaurant of your choice, observe and evaluate the type of service method in use, and write a one-page summary of your experience.

CHAPTER 4

Service Readiness

INTRODUCTION

This chapter introduces the new server to service preparation techniques that will maximize guest service and reaffirm the importance of service readiness for the experienced server.

Once the server has mastered their many duties and responsibilities, they can provide the ultimate in service. The server is often the only individual who comes in contact with the guest; therefore, the guest expects the server to be fully knowledgeable about menu items and restaurant operations.

The server is responsible to ensure that everything that is needed to serve guests efficiently is in place before the guests arrive and after the guests leave, most commonly referred to as opening and closing *side-work*. Side-work is assigned to each server and should correspond to the station or tables that they will be serving during their shifts. Opening side-work helps the

servers prepare themselves for their shift. Closing side-work helps the restaurant prepare for the next shift.

In addition to side-work, there are ongoing duties during service that helps the restaurant run smoothly. This includes a detailed organization of each station and work area so that the server is better organized and able to provide quick and efficient service.

The server's efficiency will be measured by the care they take in performing those duties before guests arrive, during the meal service, and at the close of the server's shift. Additionally, *side-work* includes housekeeping chores that will ensure that every aspect of the restaurant is clean and spotless at all times. These can be done daily, weekly, or monthly. It also includes a detailed organization of each station and work areas so that the server is better organized and able to provide quick and efficient service.

CHAPTER 4 LEARNING OBJECTIVES

As a result of successfully completing this chapter, readers will be able to:

1. Comprehend the responsibilities that support good service.

2. Understand the importance of opening and closing side-work.

3. Describe the atmosphere and setting of a dining room ready to serve guests.

4. Understand how a menu is designed and functions.

5. Recognize guest's menu expectations.

6. Explain what a server should learn about a menu in order to best serve guests.

7. Understand the consequences of a dining room not fully prepared and ready to serve guests.

CHAPTER 4 OUTLINE

Responsibilities that Support Good Service

Opening and Closing Side-Work

Closing Procedures

The Dining Room

The Menu
    Breakfast Menu
    Brunch Menu

    Lunch Menu
    Dinner Menu
    Dessert Menu
    Tablet Menus
    Wine List

The Guest and the Menu

The Server and the Menu

Responsibilities that Support Good Service

Learning Objective 1
Comprehend the responsibilities that support good service.

The dining room manager, maître d', or host divides the dining room into work areas known as stations. The stations may vary in actual number of tables, but each station usually has approximately the same number of seats. Most restaurants have a diagram of the dining room showing each station according to a number such as #1, #2, #3, and so on. A number is assigned to each table and each guest's seat to ensure the correct food is served to guests. A server is assigned to a station and is responsible for a list of opening side-work duties at that station to prepare for serving guests. The server must also maintain that station during the shift (the meal period) and be certain to follow the list of closing side-work duties at the end of the shift.

Many restaurants rotate station assignments on a regular basis, even daily. The typical restaurant may have certain areas that are more desirable because of a view or location within the restaurant. Therefore, the station will generate more activity due to guests' requests. Some stations may include booths or counters or private dining areas that can seat groups up to 12 or more at one table. New, contemporary designed restaurants have often achieved ideal seating throughout the restaurant. For those guests who request the same server, seating is usually not a concern. New servers are often assigned to smaller stations or a station with less activity as they gain experience and confidence in handling larger numbers of guests and moving at a faster pace. Some restaurants have permanent station assignments for servers with seniority or for all servers based on good performance reviews.

As the dining room's business demands slow down, the number of servers on the floor is reduced to manage labor costs. Terms used for letting servers close out at different times during the shift are commonly known as *phasing* or *cutting* the floor. Zone coverage comes into play, as the remaining servers pick up tables in addition to their assigned station. In some instances, the dining room manager will close areas of the dining room to seating and seat only in areas where there is a server available.

The French term *mise en place* is occasionally used in fine-dining restaurants and means "put into place." The actual translation is the preparation of equipment and food before service begins. Specifically, each server is responsible for their assigned station and should check it thoroughly with a visual inspection before guests are seated, during the shift, and at the end of the shift. One should look from top to bottom that includes the following:

- *A quick glance up at the ceiling—a cobweb or birthday balloon may need to be removed.*
- *Ledges may need to be dusted or a foreign object removed.*
- *Light bulbs may need to be replaced.*
- *Shelves should be stocked with appropriate serving supplies.*
- *Countertops and tabletops should be immaculately clean with spotless table settings.*
- *Table bottoms should be completely free of any gum or sticky substance.*
- *Chairs, booths, booster chairs, and high chairs should be wiped clean and free of any crumbs, food particles, or grease.*
- *The floor should be swept or vacuumed and always safe, with nothing that a guest could slip on or trip over.*

Opening and Closing Side-Work

The importance of opening and closing side-work duties cannot be overemphasized. Many times, up to half of a server's time will be spent on these items that help to ensure better service for guests. This preparation always pays off during rush periods.

STATION 1
• Make coffee and tea—using diagram in pantry
• Fill creamers and place in refrigerator
• Place four underliners next to coffee machine
• Stock all coffee cups, saucers, and spoons

STATION 2
• Restock all paper products
• Put ice in all ice bins
• Fill the pepper grinders
• Polish water glasses; leave in racks

STATION 3
• Organize the pantry—see diagram in pantry
• Stock coffee and tea in drawers
• Cut four lemons—see diagram in pantry
• Turn bread warmer on and stock bread in warmer

STATION 4
• Polish flatware; fold napkins
• Clean and stock trays and tray stands
• Fill sugar caddies, salt and pepper shakers, and stock condiments on shelf

TABLE 4.1
Opening Side-Work

Learning Objective 2
Understand the importance of opening and closing side-work.

It can make the difference between efficient and inefficient service. Most restaurants have a checklist of opening and closing side-work duties, as shown in Tables 4.1 and 4.2. It is important to recognize that most restaurants will have side-work duties that are standard within the industry, along with duties that are unique to the individual restaurant. Servers must fully understand that side-work must be entirely completed in a timely manner. It is inappropriate for servers to complete side-work after the guests arrive. It is also unprofessional for a server to be catching up on side-work instead of giving the guests undivided attention. The sense of timeliness is a must for anyone who wants to be a successful server. A server should avoid the appearance of being rushed when guests are coming into the restaurant to dine. All opening side-work should be completed before the restaurant opens for business.

Each restaurant varies in what supplies are in inventory and what is kept at each service stand. Figure 4.1 shows an example of a typical service stand. The

STATION 1
• Return all coffee cups, saucers, and creamers from the dishroom
• Wipe all trays with sanitizer and stack to dry
• Wipe down shelves and drawers in beverage station. Remove glass mats and run through the dishwasher

STATION 2
• Clean coffee and tea machines
• Wipe walls and sweep floor in service station
• Clean coffee pots and tea pitchers

STATION 3
• Wipe the back of all chairs in the dining room
• Wipe the legs of all tables in the dining room
• Vacuum the dining room
• Stock all miscellaneous items

STATION 4
• Clean and sanitize all high chairs and booster seats

TABLE 4.2
Closing Side-Work

FIGURE 4.1

Service Stand. Photo by Gerald Lanuzza.

server should check that the correct items in the correct amounts are in a service station before the shift begins. If items are low or out, they should quickly be replenished. Proper planning helps to eliminate wasted time in having to fetch items during rush periods. The work area should be arranged to allow for the maximum efficient service with the minimum amount of wasted time, energy, and effort. Everything should be easily accessible. This will reduce or eliminate the amount of unnecessary bending, reaching, twisting, and stretching. Utensils and supplies should always be kept in the same place at all times and returned to the appropriate place after each use. This allows the server to pick up items without deliberate thought or effort during the height of busy times, increasing efficiency and conserving time and energy. The service stand will typically include some or all of the following items:

- *Beverages*: ice, water pitchers, glassware, straws, coffee, tea bags, teapots, cups, saucers, cream, half-and-half, sugar, honey, soft drinks, lemons, and limes.
- *Flatware*: salad/dessert forks, dinner forks, knives, steak knives, teaspoons, soupspoons, iced-tea spoons, serving spoons, ladles, tongs, and seafood (cocktail) forks.
- *Condiments*: ketchup, mustard, Dijon, Worcestershire sauce, A-1 sauce, Tabasco sauce, salt, pepper, sugar, and sugar substitute.
- *Breakfast*: jams, preserves, honey, and syrups.
- *Bread, Butter, and Crackers*: bread, rolls, crackers, bread and cracker baskets, bread plates, and butter pats.
- *Linens*: tablecloths, place mats, napkins (linen or paper), beverage napkins, children's bibs, and bar towels.
- *Miscellaneous Items*: pens, pepper mills, corkscrew, bottle opener, to-go containers, and guest check presenters.

The functionality of side-work coincides with the nature of the shift. The tasks, while similar, can vary in details from shift to shift; for example, baskets for jams and preserves during the breakfast shift could be used for bread or rolls at the lunch or dinner shifts. Servers will be assigned specific tasks for each shift to make the transitions smooth and efficient. Each restaurant will have guidelines for side-work, with some more formal than others. Assignments might be delegated by station or by the sequence in which servers start or end their shifts. In the long run, it takes organization and teamwork to get all the bases covered throughout the day's shifts.

Typical issues that may occur when *side-work* is not completed are as follows:

- During the lunch rush on a hot day, the iced tea runs out because the opening side-work function of brewing a 4-gallon backup was not completed.
- The guest wants A-1 steak sauce but it was not stocked in the service station the night before, so the server has to run to the storage room to get it and to bring out the correct number of backups.
- The server is getting three waters for a table but the glass rack was left empty in the service station. The server responsible for ongoing side-work during the shift is not paying attention to stock levels, not to mention whoever took the last glass and did not replace it with a full rack.
- The guest tries to use the pepper mill but it is empty. The server from the preceding shift did not complete the side-work of refilling all the pepper mills.
- A guest orders coffee but all the creamers are empty because the server responsible for filling 12 only filled 6.

Closing Procedures

These procedures are basically the same as the *mise en place* steps described under the subject of dining room preparation in reverse. Ultimately, the goal is to restock everything used and to clean the restaurant. Food and beverage products should be placed in their appropriate storage locations and food storage safety regulations should be followed. Primary attention should be given to securing the facility regarding safety issues: fire, water sources, security, and especially safe food storage. Again, these tasks would be assigned as described previously.

The Dining Room

Learning Objective 3
Describe the atmosphere and setting of a dining room ready to serve guests.

The dining room atmosphere can enhance or take away from the guests' overall experience. It is very important that each table in the dining room is checked before guests are seated. All tabletop items must be clean, stain-free, sanitized, and properly placed on each table as follows:

- *Tabletop tablets, as discussed in Chapter 8, The Technology of Service (if being used), should be clean and sanitized.*
- *Tables must be immaculate and firmly in place—they should not wobble to avoid any possibility of an accident occurring.*
- *Chair seats should be checked for stains or crumbs.*
- *The salt and pepper shakers should be clean and placed facing all the same direction.*
- *Flatware and glassware should be polished to avoid any spots and placed on the table according to the restaurant standard.*
- *Tablecloths and napkins should be uniform throughout the dining room.*

Once all the elements of the dining room are checked and meet standards, the restaurant is ready to open.

The Menu

Learning Objective 4
Understand how a menu is designed and functions.

The menu is the focal point of a restaurant operation. It is the number one selling tool and the first thing that a guest reads when determining what to order. Therefore, the menu should reflect the quality and style of the restaurant, use color appropriately, and look attractive. When a menu is professionally designed, it can further support the restaurant's general appearance and ambiance, thus creating a positive first impression. The menu should be well written, clearly organized, and include clear descriptions of the menu items. When selecting a menu font, the restaurant should consider the clarity and size of the font for easy readability. If a menu is soiled, frayed, bent at the edges, or poorly printed and hard to read, it can create a negative first impression. Therefore, the menu should always be written, designed, and printed in the best possible manner to achieve its intended objective, and it should always be crisp and clean when presented to the guest. Before the meal shift begins, a maître d' or host should look carefully through each menu and dispose of any menus that are unacceptable.

Common menu designs are bifold, tri-fold, or a one-page menu that always lays open in front of the guest. Each menu design has its advantages, but menus represent a sales tool to entice guests to order. The most profitable menu items are placed on the menu where they will be noticed and ordered by guests. The guest's eyes naturally go to the top and bottom of menus and to the right of a bifold menu. Special items are often highlighted by the use of colorful, creative fonts or boxes so that they stand out and are recognized as special. The way prices are placed on a menu is also very important; for example, if prices are placed in a column it makes it easier for a guest to look for the least expensive item, although some menus have prices following the description of each of the menu items. A restaurant will choose a menu design that best suits its needs. Menus can be an expensive item for a restaurant to purchase, so they must be carefully designed and well taken care of by the restaurant's associates.

Although management can create an effective menu, the individual who really determines the effectiveness of the menu for the guest is the server. It is up to the server to see that the guest understands what is on the menu. The server should be able to answer any questions the guest may have about menu items. Many guests rely on the server to offer suggestions that will enhance the enjoyment of their meal. A server should be comfortable with this task since it is a sign of menu mastery and effective training. Using sales techniques to sell the menu is one of the most important tasks the professional server has.

The server needs to be very familiar with the menu in order to guide and help the guest in making a selection. The server needs to know important details about each and every item on the menu—for example, the method of preparation, the major ingredients, and when and if substitutions are allowed. Furthermore, the server should know how to pronounce all of the words on the menu and be able to interpret them for their guest. Many restaurants have menu-training programs to ensure that each server understands and is able to communicate the menu to the guests. Basic verbal and written tests are used to gauge the server's understanding of the menu. This is an excellent and affective training program for any style restaurant.

Breakfast Menu

Most restaurants have a separate breakfast menu, unless breakfast is listed and served 24 hours a day or all of the hours that the restaurant is open. Generally, the menu consists of two sections. The first lists a combination of food items served at fixed prices, and the second lists items that may be ordered individually.

FIGURE 4.2

Brunch Menu. Courtesy of Dirt Candy; New York, NY.

Brunch Menu

The brunch menu typically includes breakfast and lunch items and may also include a selection of alcohol juice drinks and other beverages, as shown in Figure 4.2.

Lunch Menu

The lunch menu may have food categories such as appetizers, soups, salads, sandwiches, several complete entrées, desserts, and beverages. The menu selection typically includes several price levels, which are planned to cater to the wishes of different guest categories. Many restaurants feature special lunches such as the business lunch, lunch special, chef's suggestions, manager's special, or *du jour* (of the day) menu. These items can be printed on a daily menu, restaurant reader board, tabletop tablet menu, or announced to guests when they are handed the menu by the host or server. It is important that the server practices good communication skills when reciting any special menu items.

Dinner Menu

The dinner menu has an appetizer section and may list prices for complete dinners that include soup or salad and the entrée. There may be choices, of a starch, such as mashed, baked, French fried potatoes or rice, along with a choice of vegetables and possibly a selected seasonal vegetable offering. Also, the menu may have à la carte appetizers or add-ons that are individually priced, such as a signature soup or fresh sautéed mushrooms. Complete à la carte menus are becoming more popular; this type of menu allows the guest to order the exact side dishes that they like. The menu has a protein section, a starch section, and a vegetable section, from which a guest will select each item separately. Some guests may select one side, while some may select several. Some fine-dining restaurants offer a table d'hôte menu (prix fixe) or a tasting menu that is a several course meal for a predetermined price, as shown in Figure 4.3. A restaurant may also offer early bird specials in the late afternoon, with menu entrées reduced in price or a few different entrées offered at a price lower than normal. A restaurant may also feature dinner specials that could include chef creations or the fresh fish catch of the day. The host or server normally announces these items when the menus are handed to the guests, or the items may be listed on a reader board.

Dessert Menu

The dessert menu is typically presented in a way that is very enticing to guests. The description of each dessert item can tell a tale of great delight, and may include photos of the items as they look when served. The dessert menu often presents creative items from the restaurant's pastry chef along with suggested beverage pairings. Figure 4.4 is an example of a dessert and beverage menu that also includes after-dinner drink offerings.

Tablet Menus

Paper menus have been around since the mid-eighteenth century, and continue to dominate the restaurant industry today. However, as technology advances many restaurants are exploring the use of tablet menus to create an interactive experience between the guest and server that advances the service for the guest. This is further discussed in Chapter 7, Guest Communication, and Chapter 8, The Technology of Service.

There are many advantages to a tablet menu. A tablet can store much more information than a paper menu including detailed ingredients, a picture, and suggested beverage pairing. This information can increase the guests' confidence and leads to them ordering more than they may have originally set out to order. The use of high-resolution photos may entice guests to order things they may pass up on a paper menu. There are several devices that can be used to self-order, from a smartphone to tabletop tablets. Figure 4.5 is an example of a tabletop tablet.

Heirloom Tasting Menu

March 1, 2016

12-Courses $120 / 9-Courses $90 / 7-Courses $70 / 5-Courses $55 / 3-Courses $35

Vegetarian & Vegan Options Available By Request / All Courses Available A la Carte

1st Course

Cottle Farm Beets

Cackleberry Farm Yogurt, Terrece Orchard Pecans, Lucky Clay's Red Watercress,

Deal Orchard Cherry Vinaigrette ~ 7

Suggested Pairing: Shelton Riesling

2nd Course

Ayecock Brothers Baby Red Russian Kale

Cottle Farm Turnips, Cackleberry Farmstead Cheese #9,

Chef Foraged Black Walnuts, NC Red Miso Vinaigrette ~ 8

Suggested Pairing: Shelton "Bin 17" Chardonnay

3rd Course

NC Potage

Rosemary Pete's Kabocha Squash, Cottle Farm Turnips, Boyle Farm Onions,

UAV Browned Butter, Sunshine Cove Baby Kogane ~ 7

Suggested Pairing: RayLen "Carolinius"

4th Course*

Jarret Bay Oysters

"The Chef's Farmer" Ramp Vinegar Pearls, Sunshine Cove Baby Celery ~ 9

Suggested Pairing: Biltmore Blanc de Blanc

5th Course*

Napa Cabbage Wrap

Rosemary Pete's Napa Cabbage, Rowland's Row Grilled Chicken, Raven Rock Farm Black Radish, Cottle Farm Dill Pickled Yellow Wax Beans, House Made Gochujang ~ 12

Suggested Pairing: Shelton Sauvignon Blanc

Split Charge for Parties Larger than Two is $10 Per Guest

FIGURE 4.3

Prix-Fixe Tasting Menu with Suggested Beverage Pairings. Courtesy of Heirloom; Charlotte, NC.

6th Course

Harmony Ridge Egg Yolk Ravioli

Mountain Top Rabbitry Braised Rabbit, Rabbbit Jus, OBX Sand Cured Hoffman Farm Carrots, Sugar Creek Garden Henbit, Boyle Farm Red Onion ~ 16

Suggested Pairing: Biltmore Cabernet Sauvignon

7th Course*

Carolina Classic Catfish

ASU Biodynamic Farm Painted Corn Grits, Rosemary Pete's Chinese Garlic, Thai Chili Fish Sauce ~ 16

Suggested Pairing: Raffaldini Vermentino "Superiore"

8th Course

Carolina Heritage Cheshire Pork Scallopini

Dover Farm Kohlrabi Puree, Rosemary Pete's Spinach, Rowland's Row Put Up Tomato Sauce ~ 17

Suggested Pairing: Childress Sangiovese

9th Course*

Harmony Ridge Duck Breast

Dover Farm Crowder Peas, Coto Family Farm Carlton, Duck Jus ~ 18

Suggested Pairing: RayLen Eagles Select

10th Course

Cackleberry Farmstead Cheese #7

Deal Orchard Cherry Chutney, Herbed Flatbread, Sunshine Cove Baby Red Russian Kale ~ 9

Suggested Pairing: Shelton Port

11th Course

Spring Forward

Dover Farm Put Up Strawberry Cheesecake, Southen Belle Blueberry Compote, Graham, Lucky Clay's Lavendar Chantilly ~ 9

Suggested Pairing: Childress "Starbound" Blueberry Dessert Wine

12th Course

Chocolate Cake

Lineberger Farm Blackberry Chocolate Gelato, Blackberry Fluid Gel, Chocolate and Kumquat Sauce ~ 9

Suggested Pairing: NODA Brewery Coco Loco Porter

*Items are served raw or undercooked, or contain (or may contain) raw or undercooked ingredients.

Consuming raw or undercooked meats, poultry, seafood, shellfish, or eggs may increase your risk of foodborne illness

FIGURE 4.3

(continued)

Beverages

coffee

Coffee	$3
Decaf Coffee	$3
Espresso	$3
Americano	$3
Macchiato	$4
Caffè Latte	$5
Cappuccino	$5

We serve Intelligentsia coffee

selection of tea $3

Peppermint
SUPER MINTY

The du Hammam
FLORAL GREEN TEA

Grand Yunnan
Imperial
SMOKY AND MOCHA

Rooibos des Vahines
HERBAL RED-LEAF TEA

after dinner drinks

Bodegas 501 Cream Zurbaran THIS SHERRY DELIVERSA SAVORY, CARAMEL TASTE.	$12
Standing Stone Vidal Ice LIKE AN ICE WINE, BUT HARVESTED EARLIER, IT'S ALL HONEY & PEARS.	$14
Casa de Santa Eufemia 1973 Reserve Especial Blanco Port NV A 43-YEAR-OLD ORGANIC WHITE PORT, IT'S BRIGHT AND CRISP WITH HAZELNUTS AND CARAMEL.	$15

Single Malt Scotch

Macallan 12 year	$13
Bruichladdich Port Charlotte	$15
Balvenie 14 year Caribbean Cask	$19

Digestifs

Fernet Branca	$12
Amaro Ciociaro	$10
Pierre Ferrand Cognac	$16
Pear Williams Purkhart Eau de Vie	$12

FIGURE 4.4

Dessert and After-Dinner Beverage Menu with Suggested Beverage Pairings. Courtesy of Dirt Candy; New York, NY.

FIGURE 4.5

Tabletop Tablet that Allows Guests to Visually See Menu Offerings. Courtesy of Ziosk.

Wine List

Wine continues to grow in popularity and many restaurants have excellent selections of wine. Wine lists can be organized in many ways. A wine list can be organized according to the style of the wine, which means the wines are in categories such as red, white, rosé, sparkling, dessert, and fortified. A wine list can be organized according to the region or place that the wine comes from—for example, Champagne, Bordeaux, Burgundy, Alsace, and Rhone Valley; another way is to list based on the place of origin—France, Germany, Italy, the United States, or New Zealand. A wine list could be organized by how it tastes; a younger market may embrace and understand and appreciate this organizational method. The wine list will describe the flavor of the wine, such as dry, fruity, full-bodied, light, heavy, or smooth. A wine list may be the traditional paper menu or could be tablet-based to include more information on each of the wines. Some restaurants will employ a sommelier whose responsibilities include dealing with all aspects of wine and the wine list. The sommelier would be responsible both before and during service for the wine and wine list. Before service, the sommelier would select the wines for the list, order the wines, inventory the wines, and educate the servers on the wine list. During service, the sommelier would help the guests select the appropriate wine for their meal. The server should be knowledgeable about the wines and able to suggest appropriate wines to accompany the guest's meal, as discussed in Chapter 6, Beverages and Beverage Service.

The Guest and the Menu

Learning Objective 5
Recognize guest's menu expectations.

Guests naturally feel that the server should be able to answer their questions about the menu, such as, "What are the ingredients in a certain menu item or entrée? What does it include? How is it cooked and plated and how long will it take to prepare?" A guest may even ask how to pronounce the name of a menu item or sauce if the menu uses unfamiliar vocabulary. Therefore, the server is expected to have a comprehensive knowledge of the restaurant's menu, being able to answer questions and offer suggestions. The common menu terms (Glossary) lists many of the most commonly used terms to describe menu items and cooking procedures.

When new menu items and/or terms are introduced, the server should be eager to learn about them. The restaurant owner or manager should also schedule time for "menu meetings," informing the servers about the new items, and the daily specials that may be offered. These meetings usually take place 15–30 minutes before the meal period. This is a good time to allow the servers to taste any new menu items or the special of the day. This is an opportunity to have the kitchen and service staff communicate with each other and to discuss each other's needs. This is an important training tool that will give each server a personal reference for the restaurant's menu items, thereby making them an informed and enthusiastic salesperson.

If a guest wants only a light meal, the server should know the menu well enough to suggest an appropriate item. The same is true for guests who say they are very hungry and want a full-course dinner. Also, if the guest is in a hurry, the server should be able to suggest an item that will not take much time to prepare, which means that the server should know how much time it takes to prepare each item on the menu.

There are special types of menus that restaurants may choose to offer. A restaurant may want to participate in programs that identify the healthy choices on its menu. These programs list nutritional values, and grams of fat and sugar. There has been an interest by many restaurants to have smaller portions and healthier food items in response to guests' requests. Also, gluten-free and vegetarian choices continue to gain in popularity.

In addition to healthy menus, there may be a separate children's menu. If there are children seated at their table, a server should inquire if the guest would like to see the children's menu. A children's menu will have food items that appeal to kids. They are items that may also have quick preparation times so that small children can be served first. In addition, a restaurant may have selected child's portions from the regular menu at a special price. If a child orders an expensive item from the regular menu, the server should get a parent's approval by asking if this is all right. Parents usually appreciate this. If it is not all right, the server should be prepared to quickly suggest another item or two from which the child can choose.

There has been an increase in allergies; therefore, a good restaurant practice is to ask guests if they have any allergies or dietary needs when they make their reservation. Some of the most common allergies are from seafood, dairy, nuts, soy, and gluten. These ingredients are widely used in many menu items. Guests will ask servers many questions about ingredients to avoid an allergic reaction. A server should be aware of these ingredients and should always check with the kitchen for recommendations to make sure that the ingredients are not present in a guest's food. It is easy to make some adjustment to accommodate the guest. When transmitting a check to the kitchen, make it clear that the guest has an allergy to a specific item. It is always a good idea to double-check with the kitchen to make sure they leave off that ingredient. When serving the guest their meal, repeat to them that the ingredient has been left out of their food. For example, if the guest is allergic to dairy you can say, "Club sandwich no cheese." This was an easy accommodation that will help illustrate good customer service. It is important to have an allergy statement on a restaurant menu. A common restaurant allergy statement would be, "We will try and accommodate allergy needs, please inform your server if you have an allergy need." A menu may also have a statement about undercooked or raw foods: "Consuming raw or undercooked meat or seafood may be hazardous to your health."

Some menus may include a short history of the restaurant, the chef's background, the origin of some of the house specialties, historic sites, and information about the community that may be of interest to tourists, and perhaps a list of nearby recreational areas or activities. The server should be able to answer any questions that a guest may have about such things. Some local and regional tourist associations offer complimentary maps for restaurants to give to guests. This allows a server to offer additional service and help.

If a server cannot adequately answer a guest's questions about the menu, it weakens the guest's confidence in the server and reduces the opportunity for the server to suggestively sell other menu items such as wines, appetizers, salads, and desserts. The server may be reduced in the guest's mind to just an order taker. Therefore, the opportunity to increase guest sales and tips is lost. Some questions that a server may need to be prepared to answer are as follows:

"How is the pork tenderloin prepared?"

"What does the balsamic basil dressing taste like?"

"What is in the Satay sauce?"

"Can I substitute onion rings for French fries?"

"What is the difference between a New York steak and a Rib Eye?"

"What is in the Béarnaise sauce?"

"What are capers?"

"How do you pronounce 'gazpacho'?"

"What type of oil do you use for frying?"

"Flan sounds good, what is it?"

"Do you have a vegetarian entrée alternative on your menu?"

"How long will it take for the rack of lamb to cook?"

The Server and the Menu

Learning Objective 6
Explain what a server should learn about a menu in order to best serve guests.

The guest assumes the server knows everything about the menu. Therefore, the server should take the initiative to master the menu in order to be prepared to answer questions and give explanations. Here are some tactical points to consider when learning a menu.

- Begin by mastering the menu by categories. That is, know where the signature (house specialty) items, appetizers, salads, sandwiches, entrées, features, à la carte items, beverages, and desserts are located on the menu. As you respond to a menu item question, point to the specific item on the menu. As you read, the guest will "read along," following your finger as it moves across the menu description. Reading the menu description eliminates the potential of describing the item incorrectly, and through repetition, the server gradually gains a confident and comprehensive knowledge of the menu.

- Be able to identify the menu items that include soup and/or salad and the cost (additional charge) of the add-on items such as adding shrimp or chicken to the house salad that may be included with a dinner entrée.

- Know what (if any) beverages have complimentary refills, such as soft drinks or iced tea. Also, there may be a corkage fee when a guest brings in a special bottle of wine or champagne to be served with dinner.

- Understand cooking and preparation times. Since each item on the menu takes a different amount of time to cook, it is important to keep guests informed. An easy tip to remember is that items such as thick meats require lower heat and a longer time to cook than pasta items, for example. Also, the degree of doneness of meats can change the cooking times, such as a steak cooked rare (10 minutes) or well done (20 minutes). A server can quickly learn the cooking and preparation times through experience with the kitchen.

- Be able to identify when and if ingredients such as lettuce, tomato, onion, mayonnaise, pickles, and mustard are automatically included with sandwiches and hamburgers. If they are, mention it to the guest at the time the order is placed. The guest may choose not to have some of these ingredients or may prefer to have them served separately.

- Learn the ingredients of sauces and be able to describe their flavors. If a guest seems unsure about a sauce, offer to have the kitchen put it in a cup to be served on the side.

- Memorize the restaurant standard for the varying degrees of doneness in meat. Then be able to describe the degrees of doneness by color, such as the following:
  1. *Rare*—brown, seared crust with cool red center.
  2. *Medium Rare*—brown, seared crust, warmed through with a red, warm center.
  3. *Medium*—outside well done, dark brown with reddish pink hot center.
  4. *Medium Well*—outside dark brown, inside cooked through with little juice left.
  5. *Well Done*—outside black-brown and inside brown throughout with no pink.

- Become thoroughly acquainted with the portion sizes of menu items; for example, three large pancakes as big as the breakfast plate, shrimp cocktail served with five jumbo shrimp, broiled lamb chops with a serving of three 4-ounce lamb chops, or a hot fudge sundae with two large scoops of vanilla ice cream. A guest who expects a different portion size may be either disappointed or overwhelmed. Therefore, you should be prepared to describe the portion size when asked by the guest or when you anticipate the need to do so. For example, you should know that a full-size sub sandwich is 12 inches long. If a guest states that he is full from dinner and cannot pass up that hot fudge sundae, it may be appropriate to describe its size—two large scoops of vanilla ice cream. You do not want the guest complaining, "Why didn't you tell me it was so big?"

- Be able to identify what appetizers and entrées can be split for guests. Also, inform the guest if there is an additional plate charge when providing this service. An example might be when two guests are splitting an entrée such as a 10-ounce halibut steak, and they prefer not to split the baked potato, but request an additional potato. An additional charge of $5 may be appropriate.

- Find out the restaurant's policy and pricing for extra portions and substitutions. It is not uncommon for guests to request extra portions such as double the cheese on a cheeseburger, or to ask for a substitute such as cottage cheese for French fries. When this occurs, the extra charge for the double portion of cheese may be $1. The restaurant may have limits as to what will be allowed when substituting, and may not allow onion rings to be substituted for French fries. Therefore, the restaurant should identify the most commonly asked questions regarding extra portions and substitutions and have a clear policy for servers to follow. When a guest makes an out-of-the-ordinary request, you should make every effort to accommodate the guest, but you should first ask the manager for a decision.

- Know where to access information for recipe ingredients and cooking methods. Guests with dietary restrictions will expect the server to be able to answer their questions. They may have concerns about oils, butter, fats, sugars, dairy, and low-calorie ingredients, as well as foods that may be fried, grilled, or sautéed. Also, people on vegetarian diets will be very specific about not wanting any food item that contains animal or animal by-product. Some restaurants may have it implemented into a POS system as product management software further discussed in Chapter 8, The Technology of Service. At the touch of a button, you would find a list of recipe ingredients, cooking methods, and nutritional information, in addition to other related information that could be printed on the POS printer and given to the guest. There are various types of recipe management software that can also generate the same information.

- Become knowledgeable about the restaurant's cooking methods for various menu items, as guests will expect you to be able to describe those methods. The following is a list of common cooking methods:
    1. *Baked*—food is cooked in an oven with dry heat.
    2. *Boiled*—food is cooked in boiling water.
    3. *Braised*—a combination of dry and moist heat; usually cooking meat in a small amount of liquid in a covered pan, allowing the meat to cook in the moisture created from its own juices.
    4. *Broiled*—quick cooking by direct flame or heat. (Note: *Pan broiling* is cooking in a hot frying pan or on a griddle without the addition of fat.)
    5. *Fried*—food is cooked in hot oil or fat. Food is *deep fat fried* when it is placed or immersed in oil or fat at a sufficiently high temperature to brown the surface and cook the interior of the food. *Pan frying* or *sautéing* is done with a small amount of hot oil or fat in a pan, to which the food item is added.
    6. *Grilled*—food is cooked with oil or fat on a griddle, or cooked over hot coals (*charcoal grilled*).
    7. *Poached*—food is covered in water or other liquid and simmered.
    8. *Roasted*—food is cooked in an uncovered pan without moisture in an oven using only dry heat (similar to baking).

Learning Objective 7
Understand the consequences of a dining room not fully prepared and ready to serve guests.

9. *Sautéed*—a food item is browned and cooked in a small amount of hot oil or fat in a pan.

10. *Simmered*—food is immersed in a liquid and slowly cooked over low heat.

11. *Steamed*—food is cooked in steam.

- Memorize the definitions of the menu terms that name or describe food items and cooking procedures. Also, the pronunciation of the terms should be correct. It adds flair to the merchandising description. Refer to the Glossary, Common Menu Terms.

RESTAURANT REALITY: WORK SMART OR WORK HARD?

A Saturday night dinner shift is about to begin for a 60-seat restaurant located in a busy tourist community. The host arrives 30 minutes before the shift begins, greets her coworkers, and then goes to the host stand to inspect and count the menus needed for the night. She looks at each paper menu carefully and then informs the manager that eight menus are either stained or torn and need to be replaced. The manager thanks her and quickly goes to the office to print new menus. The servers are stocking items, checking inventory, and folding napkins at the service stand. When they each finish their opening side-work responsibilities, they go to their assigned dining room stations to do a final check of tables, chairs, and table settings. The servers perform the detailed tasks that ensure a positive, inviting atmosphere for guests.

The manager and host review the reservation list and take note that three reservations indicate special needs menu requests related to food allergies. Fifteen minutes before the dining room opens, the chef describes the nightly specials to the servers and makes several menu recommendations for the guests with food allergies. This will be a

busy night and the restaurant is prepared and ready to serve their guests. The evening ended with the restaurant having served a record number of guests, the busiest night ever and the dining room operated smoothly as guests left happy. The whole staff felt good about the evening and they finished their closing duties and said—"good night!"

In contrast, the same type of restaurant a couple blocks away had a different night. The host was late, so she did not check her menus; one of the servers neglected her opening side-work and instead was texting her friends to make after-work plans; another server did not check her tables, chairs, and table settings in her station and just assumed that everything was okay. The restaurant opened and their guests began to arrive. The first hour of the shift was steady and everything was fine, but into the second hour the restaurant became very busy. The host tried to seat a table of 12 but did not have enough menus; station #1 had crumbs in the seat of a chair that the guest had to brush out before sitting down; station #2 had a wobbly table; there was not enough half-and-half for

coffee; a guest was served food they were allergic to; and glasses in station #3 had spots on them.

The servers did not complete their opening side-work that resulted in mistakes that led to the following: Four guests, to their dissatisfaction had to share two menus; the guests in station #1 were privately questioning the cleanliness of the restaurant because of the crumbs in the seat; the server in station #2 was looking for something to stabilize the wobbly table while a food order was ready to be served for another table; the coffee was getting cold while the server was getting half-and-half; the guest with the allergy was served a second entrée but was not confident and was cautiously eating; the spotty glasses in station #3 had to be replaced but not before the guest had a negative first impression of the restaurant. The servers were frustrated, embarrassed, and exhausted. Overall, the servers wasted valuable service time correcting all the little mistakes that were made before service. They worked twice as hard and were unable to meet their guest expectations. Several guests left unsatisfied and would not return in the future.

Summary

The server has responsibilities that support good service. The server is responsible for a list of opening duties at their assigned stations to prepare for serving guests. The server must also maintain that station during the shift and be certain to follow the list of closing duties at the end of the shift. These duties are commonly known as side-work. The side-work includes housekeeping chores to ensure that every aspect of the restaurant is clean and spotless at all times. Each restaurant differs in what is kept at each server station, but the server should be certain that the correct items in the correct amounts are there before the shift begins, and again at the end of the shift.

The menu is the focal point of a restaurant operation. It should be well designed and project the image of the restaurant. The server needs to be totally familiar with each item on the menu, so that they can answer questions the guests may have regarding the ingredients, preparation, cooking time, and pronunciation of a menu item or a sauce.

Generally, there is a different menu for every meal such as breakfast, lunch, and dinner, along with a wine list. Menus are priced à la carte, with a separate price for each separate item and also as full dinners, which usually include a soup or salad and the entrée. A table d'hôte or prix-fixe menu includes a complete meal, from appetizer to dessert, for a fixed price.

The server can quickly master a menu by remaining alert, attentive, and focused upon the following: Mastering the menu by categories, that is, signature (house specialty) items, appetizers, salads, sandwiches, entrées, features, à la carte items, beverages, and desserts; identifying the items that include soup and salad, and the cost of add-ons; knowing what (if any) beverages have complimentary refills; understanding cooking and preparation times; learning the ingredients of sauces and being able to describe their flavors; memorizing the restaurant standard for the varying degrees of doneness in meat; learning the portion sizes of menu items; identifying what appetizers and entrées could be split for guests; finding out the restaurant's policy and pricing for extra portions and substitutions; knowing where to access information for recipe ingredients and cooking methods; be knowledgeable about the restaurant's cooking methods; and memorizing the definitions of the menu terms that name or describe food items and cooking procedures.

Discussion Questions and Exercises

1. When a dining room manager, maître d', or host divides a dining room into work areas, what are those areas known as?
2. Explain zone coverage.
3. What does the French term *mise en place* mean and what does it specifically refer to?
4. Explain how opening and closing side-work is assigned.
5. List 10 examples of various opening side-work responsibilities.
6. Identify five different categories of items that a service stand typically includes and give examples within each category.
7. Give two examples of what can happen when side-work is not done.
8. What is the goal of an effective closing procedure?
9. List five details that should be properly checked before a dining room is ready to serve guests.
10. Why must the server be totally knowledgeable about the restaurant menu?
11. Describe the differences between an à la carte menu and prix-fixe menu.
12. List five things that a guest could possibly ask the server about the menu.
13. If a child orders an expensive item from the normal menu, how should the server react?
14. List 10 things that a server should learn about a menu in being prepared to answer a guest's questions.
15. Describe what can happen when a dining room and servers are not fully prepared to serve guests when the dining room opens.

CHAPTER 5

Serving Food and Beverages

INTRODUCTION

A restaurant's table service is developed to meet guests' expectations and designed to anticipate guests' needs. The particular demands or needs of the menu and dining room facility are also taken into consideration when selecting the type of service to use. Each restaurant will follow the method best suited for its particular dining room setting and layout; this can be defined as *protocol* for that restaurant. An example of a restaurant's particular protocol could be the type of service it uses or the way it places an order in the kitchen. Some restaurants use guéridon service, for example, to execute tableside service, whereas another restaurant would not use this type of service because it does not have the space necessary to move the cart around the dining room. Another example of protocol would be to circle the woman's seat on the guest check to assure that she would be served first. A restaurant server must learn to follow the serving protocol exactly so that service will be uniform throughout the restaurant. This chapter presents the basic service techniques that have been adopted at many restaurants throughout the country.

In addition to protocol, there are certain practices that are considered basic etiquette. This means that it is always appropriate and desirable to practice these things. Some basic etiquette guidelines would be to serve women before men and the guest of honor before the host. These basic etiquette guidelines are based on tradition, but are still appreciated by many guests, who consider etiquette an important part of the dining room experience in any type or style of restaurant.

Each meal period has its own unique dynamic and requires a server to bring their skills in a different way to match the need of the meal period. During breakfast, fast and efficient service is essential because many guests are in a hurry. Service at breakfast may be limited to juice, toast, and coffee, or it may include a complete breakfast of bacon, eggs, hash brown potatoes, and a side order of pancakes. Breakfast can be a difficult meal to serve with guest satisfaction because this is the one meal of the day that many guests prefer to be prepared exactly like it is prepared each morning in their own homes. To fully understand and replicate a home-cooked breakfast for their guests, a server must listen carefully and ask appropriate questions when necessary. There are many ways to customize the meal for the guest. A breakfast server must practice excellent listening skills to re-create the guests' breakfast for them exactly the way they like it prepared. Guests may require limited interaction if they are not fully awake or do not identify as "a morning person." In addition, breakfast foods cool quickly so it is imperative the order is delivered to the guest in a timely manner.

At lunch time, it is also essential to serve guests as quickly as possible. Many times, guests have only 30 minutes to eat and get back to work. As a result of these time restrictions, many restaurants offer special lunch menus that are quickly and easily prepared. Other guests, however, may want to order courses. If an appetizer is ordered, such as a cup of soup or salad, place it in front of the guest as soon as possible. As quickly as possible after the first course is cleared, serve the entrées and side dishes. If the guest orders only a sandwich and beverage, whenever possible, serve the beverage first. It is acceptable to serve the beverage with the sandwich when the sandwich is quickly prepared and ready to be served. A server must practice their interpersonal skills such as maintaining eye contact when listening to a guest and asking the right questions so that every guest's service expectations are met.

In contrast, guests may want to linger over coffee or dessert after lunch to engage in business or celebrate a special occasion. Therefore, the server needs to exercise good judgment when asking whether a guest has any time restriction. A simple question such as, "Will there be time for a leisurely lunch today?" It is very disappointing to a guest with no time restrictions to feel rushed. The professional server must be able to accommodate guests with a range of service needs.

Dinner is generally more leisurely and allows the server to give guests special attention. However, at times guests may be attending an event later in the evening or have another engagement, and they may want to eat quickly. Therefore, the server should inquire as to the guest's time frame for dinner in the same way as the server does during the lunch hour. Often, dinner begins with a cocktail or two. Bread and butter should be served with the salad or brought to the table immediately following the order. The courses may include an appetizer, salad, soup, entrée, and a side dish. Coffee, espresso, or tea should be offered as well as dessert. The dessert can be ordered from a menu or a dessert tray. When dessert is served, beverage refills should always be offered. After dessert, the guest may want an after-dinner drink or spirited coffee.

As the guest check increases, guests' expectations will also increase. The more a guest spends on a meal, the more they will expect from a server. Therefore, each shift will require a skill base necessary to meet the guests' expectations at that meal period. For example, it would not be expected that a breakfast server would have extensive knowledge of wines and spirits, but it would be imperative that they know the many different ways eggs could be prepared. A lunch server would be expected to understand and explain basic

cooking techniques such as sauté, grilling, and poaching, but may not be expected to prepare a table side dish. A dinner server would have to have a broad and extensive knowledge of food, food preparation, food service, wines, spirits, etiquette, protocol, and, possibly, tableside cooking techniques. The dinner meal period is the one that the guest would typically spend the most money and expect to dine in a more leisurely manner. Because of all these factors, a guest's expectations for dinner are the highest.

Identifying the different serving needs at each of these meal periods helps to deliver the best possible service for the guests. A professional server will "read the needs" of their guests and exceed guest's expectations. Each meal time is unique and offers challenges for a server. By hiring well for each meal period and matching the server's skills to the meal-period requirements, a restaurant can have happy guests who return to the restaurant more often and recommend the restaurant to friends.

CHAPTER 5 LEARNING OBJECTIVES

As a result of successfully completing this chapter, readers will be able to:

1. Explain the general rules and techniques for proper table service.

2. Understand and explain service etiquette.

3. Know the procedures to follow for removing dishes and flatware.

4. Describe the proper way to serve guests seated at a booth.

5. Understand and describe the role of the bartender/server.

6. Understand, explain, and demonstrate how to correctly load and carry trays, including the large oval, small rectangular, and round beverage trays.

7. Explain and demonstrate the correct way to hold and carry wine glasses.

8. Define and recognize service priorities, including the importance of correct timing.

9. Understand and explain the responsibilities of a server's assistant.

10. Explain the procedures to follow in order to properly buss a table, using a cart or a tray.

11. Describe the proper protocol for responding to customer complaint issues.

CHAPTER 5 OUTLINE

Proper Table Service

Service Etiquette

Removing Dishes and Flatware

Booth Service

The Bartender/Server

Loading and Carrying a Tray

Carrying Glasses

Service Priorities and Timing

Server's Assistant (or Busser) Responsibilities
  Basic Responsibilities for the Server's Assistant

Table Bussing
  Bussing with a Cart
  Bussing with a Tray
  Setting Up with a Tray

Customer Complaints and Issues
  Food-Related Complaints
  Service-Related Complaints
  Guest Behavior Issues

Proper Table Service

Learning Objective 1

Explain the general rules and techniques for proper table service.

Professional servers traditionally serve food and beverages according to the following general rules and techniques:

1. ***Serve plates with the right hand,*** *approaching the table to the right of the guest.* Serving in this manner helps avoid accidents caused by a guest coming in contact with a server's arm when plates are being served. This practice avoids the server's arm crossing over or in front of the guest. Note: ***Plates will be served with the left hand,*** *approaching the table to the left of the guest* in many fine-dining restaurants where food is plated in the kitchen and brought to the table on a serving tray; refer to Figure 5.1. These restaurants serve all food items to the left of the guest with the left hand and all liquids (soups and beverages) to the right of the guest with the right hand.

   • Serve all plates by placing the thumb up or to the side of the outer rim of the plate and never inside, as shown in Figure 5.2a and b.

   • The way a server will transport a plate to the guests' table will be influenced by several key factors. If the plate is hot, a server should use a

FIGURE 5.1
Plate Being Served with the Left Hand in Fine Dining. Photo by Dwayne Philibert.

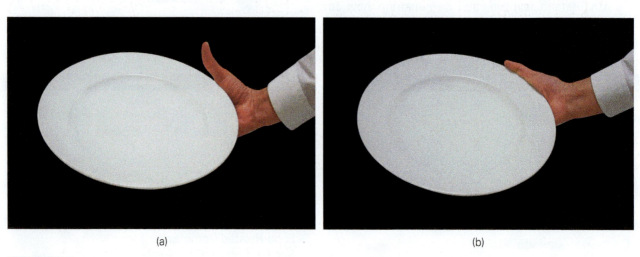

(a)   (b)

FIGURE 5.2
(a) Plate Handling with Thumb Up; (b) Plate Handling with Thumb to the Side of the Outer Rim. Photos by Dwayne Philibert.

service towel so that they do not burn their hand. The plate should be carried so that it is placed down in front of the guest with the entrée protein or main item at the 6 o'clock position. When an appetizer or dessert is served, it is placed directly in front of the guest.

Transporting multiple plates to the guests' table. Depending on the style of the restaurant, a server will have to transport plates to the guests' table. The server may use a large oval tray or hand-carry multiple plates as a function of service.

- Hand-carrying multiple plates is a skill that many restaurants expect their servers to use. It can be intimidating at first but it easily can become a skill that a server can master. The easiest method for hand-carrying plates is shown in Figure 5.3a–d, where a server prepares to hold three plates. The server could also carry a fourth plate in their right hand.

2. ***Serve liquids with the right hand,*** *approaching the table to the right of the guest.*

   Serving Soup. A cup or bowl of hot or cold soup is always placed on an appropriate sized serving plate and then placed in front of the guest.

   - The soup course is served after appetizers but before salad during a meal with many courses.

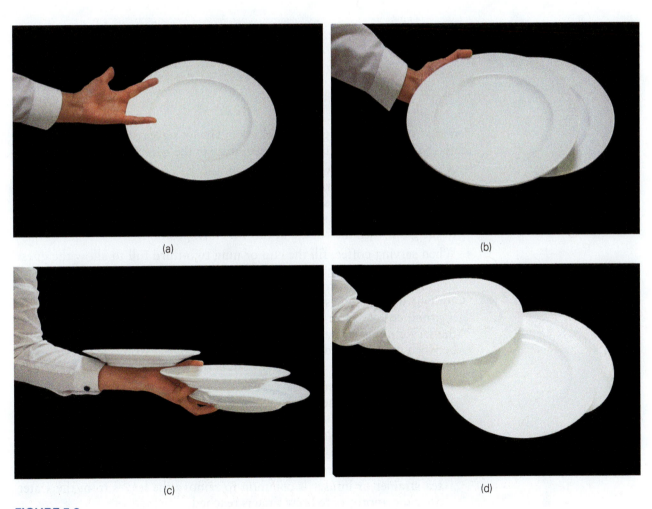

(a)   (b)   (c)   (d)

FIGURE 5.3

Holding Three Plates. (a) The First Plate is Held by the Middle and Second (Ring) Fingers; (b) The Second Plate is Placed on the Pointer Finger and Pinky and Balanced by the Thumb and Pinky; (c) The Third Plate is Placed on the Palm and Balanced by the Center of the Forearm; (d) Three Plates Comfortably Balanced on the Left Arm. Photos by Dwayne Philibert.

FIGURE 5.4
Coffee Server Pot. Courtesy of Service Ideas, Inc.

Serving Coffee or Tea. A good practice is to always serve coffee or tea in a warm tempered cup or mug so that the temperature of the beverage is maintained.

- A *coffee or tea cup* with a saucer should be carried by the saucer and should be placed in front of the guest with the handle in the 4 o'clock position; a teaspoon should be placed to the right of the guest or on the saucer. A *coffee mug* should be carried by the handle and placed in front of the guest with the handle in the 4 o'clock position.

- When serving coffee, fill the cup or mug two-third full to allow the guest to add cream and sugar, if that is their preference. Since it is the protocol of most restaurants to offer coffee refills, a server should first make eye contact with the guest and ask them if they care for more before refilling their coffee. To protect the guest from being splashed with hot coffee, the server holds a clean folded napkin or service towel with the left hand between the guest and the hot coffee being poured from the coffee server pot. An example of a coffee server pot is shown in Figure 5.4.

- When serving tea, identify the type of tea served and the restaurant's procedure for serving it. The most popular types of tea are white, green, oolong, and black. Tea can be served from loose leaves or tea bags. For both types of tea, the common accompaniments would be honey, sugar, lemon, and milk.

  - *Loose tea* would be infused in a pot of heated water with a warm tempered cup as shown in Figure 5.5. When serving loose tea, the use of a tea strainer or infuser is common to remove the leaves from the water after the appropriate brew time is reached.

  - When using *tea bags,* the restaurant may or may not have a tea box for the guests to select their packaged tea bags, according to tea preference, from the tea box. Then a warm tempered tea pot with heated

FIGURE 5.5
Tea Infuser. Courtesy of Steelite International.

water and a warm tempered cup with a teaspoon would be served to the guest. A small plate would be presented for the used tea bag.

Serving Iced Coffee, Tea, or Wine from the Bottle. There are many different types of glasses and each type requires a different service procedure. ***Stemless*** glasses, such as a highball glass or a stemless wine glass, should be carried by the base. Any ***stemmed*** glass, including a stemmed water glass or wine glass should be carried by the stem.

- Once glassware is placed in front of the guest, it is a good practice to refrain from picking it up to refill the glass. When refilling the glass, a server should use a splash guard (clean folded napkin or service towel) and refill the glass on the table (water, iced coffee, tea, or wine from the bottle) or bring a fresh drink in a fresh glass when applicable (cocktails, soda, or wine by the glass).

Serving Wine. Wine service is an important part of a meal and great care should be taken when serving a bottle of wine. After the guest orders wine for the table, a professional serving procedure follows.

a. The server presents the bottle of wine to the guest by showing the label. The server should then recite the name, vintage, producer, classification, and type of wine for the guest's approval.

    b. The bottle is then opened and served to the guest (who ordered the wine for the table) first by pouring about 1 ounce for tasting. Once the guest has approved the wine, it is poured for other guests, filling each glass half way full, beginning with the female guests, then male guests, with the guest who ordered the wine being served last.

- If the wine has been selected prior to the meal, as in the case of a banquet, the wine is served just before the main course. If more than one wine is served, the appropriate wine is served just before its designated course. Refer to Chapter 6, Beverages and Beverage Service, for additional information about serving wines and wine temperatures.

3. *Serving Bread or Rolls.* Restaurants will have their own protocol for serving bread, rolls, or crackers.

- When serving bread or rolls in a basket, the basket should be lined with a napkin. Bread could be served on a cutting board or placed on each guest's bread plate using tongs or the pincing method discussed in Chapter 3, Table Service, Table Settings, and Napkin Presentations.
- When serving butter to accompany bread, a fork, ice tong, or spoon is used.

4. *Serving Side Dishes.* Side order items such as a side salad, side of mushrooms, or baked potato would be placed to the left of the fork when served.

- When a salad is served as a course before the entrée and the guest desires to finish their salad with the entrée, then the salad should be placed to the left of the fork before the entrée is served, and a side dish would then be placed in a convenient location on the table for the guest.

5. *Serving Condiments.* The appropriate way to serve condiments would be on a small plate with a doily and placed in a convenient location on the table.

- The server should always ask the guest if they would like any condiments that might accompany the meal, such as ketchup, mustard, Dijon, Worcestershire, or steak sauce.
- Place any jarred or bottled condiment on a small plate topped with a paper doily. This will allow the guests to easily pass the condiments to each other. The use of a plate with a paper doily should also be applied to any items that more than one guest at the table will use—an example would be cream for coffee.
- When serving lemons, relishes, pickles, olives, or cheese, serve with a fork or spoon.

6. *Serving Shellfish.* A shellfish entrée requires a waste plate (or bowl) for the shells. The waste plate is placed above and slightly to the left of the entrée plate. The bread plate would be placed to the left of the fork.

- When serving lobster, place the lobster cracker to the left of the fork and the seafood (lobster) fork and place the pick to the right of the teaspoon. If a pick is not used, place the lobster cracker to the right of the seafood (lobster) fork. Place the dish of melted butter above and slightly to the right of the lobster entrée plate.
- When serving mussels or clams in a broth, a waste plate, cocktail fork, and spoon are needed.
- When serving an entrée with shellfish such as paella, a cocktail fork and waste plate are needed. Serving bouillabaisse would need a cocktail fork, waste plate, and spoon.
- When serving a shellfish appetizer on the half shell such as clams or oysters, a cocktail fork is placed to the right of the guest. A waste plate is not needed.

Finger bowls may be used at the end of the meal. Formal dining may include the use of finger bowls after shellfish or finger foods have been served. A small bowl filled with warm water on small plate garnished with a lemon slice is placed to the left of the guest. An additional napkin is also provided for the guest to wipe and dry their hands.

– Hot towels or packaged, moist hand-wipes may also be used.

7. *Serving Desserts.* A dessert is served by placing the item in front of the guest along with the dessert fork or spoon to the right of the dessert.

• Desserts may be ordered from a dessert menu or selected from a dessert tray. After the guest has indicated a choice of dessert, the server should appropriately serve the dessert from the kitchen or tray.

Service Etiquette

Learning Objective 2
Understand and explain service etiquette.

A professional server will always be aware of the host of the table and take great care to follow the guidelines for proper service etiquette. The host may or may not be predetermined. The host is typically the person who made the reservation.

• Everyone at the table should be served the same course at the same time, but a woman or older guest is served first as a matter of etiquette. When there is more than one woman or older guest present, the woman or older guest on the table host's right is first served. Then continue serving around the table clockwise, serving the table host last.

• When serving children, they should be treated the same as adults, but serve them first if the parents request they be served first.

• Always check the table setting for each guest to make sure that they have the necessary flatware for each course being served before they are served the food.

• The table host will be the person presented with the check upon conclusion of the meal.

Removing Dishes and Flatware

Learning Objective 3
Know the procedures to follow for removing dishes and flatware.

Some guests like to have their plates cleared immediately while others prefer a server to wait until all guests at the table have finished eating. It is best to ask the guest if you may clear their plates. The use of observation can also be helpful. Look for flatware that is placed in the closed position to know if the guest is finished. The closed position is when both fork and knife are laid across the plate on the right side. If a guest is resting between eating, the knife would be laid across the right side of the plate and the fork across the left.

• Dirty dishes should be taken to a side stand, a tray on a tray stand, or directly to the dishwashing area, and never scraped or stacked in front of guests.

• Completely clear all dishes, glasses not in use (leaving the water glass), salt and pepper shakers (if not normally left on the table), and condiments before serving dessert.

• Tables should be cleared of all crumbs before presenting the dessert menu or serving dessert. This is done by using a crumber (handheld scraper), a mechanical handheld vacuum, or a clean napkin. When using a napkin, it should be tightly folded or rolled; then remove crumbs or food particles by sweeping onto a plate, small tray, or into another napkin, not into the other hand.

Remove dishes and flatware from the right when each course is finished, using the right hand; then serve the next course from the right using the right hand. Exceptions to this rule are as follows:

a. When it will be inconvenient to the guest.

b. If the guest is leaning to the right to talk with another guest.

c. When serving a guest seated at a booth or next to a wall.

d. If there is a bread-and-butter plate on the right of the guest.

Booth Service

Learning Objective 4
Describe the proper way to serve guests seated at a booth.

Serving guests seated at a booth or next to a wall requires the server to stand at the end of the booth or table and serve the guests seated farthest away first. Therefore, the guests seated on the right would be served with the left hand and the guests seated on the left would be served with the right hand. This reduces the possibility of the server accidentally elbowing a guest. Refilling water glasses or coffee cups may require the server to pick up the glass or coffee cup to be able to pour safely.

The Bartender/Server

Learning Objective 5
Understand and describe the role of the bartender/server.

Many restaurants are experiencing an increase in the number of meals being served at their bars. A guest may be alone or with one or more friends who are drawn to the bar atmosphere for the possible view or just the "energy" of the bar itself. It may represent a faster service or simply an active setting that guests find enjoyable along with having the opportunity to, perhaps, share a brief conversation with the bartender. Some restaurants have guests who repeatedly sit at the bar for lunch or dinner because they find it to be a comfortable place. Guests enjoy the bar atmosphere many times because they are interested in sporting events that are on the bar's flat screen television. The bartender should know the restaurant's menu and be fully trained in basic service, including flatware placement, all types of beverage service, and dessert service.

Professor James Reid, Hospitality Management Program, New York City College of Technology, has worked many years in the hotel and restaurant industry, and has served as director of training and development for the New York Waldorf Astoria Hotel and general manager of food and beverage operations at the Sheraton Manhattan. He offers the following observations:

Bartenders are most often excellent listeners and communicators with likable personalities. So, it is not uncommon to see guests frequenting a bar for more than just an alcohol beverage. And with more restaurants currently making their complete menu available at the bar, it is no surprise that this has become a growing area of business.

The experienced bartender has the ability to connect with guests in a casual way that can foster the good feelings that are associated with a friendship. When that relationship is supported with outstanding customer service, it becomes a winning formula for repeat business and generous tips. During the peak lunch and dinner time periods, the seats at the bar can turn very quickly with guests who have the need for fast service. When this fast turnaround occurs and the bar operation is staffed with professional bartenders/servers and server's assistants/bussers, the tip income can be substantial.

The hotel and restaurant operators that have identified this as a growing trend within their establishments are inviting bartenders to join their server-training programs to advance server skills at the bar. Bartenders also join in menu sampling/tasting sessions just as dining room servers join in wine sampling/tasting in order to become more knowledgeable to better serve their guests. It's all about superior guest service in the hotel, restaurant, and the bar.

Loading and Carrying a Tray

Learning Objective 6
Understand, explain, and demonstrate how to correctly load and carry trays, including the large oval, small rectangular, and round beverage trays.

There are various types of trays in general use, such as the **large oval** for bigger loads, **small rectangular**, and **round beverage trays**. Large oval trays are used when there are tray stands or side stands available to the server so that they can put the tray down before serving the guests. Rectangular trays are used for smaller amounts of food or for glasses. The round beverage trays are used for serving wine and cocktails. Restaurants that expect servers to handle full dinners for large parties generally use trays and tray stands. As a rule of professional service, a tray should not be placed on guest tables.

The following guidelines should be followed when loading and carrying an **oval tray**:

- Make sure the tray is clean, top and bottom.
- Unless the tray has a nonskid surface of cork or similar material, cover the inside of the tray with a damp service cloth to prevent dishes or glasses from sliding.
- In most serving situations, hot and cold items will be loaded on the tray. Position on the tray is not determined by order of loading, but by the need to:
    a. Balance the tray.
    b. Keep hot foods away from cold foods.
    c. Preserve the food's attractiveness for the guest.
- Load the center of the tray first, and then work toward the outer edge.
- Load larger, heavier pieces toward the center of the tray or at the edge of the tray nearest the shoulder when carrying.
- Load lighter, smaller pieces toward the edges of the tray.
- Do not stack or overlap hot dishes with lids on cold dishes, or cold dishes on hot dishes.
- Keep plates with sauces or liquids level with the tray to prevent spillage.
- Do not place appetizers, soups, or cups on underliners (small plates) or saucers on the tray, but stack all underliners and saucers separately.
- Place coffee and teapot spouts away from food and plates, but not hanging over the edge of the tray.
- When stacking dishes with covers, do not stack more than four high or attempt to carry more than 16. It is possible to carry five stacks of four each, if done carefully.
- Never overload a tray. This will cause breakage as well as a possible accident or personal injury and loss of the food spilled.
- Balance the tray before lifting.
- Keep open dishes away from the side that will be nearest to the server's hair.

An **oval tray** is carried on the server's shoulder, and it must be lifted to shoulder height. Since a tray may be fully loaded with covered dishes, it can be extremely heavy; therefore, it must be lifted properly according to the procedures shown in Figure 5.6 and properly carried as shown in Figure 5.7.

Note: The server should never attempt to lift more than they are comfortable handling, nor should the server ever try to lift the tray to the shoulder using only the arms. This can result in twisted back muscles.

Small rectangular trays are widely used in high-volume, limited-menu restaurants. They are used in some cocktail lounges, especially when the need to use all available space for seating leaves no room for side stands or tray stands.

A rectangular tray cannot be loaded as heavily as an oval tray, but a full breakfast or lunch for two people can be accommodated if properly loaded. The following procedures should be followed when using a rectangular tray:

- Make sure the tray is properly loaded and balanced.
- Slide the tray broad side forward onto the left forearm.

FIGURE 5.6

Preparing to Lift an Oval Tray:
1. Make sure the tray is properly loaded.
2. Position the tray so that one side of the oval extends 5 inches off the tray stand (service table of side stand) in which the tray rests.
3. Drop into a squat position by bending completely from the knees to get under the tray.
4. Firmly place one side of the shoulder underneath the edge of the tray and slide the shoulder side hand toward the bottom center of the tray as the tray is being slid off the tray stand or table, as the other hand grasps the outer rim to steady the tray.
5. Stand up, keeping the back as straight as possible, using the legs to do the lifting; then the tray can be properly carried. Photo by Dwayne Philibert.

FIGURE 5.7

Properly Carrying an Oval Tray.
When the tray has been brought to the table, place the tray on a tray stand or side stand by keeping a straight back and again using the legs to drop into the squat position so that the tray can be slid onto the stand. Remove dishes evenly from the tray to ensure the tray remains balanced on the stand, as you serve the guests. Photo by Dwayne Philibert.

- Hold the upper left arm close to the body.
- Use the right arm to carry a tray stand.
- Once the tray has been brought to the table, properly place the tray on the tray stand as shown in Figure 5.8 and serve the guests.
- When serving guests with the tray in the carrying position, unload it first from one side and then from the other in order to maintain balance.

FIGURE 5.8
Covered Tray Stand. Courtesy of SDI Brands.

Round beverage trays are best carried as shown in Figure 5.9. This enables the server to maintain balance and compensate for weight shifts while serving beverages.

When serving, slowly lift the glasses or bottles from the tray. If the tray starts to tip, quickly return the glass or bottle that caused the shift in balance. Then carefully slide the hand underneath the tray to the area that needs support, and resume serving. A good technique to keep the load steady is to make sure all items are clustered together and touching, as shown in Figure 5.10. This stabilizes individual items (tall beer bottles and wine glasses) and minimizes the possibility of a single item losing balance and knocking over the rest to the load.

Carrying Glasses

Learning Objective 7
Explain and demonstrate the correct way to hold and carry wine glasses.

It is good service practice to carry glasses on a beverage tray when serving and clearing a guest's table. Another method that applies to transporting stemmed wine glasses to a table is hand-carrying as shown in Figure 5.11a and b. It is possible for a well-trained server to carry many wine glasses to the table in one trip. It is very common for a server to carry as many as eight glasses at one time. Advanced glass-carrying skills are easily learned and then mastered with adequate practice. However, when the potential for slippage exists, the server should only use one hand to carry glasses.

FIGURE 5.9
Properly Carrying a Round Beverage Tray:
1. The palm of the hand underneath and in the center of the tray.
2. The tray is held close to the server's body to prevent spills or accidents. Photo by Dwayne Philibert.

FIGURE 5.10
Items Clustered Together on a Round Beverage Tray. Photo by Dwayne Philibert.

Service Priorities and Timing

Learning Objective 8
Define and recognize service priorities, including the importance of correct timing.

Service priorities and timing are among the most important skills for a server to possess. It is a skill that is developed through experience, and is sometimes difficult to train because it requires critical thinking skills and good judgment on the part of the server.

The server should always greet, welcome, and, if it is the protocol of the restaurant, serve water to guests within seconds from the time they are seated. The server should be alert and attentive at all times and constantly aware of what is happening at their tables in anticipation of guests' needs. This is accomplished by frequently looking at different tables and making eye contact with guests, even when engaged in taking an order or serving. Other tables may simultaneously need water or coffee refills, or may be ready to order dessert. Therefore, the server needs to cultivate

(a)   (b)

FIGURE 5.11

(a) Server Carrying Five Stemmed Glasses; (b) Holding Stemmed Glasses by the Stem. The size of the bowl of the wine glass and the size of the server's hand will dictate the amount of glasses a server can safely carry. Photos by Dwayne Philibert.

service priorities and timing that convey a sense of urgency. This can be accomplished by developing the following techniques:

- *Pivot point service is a designated starting position with all orders served clockwise from that point.* Servers should mentally number the positions at their tables with the designated starting pivot point and then go around the table clockwise as orders are taken. This allows the server to identify what each guest has ordered. The pivot point could be the party's host or, as with booths, the first person seated on the left and closest to the aisle. When serving the food order, never ask guests what they have ordered. Be accurate and correct when taking the order and exact when delivering it.

- *After placing the guests' orders with the kitchen, promptly serve rolls and butter, appetizers, salads, soups, and/or drinks.* Some restaurants have a policy of serving water as soon as guests are seated. Guests appreciate quick service and like to have enough time to finish one course before the next course arrives.

- *Hot foods should be served the moment they are ready.* The aroma, sizzle, and intensity of certain foods such as soups, seasoned sauces, steamed vegetables, and steaks last only a short time and make up part of the guest's dining pleasure. Conversely, cold foods such as seafood appetizers, fruit salads, or parfaits must be served cold.

- *Serve all the guests at the table the same course at the same time, without long lapses of time between courses.* There is a delicate balance between not rushing guests and preventing them from fidgeting and getting impatient between courses. A constantly observant server will be able to maintain the appropriate service timing.

- *Keep water glasses refilled at all times.* To some guests, nothing is more disturbing than to have an empty water glass. It is essential to check water glasses each time the server visits the guest, for any reason. For example, check water glasses when serving salads; when serving hot foods; when about halfway through with the meal; when suggesting dessert; and when serving dessert. Knowing which glass to fill first is important: for example, a wine glass or coffee cup would be refilled before a water glass.

- *Always make trips count.* Never go empty-handed. The efficient server takes something that has to be delivered or removed from guest tables; for example, delivering an order from the kitchen to one table and removing dishes from another table to prepare for dessert. This saves time and energy and increases the speed of service by focusing upon efficiency and not wasting steps.

- *Occasionally, guests take a leisurely approach to leaving after their meal.* This may be acceptable when the restaurant is not busy, but when the table is needed for the next party the guests may need a gentle hint that it is time to leave. The server may ask if the guests would like anything else, or start clearing the dessert dishes and glasses, thanking the guests and wishing them a pleasant evening.

- *Never keep a guest waiting for the check.* When presenting the check, place it in the center of the table face down, unless one of the guests has specifically asked for the check, or unless it was obvious when the orders were placed who would be paying. As soon as a credit card or money has been placed next to the guest check, the server should quickly process and return the credit card slip with the card and a pen or the change to the guest. The experienced server uses an inexpensive ballpoint pen and removes the cap. This reduces the possibility that the absent-minded guest will place the pen in their pocket. The process for guest check payment should always be quick. If it is slow or delayed, guests may be displeased. Guest check processing and payment will be further discussed in Chapter 7, Guest Communication, and Chapter 8, The Technology of Service.

Server's Assistant (or Busser) Responsibilities

Learning Objective 9
Understand and explain the responsibilities of a server's assistant.

Being a server's assistant (or busser) is an excellent opportunity to learn the restaurant business thoroughly. Because of the wide variety of duties, the server's assistant can learn about waiting on tables, cooking, dishwashing, food preparation, and a variety of other areas—a little about every job in the restaurant. The server's assistant of today is often the server of tomorrow and the managers of the future.

The server's assistant must be able to perform under pressure when the restaurant is extremely busy and fast-paced. The server's assistant should be in excellent physical condition and should want to be of service to people. They should always be courteous and respectful to guests and other staff members.

Since the server's assistant is an assistant to just about every employee in the restaurant, they may take orders from the servers, host, cooks, and management, as well as the guests. During rush periods, this may become frustrating. In the restaurant business it seems that everything happens at once, and this is a time when teamwork is essential. Through training and experience the server's assistant will be able to learn the order in which to respond to duties, always doing things that directly affect the guest first, working with speed and efficiency.

Throughout the restaurant industry, a common goal is to provide guests with quality food and good service in a clean and sanitary environment. Therefore, the role of the server's assistant is critical in providing good service and in working to maintain a clean and sanitary restaurant. The best habit that the server's assistant can develop is to clean as they work. The key is not to wait until later to clean and straighten but to consistently do it as part of the work.

The manager explains general housekeeping duties and assigns specific responsibilities to the server's assistant for each meal period during the day. Server's assistants may keep service stands equipped and tidy, replenishing supplies and ice, rolls, coffee, and other items as needed so that servers can serve guests quickly. The server's assistant works quietly, talking to others only when necessary and then in a low voice. This contributes to quiet and dignified service and in maintaining good guest relations.

Basic Responsibilities for the Server's Assistant

The focus of the server's assistant is to do their best to keep the restaurant in top operating condition. Some additional responsibilities are as follows *(Note: Porters may also be employed to perform some of these tasks):*

- During meal periods, keep an eye on the floor. Crumbs and food particles should be swept up immediately with a small mechanical sweeper. Napkins, flatware, a piece of food, or any litter should be picked up as soon as it is seen.
- Spilled liquids should be cleaned up as soon as the spill occurs. If an area with a spill must briefly be left unattended, be sure that a chair or some other obstacle is placed over it so that no one will slip. Most spills can be soaked up quickly with a clean dry towel.
- All rugs and carpets should be vacuumed before and/or after meal periods, but never during a busy time. Vacuuming near guests should be avoided. The noise and activity can be irritating.
- Restrooms need to be checked periodically for cleanliness and supplies. Restrooms may need to be cleaned after every meal period, and soap, hand towels, and toilet paper replenished.
- High chairs should be wiped clean with a safe sanitizing solution after every use.
- The buss cart should be clean, orderly, and properly stocked with table setup supplies such as flatware, napkins, place mats, chinaware, etc., ready to go into use as shown in Figure 5.12.
- Server stand trash must be emptied periodically and replaced with a new trash bag liner. The station must be well equipped with supplies, and replenished with ice, rolls, coffee, and other items as needed.
- Salt and pepper shakers, sugar bowls, and table condiments (ketchup and mustard) are checked and refilled as needed between meal periods.
- Some dining rooms have table candles that need to be lit before the dining room opens and checked throughout the evening.
- A salad bar or dessert table may need to be checked and refilled frequently.
- In addition to meal-period responsibilities, the manager will assign and schedule daily and weekly housekeeping and cleaning duties. Most of these assignments should be scheduled so that the entire restaurant receives a thorough cleaning once a week. This means washing windows and cleaning all the small cracks and crevices where soil and food particles can accumulate.

In carrying out responsibilities within the restaurant, the server's assistant will often be dealing with guests. Server's assistants should be familiar with all menu items in case a guest asks a question. Courtesy is the key to good guest relations.

FIGURE 5.12
Buss Cart Stocked with Table Setup Supplies. Courtesy of Lakeside Manufacturing.

If a guest requests some service from the server's assistant, such as a water refill, it is important that the server's assistant take care of it right away. If the request is for food or something that the server's assistant cannot deliver, the guest should be advised that the server will be informed without delay.

Table Bussing

Learning Objective 10
Explain the procedures to follow in order to properly buss a table, using a cart or a tray.

As soon as guests leave, the tables must be cleared. During the meal hours other guests are often waiting for tables; they are hungry and sometimes impatient; therefore, the server's assistant needs to act immediately in clearing and preparing tables. This can be accomplished by bussing with a cart or tray.

Bussing with a Cart

Typically, a buss cart is used in casual fast-paced restaurants. Using a cart to buss tables is the fastest, most efficient method of bussing. It is essential that the cart is clean, polished, and well stocked. It should have three or four shelves equipped with two clean tote boxes (buss tubs), with or without a flatware compartment, and two clean cloths, one dampened with a sanitizing solution and one dry. Some carts may also have a refuse bin attached.

The upper shelf of the cart may have a flatware bin (tub) filled with clean flatware. The top shelf may carry place mats and/or clean tablecloths and napkins.

Using a buss cart allows the server's assistant to clear and clean a table and then set it up immediately. To properly buss a table, the following procedures should be followed:

- Pick up all flatware by the handles first, and place in a separate container.
- Put all paper and waste in a separate section.

- Put all "like" items together (e.g., glasses with glasses).
- Do not touch parts of dishes or flatware that may have come in contact with the guest's mouth. Avoid exposure to possible germs by picking up cups by the handles, glasses at the bottom or by stems, and flatware by the handles.
- Soiled napkins and place mats are rolled up and placed on the cart.
- Place condiments such as Dijon, Worcestershire, or steak sauce on the bottom shelf of the cart.
- Wipe off table, chairs, booth, table condiments (ketchup and mustard), etc. Remove crumbs or food particles by sweeping them onto a plate or into a napkin, not into the other hand. Do not allow crumbs or food particles to fall on the floor.
- Before leaving the table, check to see that the table has sparkling clean and filled salt and pepper shakers and sugar containers. Server's assistants should clean table, chairs, or booth if needed. The floor around the table should be cleaned and vacuumed if needed. Check to see that the table has been set with flatware, place mats, and/or clean tablecloths, napkins, glasses, coffee cups, etc., in the proper places according to the restaurant's policy. Also, the buss attendant should make sure that the chairs are straight and in order.
- Server's assistant should take the buss cart to the dishwashing area and separate items in preparation for washing. The flatware goes in presoak tubs, glasses and cups go in racks, and dishes are scraped and placed together by size. Trash should be placed in the proper container.
- Work fast and efficiently.

Tables properly set up will enable the server to better serve the guests when they arrive. It is preferable to have the table set up before the guest sits down, but it is essential to have the table set up before the order is taken.

Bussing with a Tray

Using a tray to buss tables would be used in many different-style restaurants, including some fine-dining restaurants and banquet settings. The tray is placed on a tray stand next to the table to be bussed. The dishes are stacked on the tray according to size—large plates together, small plates and saucers on top of large plates or on the side of the tray, and glasses and cups around the edge of the tray as close to the plates as possible. Flatware should be placed together along the side of the tray. Stack the heaviest dishes on the side of the tray that will be carried on the shoulder. Lighter pieces can be placed around the edge. Soiled napkins and place mats are rolled and placed on the tray, unless it is the policy of the restaurant to place napkins and place mats on a separate tray. Care must be taken not to accidentally wrap any flatware in paper or it will end up in the trash instead of the dishwashing machine. Follow the procedures listed above to properly buss a table. Then lift the tray according to the loading and carrying steps previously discussed, remembering never to lift more than you are comfortable in handling.

Setting Up with a Tray

Setting up can be done with a tray. A rectangular tray is often used in the following manner. A linen napkin can be unfolded on the tray to serve as a liner. Clean flatware (forks, knives, and spoons) is spread on the tray. Glasses and napkins are also included. This allows the server or server's assistant to quickly set up tables. All tables should be set up as soon as they are bussed.

Customer Complaints and Issues

Learning Objective 11
Describe the proper protocol for responding to customer complaint issues.

When confronted with a customer complaint or behavior issue, the server must maintain a positive attitude and resolve the issue as quickly and efficiently as possible. The server needs to be confident in their abilities and remember that customer satisfaction comes before anything else. The following are examples of situations that occur most often, along with suggestions for effectively solving them.

Food-Related Complaints

- **Guest complains that food is cold or undercooked.** The server should apologize and immediately remedy the problem by returning the food to the kitchen to be warmed or fully cooked. If the food is half eaten and the guest refuses to have the remaining food returned to the kitchen for additional cooking, some restaurants may authorize the server to offer the displeased guest a complimentary dessert.

- **Guest says food is overcooked or burned.** The server should follow the restaurant policy for how to handle this type of problem. A substitution may be offered or the food item can be replaced.

- **Guest states that the portion size is too small.** If the server recognizes that the portion is smaller than normal, the server should apologize and immediately take the guest's plate back to the kitchen for the correct portion amount. Most restaurants have standard portion sizes and a manager is the best person in the restaurant to address this issue.

- **Guest is very dissatisfied with food and does not want to wait for a replacement.** The server should apologize and suggest another entrée that is already prepared or is easily and quickly prepared. If the guest refuses, the server should promptly inform the manager. The best decision may be not to charge the guest for the meal.

- **Guest finds a foreign object in the food.** This is among the worst possible situations. If a guest finds a piece of metal or glass, a Band-Aid, a bug, or anything else that would be dangerous and unappetizing, the server needs to immediately apologize and remove the plate, inform the kitchen and the manager, and return with fresh food for the guest. Most restaurants have a policy of not charging the guest for the meal along with offering the utmost apology for the unfortunate occurrence.

Service-Related Complaints

- **Guest says that the order is wrong.** When this occurs, it is not important who is at fault; what is important is for the server to apologize and promptly correct the mistake. The error should be noted in the POS system followed by entering the correct order. The manager may want to visit with the guest to further apologize.

- **Server forgot to place the order with the kitchen.** This might happen during a very busy shift where the server forgot to enter an order at the POS terminal. When it is discovered, the server should immediately place the order and alert the kitchen and the manager of the problem. Then explain and apologize to the guest for the delay. Sometimes, a complimentary drink, appetizer, or beverage refill is necessary to appease the guest.

- **Food is slow coming from the kitchen.** Occasionally, a kitchen may be temporarily backed up with orders. When this occurs, the server should explain the reason to guests—for example, a large party just arrived, or a tour bus just dropped off a large group. Most people are understanding and patient if they know why they have to wait and if they are not forgotten. The server needs to keep the rolls and butter replenished, water and beverage glasses full. If the delay is prolonged, some restaurants have a policy of providing guests with complimentary beverages, appetizers, or desserts.

- **Server is informed that the kitchen is out of the food item ordered by the guest.** When this happens, the server should apologize to the guest for the inconvenience and suggest some comparable choices. It may be necessary to return the menu for the guest to review. Once the kitchen has run out of an item, the servers should be informed immediately. This will avoid or minimize the possibility of having to disappoint a guest once having placed the order versus being told ahead of time that the item is not available.

- **Server spills food or drink on the clothing of a guest.** When a spill accident occurs, the server should react immediately by doing the following: Apologize and be certain that the guest was not hurt; assure the guest involved that the restaurant will clean the garment or replace it if necessary; replace the item that was spilled and alert the manager; and clean up the mess as quickly as possible.

- **Guest is unhappy and has a bad opinion of the food and service.** The server should apologize and try to satisfy the guest in a reasonable manner. If that is not possible, the manager should be asked to resolve the situation. Some guests are never satisfied, and some are attempting to get a free meal. They still have to be treated with respect and dealt with fairly.

Guest Behavior Issues

- **Guests allow their children to wander the floor.** Children should be brought back to the table for adult supervision. They would otherwise be at risk for getting knocked over, accidentally tripping a server, or annoying other guests.

- **Guest leaves shopping bag or backpack in the aisle.** The server needs to politely suggest that the guest move the bag or backpack out of the way of traffic to avoid possible trips or falls.

- **Guest is intoxicated.** The server should promptly inform the manager. If the guest becomes loud, obnoxious, or abusive, the manager may ask the guest to leave or may have to take other measures in having the guest escorted out of the restaurant. With the increase of liquor liability and laws passed specifically affecting alcohol service, the responsibility of monitoring alcohol beverage service falls directly upon the server. The server should be completely informed about the legal statutes and house policies regarding intoxicated patrons. This is further discussed in Chapter 6, Beverages and Beverage Service.

- **Guests attempt to leave without paying.** The server should immediately inform the manager of the situation. The manager should approach them and ask whether they paid, being polite but firm.

STEPS TO RESOLVE A CUSTOMER COMPLAINT OR ISSUE

1. Listen—the most important step in solving a difficult situation is to allow the guest to feel they have an opportunity to explain themselves. Many guests want to be heard first and foremost.
2. Understand—a guest wants you to understand why they are upset. Showing understanding can diffuse a difficult situation. Understanding the exact problem is very important for the future, so allow the guest to completely explain themselves.
3. Apologize—let the guest know you are sincerely sorry for the things that you have control over.
4. Resolve—each guest will need or want something different from you. The ultimate goal is to get the guest to return and have a better experience. So, make sure you know exactly why they are unhappy and then try and match the solution to the complaint.

QUICKLY RECOVER FROM CUSTOMER COMPLAINTS

Fiona Cameron is a hospitality consultant and educator and is the founder and president of FCW Hospitality and Private Residence Consulting, Inc. in New York City. Ms. Cameron has a Master of Business Administration degree from Les Roches School of Hotel Management and is a Certified Etiquette and International Protocol Consultant. Her experience includes recruiting and training teams of superior service professionals in Europe, Asia, and America. Ms. Cameron offers the following:

When confronted with a guest complaint or issue the immediate focus must be to quickly recover by taking the necessary action to immediately resolve the complaint or issue for the guest. Having worked in foodservice environments ranging from casual dining, theme restaurants specializing in the authentic cuisine of a particular culture, to the ultimate in fine-dining in Europe, Asia, and America, there is one scenario that does not differ no matter what the environment—*Customer Complaints.*

Whether a guest has ordered a modest lunch or an extravagant dinner they have expectations with regards to the quality of the food being offered and the service being provided. As hospitality professionals we know that there are occasions when something goes wrong or just happens. It may be a mistake or error in the kitchen when preparing a food item or perhaps the server accidently gets bumped and spills a beverage, and it can occur at the most awkward of times.

Whatever the situation or circumstance may be, **the server must have the genuine desire to satisfy the guest**. The guest may have a simple misunderstanding regarding the food or service or perhaps it is a blatant error that occurred. The fact remains that when the guest expresses a dissatisfaction to the server, an immediate and satisfactory solution must be provided.

Guests can be forgiving when they experience a sincere apology accompanied by the server's immediate action that resolves their complaint. When a professional server possesses the genuine desire to serve guests, they can quickly turn a customer complaint into a memorable positive experience for the guest.

RESTAURANT REALITY: COMPLAINTS ARE NOT ALWAYS REASONABLE BUT ALWAYS HAVE A SOLUTION

Ms. Kane is a young and enthusiastic restaurant manager in a large four-star hotel in a beautiful city near the sea that attracts tourists from all over the world. She works hard and has a true understanding of hospitality. Despite working many hours a day, she always arrives at work with a cheerful disposition. She truly likes to see her guests happy and goes out of her way to please the hotel's guests.

Tourist season is in full swing, the hotel is booked solid for three consecutive weeks, and all managers are working many hours a day and six-day workweeks. Ms. Kane recognizes a table of guests in the restaurant. They have eaten in the restaurant three out of the four days since check-in at the beginning of the week. She approaches the table and asked if they are enjoying their meal and more importantly their stay in the hotel. Their response is very complimentary and Ms. Kane is delighted. She excused herself as the guests' next course arrived. The restaurant is busy but everyone in the dining room looks as though they are enjoying themselves. Ms. Kane checks on other tables and helps her staff with anything that they needed. Time is flying by as it does in a busy restaurant. Ms. Kane notices the regular customers finishing their dessert and she walks toward their table to say good-bye. While she was saying good-bye to her guests, a server approaches the table and asks for help. Ms. Kane excuses herself and goes to another table where the server is having a difficult time with a guest. Ms. Kane introduces herself and asks what she could do for the guest. At this time, the gentleman sitting at the table in a loud voice bellows, "These are the most uncomfortable #$@^ chairs I have ever sat in my entire life, something needs to be done about it immediately." Ms. Kane is flabbergasted; she had never heard such a vulgar complaint about the restaurant's very expensive chairs. She composes herself and knows she has her hands full. She tells the guest that she will be right back. She gathers six

throw pillows from the lounge area and races back to the restaurant. She offers the guest one, then two, then three of the pillows. He is still not satisfied. She offers him four, then five. He positions himself in the chair and is finally comfortable. Ms. Kane smiles broadly at the server and thanks her. The guest is happy the rest of the night and everything goes smoothly.

Ms. Kane felt good about the outcome of the complaint. Although she knew that the chairs were designed and chosen for their elegance and comfort, she did not make an issue of it with the guest. It was more important to Ms. Kane to display true hospitality than if the guest's complaint was valid. The guest may not always be right but they must always be satisfied.

Summary

The general rules and techniques of proper table service are presented in detailed procedures that apply to most restaurant operations. The correct methods of loading and carrying various trays are explained; every server should be competent in these methods.

The server needs to cultivate service priorities and timing that convey a sense of urgency in meeting the needs of the guests. They must also follow what is called *protocol* of the restaurant that encompasses the procedures that work best in the style and layout of the restaurant. This is accomplished by developing techniques that include the following: Greet, welcome, and serve water to guests as soon as they are seated (unless the policy of the restaurant is to serve water only if requested by guests); always make trips count; hot foods are to be served the moment they are ready; after placing the guests' orders with the kitchen, promptly serve rolls and butter, appetizers, salads, soups, and/or drinks; serve all of the guests at the table the same course at the same time, avoiding long lapses of time between courses; when delivering the food order, never ask guests what they have ordered, develop a method to remember so that the delivery will be correct; keep beverages refilled at all times; serving procedures should be smooth, efficient, and convenient for the guest; and never keep a guest waiting for a check.

Never lose sight of the fact that the guest is the real "boss." If guests are not happy and satisfied today, they will not return tomorrow. Even worse, they can and will persuade friends to stay away, too. One of the server's functions is to create and maintain the goodwill of the guests. When a guest complains about the food, the server needs to understand the complaint correctly and take care of it immediately. Most complaints can be handled through the server or the manager. When a guest is dissatisfied, first and foremost they want to be heard. Good listening skills will help resolve the complaint in an effective and timely manner. Several of the most common difficult situations that might occur in a restaurant are discussed in the chapter along with solutions and corrective actions.

The server's assistant or busser has an important function in every restaurant. The most important duty is to please the guest. Nearly everything that a server's assistant does is aimed toward that goal either directly or indirectly. "Clean as you go" is one of the best habits that a server's assistant can develop, as this always contributes to a clean and efficient restaurant. The server's assistant or busser is responsible for bussing and setting tables, replenishing supplies at the server's stand, and performing other responsibilities as assigned by the restaurant manager.

While it is important to follow the basic rules and techniques for proper service, successful servers focus on smooth, efficient serving procedures that are convenient for the guest, and that do not interrupt the guest's comfort.

Discussion Questions and Exercises

Note: An actual restaurant dining room setting or mock setup should be used in order to allow the student to demonstrate procedures, techniques, and functions that were presented in this chapter. Students can be asked to describe what they feel is excellent service.

1. Explain and demonstrate the general rules and techniques of proper table service.
2. When there is more than one woman or older guest present at a table, whom would you serve first as a matter of traditional etiquette?
3. Explain the procedure for removing dishes and flatware.
4. What should the server do if they continue to notice water spots on the flatware?
5. Explain the procedure to follow when serving guests at a booth or next to a wall.
6. Explain and demonstrate the procedures for correct plate handling.
7. Explain and demonstrate the correct way to hold and serve a plate.
8. Explain and demonstrate the correct way to hold and serve beverage glasses, wine glasses with stems, and cups and mugs with and without saucers.
9. What is the procedure to follow when serving coffee or tea?
10. Explain the procedure to follow when wine is being served.
11. What additional items are brought to the table when specialty foods such as lobster are served?
12. How is a finger bowl prepared for use, and when should it be used?
13. Explain the ways that crumbs and small food particles can be removed from a table.
14. Explain or demonstrate the correct way to load and carry a large oval tray.
15. Explain or demonstrate the correct way to load and carry a small rectangular tray.
16. Explain or demonstrate the correct way to load and carry a round beverage tray.
17. Explain the correct procedure for carrying multiple plates. Demonstrate the basic technique.
18. Identify and discuss six techniques that a server could develop to help improve serving priorities and timing.
19. Discuss how the following difficult situations could be handled:
    - Guest complains that food is cold or undercooked.
    - Guest says food is overcooked or burned.
    - Guest states that the portion size is too small.
    - Guest says that order is wrong.
    - Guests allow their children to wander the floor.
    - Guest is very dissatisfied with food and does not want to wait for a replacement.
    - Server forgot to place the order with the kitchen.
    - Guest is unhappy and has a bad opinion of the food and service.
    - Guest is intoxicated.
    - Guest leaves shopping bag or backpack in the aisle.
    - Server spills food or drink on the clothing of a guest.
    - Food is slow coming from the kitchen.
    - Server is informed that the kitchen is out of the food item ordered.
    - Foreign object is found in the food by guest.

20. Define some of the responsibilities of a server's assistant.
21. How should a bussing cart be equipped?
22. List the procedures for properly bussing a table.
23. Explain how a server's assistant or busser would use a tray to buss a table.
24. How would a small rectangular tray be used in the process of setting up tables?
25. Explain why some guests may prefer to dine at the restaurant's bar.

CHAPTER 6

Beverages and Beverage Service

INTRODUCTION

Beverage service is an important aspect of an enjoyable dining experience, which includes a wide variety of alcohol and nonalcohol beverages. The server needs to learn the proper way of serving these beverages and must acquire basic knowledge of wines, liquors, beers, and cocktails, as well as nonalcohol options.

A meal can begin with a guest's favorite sparkling water, a tasty cocktail, and a special bottle of wine, and it can end with the perfect cup of coffee or tea. Each type of beverage requires a server to be knowledgeable in several key areas. The server should know the origin of the beverage, the proper technique to serve it, the correct serving temperatures, the glassware or china it should be served in, and, most importantly, the responsible way to serve alcohol beverages.

CHAPTER 6 LEARNING OBJECTIVES

As a result of successfully completing this chapter, readers will be able to:

1. Understand the legal responsibility when serving an alcohol beverage.

2. Know the fundamentals of wine and wine service.

3. Understand the importance of wine temperatures and the recommended serving temperatures of various wines.

4. Describe how and when to use an ice bucket.

5. Understand and explain the correct way to present and serve a bottle of wine to a guest.

6. Know the correct way to open and serve a bottle of champagne or sparkling wine.

7. Explain the process of decanting wine.

8. Identify different wine and beverage glasses.

9. Explain the popular styles of wine.

10. Understand that the climate in which grape varietals are grown affects the taste and color of wine.

11. Describe various food and wine pairings.

12. Identify and describe popular distilled spirits and cocktails.

13. Understand and explain the difference between beers, lagers, and ales.

14. Know the correct procedure for serving bottled water.

15. Explain the different types of coffee drinks.

16. Describe how tea is prepared and served.

17. Understand the various food and tea pairings.

18. Recognize the popularity of specialty and customized cocktails.

CHAPTER 6 OUTLINE

Responsible Alcohol Beverage Service
Wine and Wine Service
Proper Temperatures for Serving Wines
Ice Bucket Usage
Wine Presentation and Service

Opening Champagne or Sparkling Wine
Decanting Wine
    Steps to Decant a Bottle of Wine
Wine Glasses
Styles of Wine

Responsible Alcohol Beverage Service

Learning Objective 1

Understand the legal responsibility when serving an alcohol beverage.

The Alcohol and Tobacco Tax and Trade Bureau is the federal bureau under the Department of Treasury that collects the taxes on alcohol, tobacco, firearms, and ammunition; they protect and prevent unfair and unlawful market activity for alcohol and tobacco products. In addition to the federal regulations and taxes, each state has its own rules and regulations regarding the issuing of liquor licenses that fall under the Alcohol Beverage Control (ABC) agency within each state. The ABC regulates the sale and distribution of liquor. Some states have license quotas limiting the number of places that can sell alcohol within the state, at any given point in time. Towns may also have quotas in place. It is important to know if there are any available licenses for your state and town. There are also several types of licenses available through the state. There are on-premise and off-premise licenses that govern the sale of alcohol beverages. An on-premise license allows a business to serve alcohol on site only. An example would be a restaurant or bar where a guest consumes the beverage while in the establishment. An off-premise license allows a business to sell a customer alcohol products that they will take away from the business. An example would be a liquor store. Once a license is issued, a business owner would be responsible for paying an annual renewal fee and following the regulations within the license.

A serious responsibility comes with the privilege of having a liquor license issued by an ABC agency. A liquor license can be revoked if the terms of the license are violated. Therefore, it is in every restaurant's best interest to be vigilant in protecting that license. Stringent standard operating procedures are necessary to prevent harm caused by an intoxicated person acting irresponsible, the loss of the license, or a lawsuit that could devastate the business.

Dram Shop liability refers to a body of law that governs the liability of bars, taverns, restaurants, and other establishments that sell alcohol beverages to visibly intoxicated persons or minors who may cause death or injury to third parties (persons not having a relationship to the bar) as a result of alcohol-related car or other type of accidents. The name *Dram Shop* originated with reference to a shop where spirits were sold by the dram, a small unit of liquid. Dram shop is a legal term referring to a bar or establishment where alcohol beverages are sold.

Those who serve alcohol beverages are increasingly legally obligated to the *Prudent Person Rule* that asks, "*What would a prudent person do in this or a similar situation?*"

The basic answer to the question is that a prudent person would not serve alcohol to someone who is intoxicated. Nor would a prudent person allow someone who is visibly intoxicated to drive a vehicle anywhere.

Management proves that it is a responsible provider of alcohol beverages when it puts the following guidelines in place.

1. *Establish and enforce a house policy that specifically states the house rules concerning underaged and visibly intoxicated persons.* The house

policy would be posted in a conspicuous place in order to allow access for everyone to read the policy. An example of a house policy is one that would simply state the following: This establishment maintains a zero tolerance policy that includes checking identification to avoid serving underage guests and never serving a guest who is visually intoxicated. Rules governing alcohol beverage service are set forth by individual State Liquor Control agencies.

2. *Support an alcohol beverage server training program for beverage managers and all servers.* A certified alcohol server training program, ServSafe Alcohol Responsible Alcohol Training, is available from the National Restaurant Association Educational Foundation. Other alcohol server training programs may be available in various states. Although responsible alcohol service training courses are not mandatory, the benefits to a restaurant include the following: educates managers and servers to recognize signs of intoxication and take the appropriate action, heighten skills and professionalism of employees, and may help with lowering liability insurance premiums. Everyone involved with the preparation and service of alcohol beverages should go through an alcohol server training program before beginning to work in a beverage operation.

3. *Review reports from POS (point-of-sale) systems that may provide information regarding the number of items sold, specific quantities, dates, and times.* This keeps management informed of any irregularities or out-of-the-ordinary occurrences that may give cause for concern that might result in additional or renewed alcohol server training. For example, if customers are reordering drinks in a short amount of time it may inform management that the servers need to slow the pace of service to control a person from becoming intoxicated.

4. *Complete an incident report for any problem occurring with a customer.* This is a form used to record incidents that occurred when serving customers or denying service to them due to irresponsible behavior.

5. *Possibly the best defense, as part of a third-party liability claim, if ever sued, is to complete an incident report.* The incident report is used to record a description of any episodes that occur and is signed by the person reporting the incident, employee(s) involved, manager, and any witnesses. The report effectively documents irresponsible behavior and helps an establishment avoid a lawsuit. Figure 6.1 is an example of an incident report.

Responsible alcohol service begins with the server verifying that the person ordering the alcohol beverage is of the legal age of 21. For proof of age, servers should accept only stand-alone identification such as a valid driver license with photo, passports, military identification, or state-approved identification. The responsible server takes this task seriously and checks identification for all their guests. The server realizes that this is an important part of the server duties and ensures a pleasant dining experience for all guests.

Servers should always be conscious of taking good care of their guests and protecting them from the effects of alcohol misuse. Along with being a legal obligation, responsible alcohol service constitutes good business, and is the "morally correct" thing to do. Therefore, the server should be aware of the number of drinks a guest has been served, and should know and recognize the signs of visible intoxication such as glassy or bloodshot eyes, slurred speech, impaired motored skills, lowered inhibitions, and slowed reaction and reflexes. The server should have a brief chat with the guest before serving, and at each visit to the table determine if the guest is intoxicated or at risk of intoxication because of mood, fatigue, medications, or changes in behavior.

Incident Report

Date: 01/11/XX   **Shift:**   5:00 P.M. to 1:00 A.M.

Reported By: Rick V., Bartender   **Manager:**   Harry M.

Employee(s) Involved	Position	
Betty S.	Server	

Customer(s) Involved	Address	Phone #
David D.	?	?

Witnesses	Address	Phone #
Fred W.	123 Central Ave, City, State, ZIP	(555) 555 5555

Description of Incident
Drink order refused to David D. who was acting belligerent and appeared visibly intoxicated. Server tried to call a taxi but customer refused any help and would not give address or phone number. David D. left.

FIGURE 6.1
Incident Report

Wine and Wine Service

Learning Objective 2

Know the fundamentals of wine and wine service.

History tells us that humans have been making, offering, and accepting wine since the beginning of documented time. Cave and tomb drawings, spanning ages, depict man in the company of a jug of wine. These early peoples did not have the glassware from which to sip nor the bottles to house wine in, but their traditions, superstitions, and earthenware amphorae (jars) and cups were the precursors to the culture of wine and service we offer today.

Wine has always been a great partner for food but in recent years the interest in wine and the number of wine enthusiasts have increased dramatically as reflected in an industry-reported annual increase in wine sales. Many people have become interested in wine as a hobby or have embraced wine for its newly discovered health benefits, which make wine and wine service an important addition to responsible alcohol service training. Guests will come to a restaurant with various levels of wine knowledge; therefore, a prepared server can offer a higher standard of service to the guest.

Many customers and restaurateurs alike may feel intimidated by the mystique of formal wine service. Distinctive techniques and flair of service are as abundant as talented wine servers or Certified Sommeliers. However, the true key to serving a bottle of wine to a guest is as simple as knowing a few basics. Once the server masters these basics, the server can slowly develop the time-honored skills necessary to respond to their guests' interests. Increasingly, restaurants are employing Sommeliers to oversee their beverage programs. Becoming a Certified Sommelier requires many years of study and a good understanding of the potential high profits of a beverage program within an establishment. A Sommelier has many responsibilities such as writing a beverage list, weekly ordering, proper beverage storing and inventorying, training staff, and helping guests to select beverages that would enhance their dining experience. This is considered a high-level career in the service industry especially for someone who enjoys a lifetime of learning and interaction with people.

The professional server needs to understand the restaurant's wine list and allow the guest to feel comfortable in making a wine selection. If a guest does not have experience with wine, the server should be able to offer helpful suggestions and responses to questions from the guest. Furthermore, for the guest to thoroughly enjoy the wine, it must be served properly.

Proper Temperatures for Serving Wines

Learning Objective 3

Understand the importance of wine temperatures and the recommended serving temperatures of various wines.

Serving wines begins with the knowledge of proper serving temperatures. A bottle of overchilled wine will mask desirable or undesirable qualities of the wine instead of highlighting the best that the wine has to offer. A wine that is too warm may taste heavy and lack finesse, creating an unpleasant experience for the guest. The vapors that are released from wine vary depending on its relative volatility. Red wine has higher molecular weight than white and is therefore less volatile. The aromatics of a red wine require a warmer room temperature to vaporize the wonderful aromas that are desired. Because lighter white wines and rosés are more volatile, they release their perfume at a much lower temperature. Generally speaking, white wines and sparkling wines should be served between 45° and 50°F. Dessert wines should be served slightly cooler at 40–45°F. Cooler temperatures definitely contribute a perception of balance to sweeter white wines. Red wines are best enjoyed at a cellar temperature of between 50° and 65°F, with the exception of very light red wines, like Beaujolais, which can be served at 50–55°F. We sometimes refer to red wines being served at room temperature, which is hard to calculate due to climatic and seasonal differences. For example, room temperature in May in Florida varies from the cooler room temperature at the same time of year in Vermont. A restaurateur needs to consider this when serving and storing wine. Therefore, the server always needs to be aware of correct serving temperatures and make the necessary temperature adjustment prior to serving the wine.

Some restaurants are guilty of keeping their white wines in multipurpose coolers set at 40°F. If this is the case, the wine should be removed a few minutes prior to service to ensure that the wine has reached its proper serving temperature. Likewise, red wines can often be found housed in warm kitchens. Here, a quick chill in an ice bucket can revive a light-style red before it is served. Table 6.1 provides a quick reference for wine serving temperatures.

A great wine can be a wine that has some sweetness, some acidity, and, if it is a red wine, some tannin, or a wine that the guests prefer and enjoy with their meal. Wine is very subjective; therefore, servers must communicate and listen to their guests. All guests have their own personal taste in food and wine. Asking a guest what type of wine they prefer at home is an excellent way for a server to understand what style of wine that guest would enjoy. In addition, it is very important to know what type of food the guest has selected from the menu. Heavy wines are not recommended with light food because they can overpower the food and disguise the flavors intended by the chef.

Dessert and Sparkling Wines	40–45°F
White Wines, Rosés, Sherries, and Champagnes	45–50°F
High-Quality Dry Wines, Light-Style Red Wines	50–55°F
Lighter-Style Red Wines	55–60°F
Full-Bodied Red Wines	60–65°F

TABLE 6.1

Wine Serving Temperatures

(a)   (b)

FIGURE 6.2
(a) Wine Bucket with Stand; (b) Table Wine Bucket When More Than One Wine Is Served
Courtesy of Steelite International.

Ice Bucket Usage

Learning Objective 4

Describe how and when to use an ice bucket.

Ice buckets are appropriate on many occasions. They can be used in conjunction with a stand or set on a dining table as long as they do not overwhelm the china or glassware, as shown in Figure 6.2a and b. It is a good idea to use a bucket with Champagne or sparkling wines. A special occasion deserves an exceptional presentation. White wines probably do not require a bucket unless the guest requests it. Instead, a wine chiller can be an appropriate service companion for a white wine because a wine chiller will simply maintain a wine's temperature. A wine will warm only slightly over the course of a meal, and this may even enhance its flavor. Another consideration for when to use an ice bucket is the number of people sharing the bottle of wine. Three or more will quickly empty the bottle, and thus will usually not require an ice bucket. However, one or two will take longer to consume the wine, making the use of an ice bucket appropriate. There are many styles of wine buckets available, so it is best to choose one that fits the style of the restaurant.

Ice buckets should be half-filled with shaved or cubed ice. If a bottle needs to be chilled quickly, cover it with ice then pour salt on top of the ice and let it stand for about 5 minutes. Add some water to loosen the ice and speed the chilling. Servers who choose to add water to their buckets should periodically check to make sure that the label is not sliding off the bottle. The server should also be readily available for prompt service to avoid the guests dripping on themselves or on the tablecloth. A server should be prepared with a side towel when using an ice bucket.

Wine Presentation and Service

Learning Objective 5

Understand and explain the correct way to present and serve a bottle of wine to a guest.

The person who selected the bottle of wine is "the host." After the host is identified, the server will proceed. The server should present the wine to the guest confirming the wine selection as shown in Figure 6.3. Some of the important elements to convene would be the wine producer, the grape varietal, the wine's origin, and a vintage if applicable. The host will examine the label and then instruct the server to open the bottle; after the bottle is opened "the host" tastes the first 1–2 ounce poured in the glass for approval. This ritual is very important because it ensures that the wine is acceptable before more than one glass is poured. If there is a flaw/fault in the wine, the server should get another bottle and re-present the second bottle to the guest. It is industry practice to inform your wine sales representative that there was a flaw/fault in the wine. The sales representative will replace the bottle with a new one if the flaw/fault is confirmed. There are some common flaws/faults that a server will be exposed to, each having distinct aromas or color. Flaws/faults can happen naturally and should not be of any great concern if handled properly.

FIGURE 6.3

Presenting a Bottle of Wine to a Guest
Photo by Dwayne Philibert.

The server should follow the steps of opening wine carefully. There is a systematic way to serve wine in a proper manner, and the server can easily learn it. The server should have a wine key (wine opener), a napkin, and a bread and butter plate to present the cork. The server should stand to the right of the host, present the bottle, and then proceed with the six steps to open wine.

The server should recite the producer's name, the type of wine, including either grape varietal or place of origin and vintage, in a soft but clear voice, making eye contact with the guest. Once the bottle has been approved, generally with a nod from the host, it can be opened according to the steps in Figure 6.4.

The lead or plastic capsule must first be cut below the bulge in the glass to ensure that the wine will not have any contact with the foil during pouring (make sure the knife blade is sharp); see Step 1. A traditional wine opener is excellent to use because of its versatility. It has a knife at one end for cutting, a thin corkscrew for easy insertion into a cork, and a bottle opener at the opposite end. Wipe the neck of the bottle to remove dust or microorganisms that may have developed under the foil, as shown in Step 2.

The cork should be removed by following the opening procedure. Hold the neck of the bottle in one hand, pointing the bottle away from the guest, and with the other hand insert the tip of the corkscrew into the center of the cork, as shown in Step 3 (Note: many prefer to rest the bottle on a side-stand or on the corner of the table). Twist the corkscrew into the cork for a firm grip, hold the corkscrew straight, and twist into the cork without pushing down on the cork; place the edge of the bottle opener on the lip of the bottle, holding it in place with your finger, and with a firm grip slowly pull out the cork, as shown in Step 4. Unscrew the cork from the corkscrew as shown in Step 5. Wipe off fingerprints or cork dust from the neck of the bottle with the side towel or a clean linen napkin. Practicing wine opening will build confidence in the server and will allow a server to remove even the most difficult corks without a break. Place the cork on a bread and butter plate and then pour the wine, as shown in Step 6, for the guest to taste and approve. Take care not to

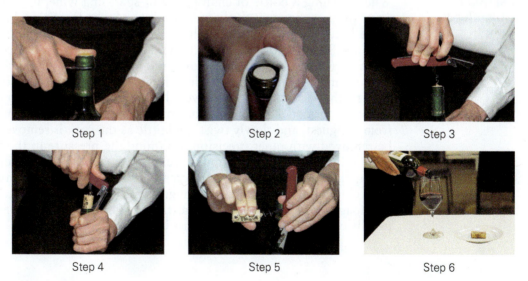

Step 1   Step 2   Step 3

Step 4   Step 5   Step 6

FIGURE 6.4

Preparing to Serve a Bottle of Wine
Step 1 Cut and remove foil with a wine opener
Step 2 Wipe the neck of the wine bottle
Step 3 Insert the corkscrew
Step 4 Remove the cork
Step 5 Unscrew the cork from the corkscrew
Step 6 Place the cork on a bread and butter plate and pour the wine.
Photos by Gerald Lanuzza (Steps 1 through 5); Photo by Dwayne Philibert (Step 6).

stain the tablecloth with the cork. A server may use a napkin as a scarf on the bottle to assist with a clean pour and lessen the likelihood of soiling the linen tablecloth.

Occasionally a cork may break. When this occurs, the server should remove whatever cork is on the corkscrew, insert the corkscrew into the center of the cork remaining in the bottle, and gently twist all the way through the cork, being careful not to push the cork further into the bottle before slowly removing the cork. Place both pieces of the cork side by side on the bread and butter plate for the guest to inspect. If the cork accidentally falls into the bottle, simply apologize and offer the guest another bottle of wine. If the guest prefers a new bottle of wine, inform the manager and return the bottle with the cork to the bar for decanting (discussed in the next section). Feeling the cork for moisture content can, in some cases, identify if the wine was stored properly, on its side. It is true that we can detect some early indications of quality by smelling or inspecting the cork. The best way to analyze a wine is by looking at its color, smelling its aroma, swirling it to release its bouquet, and best of all tasting and then savoring its unique characteristics and flavor profile.

Once the cork has been removed, and the lip of the bottle wiped with a clean side towel, the server should pour about 1 ounce of wine for tasting purposes. The bottle should be held firmly while pouring. While the host, the guest who ordered the wine, tastes the wine, the server should be holding the bottle at the base with one hand and the neck with the other hand, with the label facing the guest. After the guest has given approval, the server should pour the wine for the other guests at the table, starting with the guest to the right of the taster (or women and/or older guests first), with the taster's glass filled last. The bottle should be twisted with a turn of the wrist as poured to prevent dribbling on the table. Glasses are generally filled one-third to half-full that permits swirling to experience the full bouquet that the wine has to offer.

Opening Champagne or Sparkling Wine

Learning Objective 6

Know the correct way to open and serve a bottle of champagne or sparkling wine.

When opening a bottle of champagne or sparkling wine, it is important to understand the great pressure the bottle is under and take great care. Loosely cover the top of the bottle with a side towel or linen napkin as a safety precaution as shown in Figure 6.5a. Then remove the foil and wire cap (usually with five complete twists plus one half-twist of the wire) as shown in Figure 6.5b. If the bottle has been shaken, the cork might pop off and accidentally injure someone if the bottle is not covered. As a further precaution, the server should have a hand on top of the cork. When removing the cork, firmly hold the cork in one hand, with the bottle pointing away from the guest, and slowly twist the bottle as the cork is removed. The cork should be removed with quiet precision, retaining the pressure in the bottle that creates the bubbles. Contrary to popular belief, it is not the best practice when opening champagne or sparkling wine to create a loud pop. Always have one champagne glass close at hand for quick pouring. Occasionally, when the cork is removed, the champagne may quickly overflow as the pressure is removed from the bottle. This is usually controlled after the first glass is poured.

Decanting Wine

Learning Objective 7

Explain the process of decanting wine.

There are two common reasons to decant a wine. Young full-bodied wines typically need time to breathe, a term meaning to allow oxygen to have contact with the wine, so that the aromas and flavors are released. Decanting speeds up the process of oxidation by pouring the wine from the bottle into a decanter that is typically an elegant crystal vessel. Pouring the wine into a glass and letting it sit can also allow the wine to breathe. In addition, there are also several quick and easy wine aerators on the market that attach to the opening at the top of the bottle; they can speed up the aeration process.

(a)

(b)

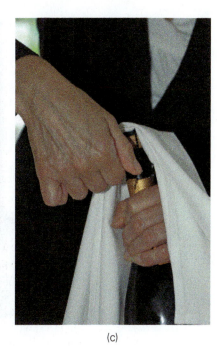
(c)

FIGURE 6.5

Opening a Bottle of Champagne
(a) Cover the top of the bottle with a linen napkin; (b) Remove the foil and wire cap.
Photos by Gerald Lanuzza.

In contrast, older wines may have a layer of sediment at the bottom of the bottle, and therefore need to be decanted to remove the undesirable sediment. Before beginning decanting, the server should be careful not to shake the bottle, to avoid activating and distributing the sediment throughout the wine. Decanting a bottle of wine may present problems to a novice server, but it is not as difficult as it may seem once the skill is acquired.

Wine is decanted by slowly pouring from a bottle to a decanter without disturbing any sediment. A light source, such as a candle or flashlight, behind the shoulder of the bottle (entire foil should be removed) will be the clue when to stop as the sediment approaches the neck. The same process would be followed for a bottle having cork particles. Another method for removing cork particles is to pour the wine through cheesecloth.

A server will first need the proper equipment to properly decant a bottle of wine: a wine key with a sharp knife (serrated works well), glass decanter, candle for the light source, and a napkin. Be careful not to agitate the sediment. After decanting the wine, ask the guest for approval and then serve from the glass decanter. An example of a glass decanter is shown in Figure 6.6. The wine bottle should always go back on the table so that the guests see what they are drinking.

Steps to Decant a Bottle of Wine

1. Stand the bottle up for several hours to allow the sediment to settle to the bottom or carefully transfer the wine in the same position as it was stored, preferably on its side, to a wine basket.
2. Remove the entire capsule with a knife.
3. Remove the cork with a corkscrew.
4. Place the candle behind the bottle to identify the location of the sediment.
5. Pour the wine gently and slowly into the decanter in front of the candle.
6. Stop pouring when you observe sediment traveling up the neck of the wine bottle.
7. Let the wine aerate in the decanter for 30 minutes to 1 hour before serving.

FIGURE 6.6
Wine Decanter
Courtesy of Steelite International.

Wine Glasses

Learning Objective 8

Identify different wine and beverage glasses.

Wine glasses ideally are clear and made of glass. Etched or colored glasses are not the best choice when one is attempting to appreciate the true color and characteristics of wine.

Wine glasses should always be carefully polished before service begins. There are many styles and shapes of wine glasses. Traditionally, wine glasses possess long stems for handling and have a wide enough bowl for swirling and smelling, as shown in Figure 6.7. Stemless glasses are quite popular especially in a casual setting; however, some wine experts feel that the temperature of your hand can heat up the wine. Most restaurants prefer a smaller bowl for white wines and a larger one for red wines. Typically, the smaller the bowl of the glass, the more aroma is directed toward the nose, thereby being easier to identify. A wider bowl with a smaller opening allows the wine to breathe, letting oxygen get to the wine and release aroma and flavors when tasted. The key is never to present the wine in a small glass that does not allow free movement of the wine.

Lengthy and multiple-course dinners often command several wine selections. The host will usually dictate which wine should be poured first. White wines usually are better enjoyed prior to red wines, younger wines before older wines, and dry wines before sweet wines.

Styles of Wine

Learning Objective 9

Explain the popular styles of wine.

Wine styles are typically defined by the grapes and the process in which the wine is produced.

White wines are usually made from white grapes, but in some cases you can make white wine from red grapes by eliminating contact with skin. There are some popular specialty wines made in this way.

Rosés are made by fermenting red grapes, skins, seeds, and juice, but only for a short time. This produces a light pink or salmon color and can yield a fruity, light wine.

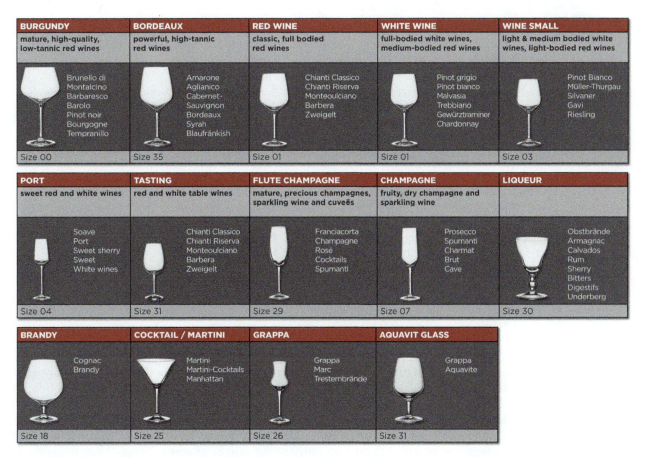

BURGUNDY	BORDEAUX	RED WINE	WHITE WINE	WINE SMALL
mature, high-quality, low-tannic red wines	powerful, high-tannic red wines	classic, full bodied red wines	full-bodied white wines, medium-bodied red wines	light & medium bodied white wines, light-bodied red wines
Brunello di Montalcino Barbaresco Barolo Pinot noir Bourgogne Tempranillo	Amarone Aglianico Cabernet-Sauvignon Barolo Bordeaux Syrah Blaufränkisch	Chianti Classico Chianti Riserva Monteoulciano Barbera Zweigelt	Pinot grigio Pinot bianco Malvasia Trebbiano Gewürztraminer Chardonnay	Pinot Bianco Müller-Thurgau Silvaner Gavi Riesling
Size 00	Size 35	Size 01	Size 01	Size 03

PORT	TASTING	FLUTE CHAMPAGNE	CHAMPAGNE	LIQUEUR
sweet red and white wines	red and white table wines	mature, precious champagnes, sparkling wine and cuveés	fruity, dry champagne and sparkling wine	
Soave Port Sweet sherry Sweet White wines	Chianti Classico Chianti Riserva Monteoulciano Barbera Zweigelt	Franciacorta Champagne Rosé Cocktails Spumanti	Prosecco Spumanti Charmat Brut Cave	Obstbrände Armagnac Calvados Rum Sherry Bitters Digestifs Underberg
Size 04	Size 31	Size 29	Size 07	Size 30

BRANDY	COCKTAIL / MARTINI	GRAPPA	AQUAVIT GLASS	
Cognac Brandy	Martini Martini-Cocktails Manhattan	Grappa Marc Tresternbrände	Grappa Aquavite	
Size 18	Size 25	Size 26	Size 31	

FIGURE 6.7
Wine Glasses
Courtesy of Steelite International.

Sparkling wines are made throughout the world by creating a second fermentation, in the bottle, in a tank, or by injecting bubbles into a wine that is already made. The best sparkling wines are made when the second fermentation takes place in the bottle because it produces the smallest and most numerable bubbles. Champagne is a place in France; therefore, according to the EU (European Union) a wine with bubbles should only be called Champagne when it originates from the Champagne region of France. It has its own unique flavor that comes from the natural characteristics of that region. It has been described as tasting creamy, yeasty, and nutty. The following terms describe the style and flavor of Champagne from the driest to the sweetest: Brut, Extra Dry, Sec, and Demi-Sec.

Fortified wine was originally made in the seaports of Spain, Portugal, Madeira, and Sicily. Seafarers strengthened wines with distilled brandies so that they could travel for months aboard ships in both hot and cold cargo bays without spoilage. Fortified wines have many applications, including using them in culinary for basic sauces, in baking for poaching or in dough, serving them as after-dinner drinks, and even as aperitifs before the meal to stimulate the appetite. The most popular fortified wines are Sherry, Port, Madeira, and Marsala.

Knowing the characteristics of a wine can help guide the server in offering suggestions to the guest who may request the server's opinion and/or recommendation for a wine selection. As a general rule, white wine is served with seafood and chicken and red wine with meat. Although there are no firm rules, ideally, the wine should complement the menu item, not dominate it. Consequently, dry wines are normally

Style of Wine	Common Characteristics	Country of Production
White	Pale to golden in color, darken as they age, fermented without skins, flavor from dry to sweet. Serve with poultry and fish.	Europe, United States, Australia, New Zealand, South America, South Africa
Rosé	Pink to salmon in color, fermented with skins for a short period of time, flavor from dry to sweet. Serve with light meats, poultry, and fish.	Europe, United States, Australia, New Zealand, South America, South Africa
Red	Ruby to purple in color, fermented with skins to extract color and flavor, mostly dry, serve with red meats and game.	Europe, United States, Australia, New Zealand, South America, South Africa
Sparkling	Can be white, will have effervescence, flavor from dry to sweet, serve before dinner as aperitif through dessert.	Europe, United States, Australia, New Zealand, South America, South Africa
Fortified	Ruby to tawny in color, alcohol is added to increase percentage of it, flavor from dry to sweet, serve dry as aperitif or sweet with cheese and dessert.	Port, Portugal; Sherry, Spain; Madeira-island of Madeira; Marsala, Italy

TABLE 6.2
Common Wine Style Characteristics

served directly with the entrée and sweeter wines with the dessert. Contemporary menus offer creative combinations of foods and sauces known as fusion foods, in which a seafood item, for example, may be accented with a sauce that would traditionally go with a meat item. The same is seen with wines such as a red wine being paired with a chicken entrée. Therefore, the server should be familiar with the preparation ingredients and accompanying sauces of menu items. Also, the time of the day can certainly dictate one's choice. A light, fruity, or even blush wine is an excellent choice for lunch. Ultimately, if the server can describe the wine's qualities, the guest will appreciate both the server's expertise and the wine selection. Table 6.2 provides a quick reference to common wine style characteristics.

Grape Varietals

Learning Objective 10

Understand that the climate in which grape varietals are grown affects the taste and color of wine.

Wine has been made for centuries and certain grapes have been the backbone of wine making throughout the world. When viewed from a distance, capturing wine knowledge can seem a daunting task. Although thousands of grape varietals exist, beginning with six and building slowly could easily lead to a mastery of dozens of varietals. Some noble grape varietals to begin with are listed in Table 6.3. The *Vitis*, or grapevine, produces a number of different rootstocks. Each rootstock gives birth to the many grape varietals. The European rootstock *Vinifera* is the family that is considered to produce the finest of the grape varietals. These types of grapes, sometimes known as noble grapes, have their origin in specific areas of Europe due to specific soil types and climates in the newer wine-growing regions of the world, including the United States, Australia, New Zealand, South America, and South Africa. In these newer regions, the wine is named by the grape varietal, which will guarantee at least 75 percent of the grape named on the label will be in the wine.

Wine guidelines have been set up for many of the wine-growing regions of the world. The European wine areas are steeped in tradition that dictates that grape characteristics are dependent on the soil, climate, and length of time ripened on the vine. This has led to their wines being named by the place that the grape is grown, which can be a town, a region, or a specific vineyard.

Grape	Style of Wine	Place of Origin	Flavor Characteristic	Other Places Grown
Sauvignon Blanc	White	Bordeaux, France	Grassy, herbal, fruity	United States, New Zealand
Chardonnay	White	Burgundy, France	Creamy, buttery, fruity	United States, Australia, S. Africa
Riesling	White	Germany	Fruity, acidic, spicy, delicate	United States, Australia
Cabernet Sauvignon	Red	Bordeaux, France	Red & black fruit, spice, vegetal	Many new regions
Pinot Noir	Red	Burgundy, France	Cherry, liquorice, plum, spice	All new regions
Merlot	Red	Bordeaux, France	Soft, plum, berry, currant	United States, Australia

TABLE 6.3
Some Noble Grape Varietals

It has also led to a term called *terrior*, which is not easily translated into English but includes the natural factors that determine the uniqueness of the grape that produces the wine from a specific place. Many people find this way of labeling easier and embrace these wines for their recognizable labels. Table 6.3 provides a quick reference to some noble grape varietals.

In choosing wines for a restaurant's wine list, the owner/manager/sommelier should take the same care that is taken with the food items that are selected for their menu. The wines should be paired with the menu items for servers to suggest to guests. A restaurateur could begin by understanding which grapes grow best in which region and which wines will enhance the menu of the restaurant. It is important to match the type of wine with the style, atmosphere, and price point of the restaurant.

Notable Wine Varietals and Food Pairings

Red

Cabernet Franc (cab-er-nay frahnk):
- Mostly used in Cabernet blending but recently has stood alone.
- Not as muscular as Cabernet Sauvignon with lovely raspberry aroma.
- Food pairing recommendations: wild game with earthy flavors, olives, and feta cheese

+Cabernet Sauvignon (cab-er-nay so-vin-yon):
- Perhaps the grandest of the red varietals.
- Big, bold, and complex with violet aromas, black currant flavors.
- Sometimes blended with Merlot (or other varietals) to "soften" the wine, making it easier to drink when young.
- Typically, a wine aged in oak.
- Has the ability to age well.
- Food pairing recommendations: chocolate, lamb, duck, beef, and strong cheeses including blue cheese.

Gamay (gam-ay):
- One of the lighter and fruitier red varietals, best known as the popular Beaujolais Nouveau, released around Thanksgiving time.
- Food pairing recommendations: Thanksgiving foods such as turkey, ham, and traditional accompaniments.

Grenache (gre-nash):
- Found in the Rhone Valley and Spain.
- Soft tannins and acids.
- Food pairing recommendations: olives, manchego cheese, and roasted lamb.

+Merlot (mur-lo):

- Traditionally, a blending grape in Bordeaux.
- Softer and rounder than Cabernet with plum notes, lush, and velvety.
- Gaining in popularity due to its ability to be consumed young.
- Food pairing recommendations: grilled meat or fish such as tuna, tomato meat sauce, chocolate, berries, and hard cheeses.

+Pinot Noir (pee-no-nwar):

- Fine, full flavored, full body with an "earthy" nose.
- Velvety and long lasting on the palette.
- Food pairing recommendations: salmon, lamb, sausage, game, and goat cheese.

Sangiovese (sang-joe-vay-zay):

- Rich garnet hue, deep when young, warm red-brick when mature.
- Can taste slightly earthy and tannic (used in Chianti and other Italian wines).
- Food pairing recommendations: Tuscan pasta, risotto, bruschetta, lasagna, and hard cheeses like parmesan.

Syrah (sir-ra):

- Full, heavy, long-lived wines of great color, scent, and body.
- Food pairing recommendations: game, mushrooms, grilled meats, and slightly pungent cheese.

Zinfandel (zin-fun-del):

- Unique to California.
- Depending on winemaking techniques, it can be made in bigger or lighter style. Berry overtones.
- Food pairing recommendations: blackened fish, spicy sausage, game, grilled peppers, and aged cheeses.

White

+Chardonnay (shar-dun-nay):

- Most classic variety.
- Pale to yellow color (aged in oak).
- Vanilla and oak flavors when aged in oak.
- Dry, rich, and fresh.
- Nutty and full bodied.
- Food pairing recommendations: shellfish, flounder, halibut, salmon, poultry, pork loin, and mild cheeses.

Chenin Blanc (shen-n-blahnk):

- A truly diverse grape, fruity with residual sugar (honeyed richness) to nicely dry.
- Has been famous for centuries in Loire Valley, growing in popularity in California, and named Steen in South Africa.
- Food pairing recommendations: fruit salsa, light cream sauces, shellfish, poultry, charcuterie, and mildly spicy foods.

Gewürztraminer (geh-verts-trah-mee-ner):

- From the German "gewurtz" or spice.
- Has a strong aroma of tropical fruit and rose petals.
- Cool climate grape with passion fruit, floral and spicy taste.
- Food pairing recommendations: slightly sweet food, spicy Asian dishes, shellfish, poultry, pork, pâté, and mild cheeses.

Muscat/Moscato (muss-kat):

- There are at least six variations of this varietal, it has become very popular for its fruity aroma and taste.
- It can produce wines of great diversity and an authentic grapiness that appeals to a diverse demographic including the millennials.
- Food pairing recommendations: cured meats, dried fruit, and mild cheeses.

Pinot Blanc (pee-no blahnk):

- Light, good sipping wine, accessible to all.
- Food pairing recommendations: fresh fruit, light cheeses, and seafood appetizers.

Pinot Grigio (pee-no-Gree-gio):

- A white mutation of Pinot Noir with good color.
- Can have a deep golden color, it has soft acid, good aroma, and spice.
- Food pairing recommendations: light meats such as veal, pork, pesto, shellfish, and mild cheese.

+Riesling (rees-ling):

- Fruity, yet elegant, wine distinguished in Germany, Alsace, and Pacific Northwest.
- Generally medium-dry with crisp acidity.
- Food pairing recommendations: spicy foods, sushi, poultry, and creamy cheeses.

+Sauvignon Blanc (so-vin-yon blahnk):

- Exceptional examples from Bordeaux, New Zealand, and California.
- Can produce big, dry, aromatic wines.
- Occasionally found in dessert wines.
- Refreshing acidity.
- Food pairing recommendations: fish, oysters, turkey, sauces with citrus, and feta cheese.

Semillon (sem-ih-yon):

- Best known in Sauternes district of Bordeaux.
- Often blended with Sauvignon Blanc to make world-class dessert wines.
- Sweetness of freshly ripened fruit.
- Food recommendations: rich pâtés and gooseliver, creamy cheeses, and fruit desserts.

Trebianno (tre-bee-ah-no):

- Dry, light table wine from Italy.
- Often blended with other less-than-noble varieties.
- Food recommendations: simple foods such as poached fish, vegetable antipasto, and light seafood pasta dishes.

Note: + indicates inclusion in Table 6.3, Some Noble Grape Varietals

Food and Wine Pairing

Learning Objective 11

Describe various food and wine pairings.

The dishes that match with the wine have come about through years of traditions in culinary preparation and wine production. The principal is to try to achieve balance, a partnership, so that the food does not overpower the food, or vice versa. A knowledgeable server will be able to gently guide guests into the combination that fits their personal desires. Many guests will drink only one style of wine, but may enjoy food that does not pair well with their preference. For example, a guest may want red wine due to its health benefits with their fish. Because heavy red wines may overpower a delicate fish, the server may suggest a lighter red wine or a meatier fish. There are some basic rules applied to food and wine pairing. The weight or body of the wine is very important. Food should not be heavier than the wine to have an ideal match. Light wines work well with light food such as poached fish or poultry. Heavy, full-bodied wines can stand up to heavy foods like grilled lamb. Tannin in red wine can be described as having an astringent or bitter flavor that comes from several places, including the skins of the grapes. They generally dry your mouth out. Tannin helps to cut through fat in food, which refreshes the palate after each bite. Therefore, red wines can be matched to richer foods. Tannins are very important in red wine when pairing with food. Wines with heavy tannins can stand up well to heavy, juicy red meats. Be aware of any sauce served with the red meat; the heavier the sauce, the more tannic wine can be paired because the wine cuts through the richness of the sauce. Dry sparkling wines like Champagne or Cava refresh the palate and work well with foods that have a salty characteristic, like cheese and cured meat. White wines are lighter in style and flavor than red and match well with lighter-style foods such as appetizers, flaky filet of fish, simply prepared chicken, and veal. Crisp white wines made from Sauvignon Blanc can stand up to dressings and light-style foods, which are from something citrus. Full-bodied wines made from Chardonnay can complement seafood, heavier fishes, and the rich sauces typically served with fishes. Sweeter white wines pair with rich and highly spiced foods; the sweetness can round out or tame the spice. Dry, acidic wines, which make your mouth water, pair best with foods such as lemon or tomatoes, which also have acid in them. Sweet foods need sweeter wines so that they will not taste acidic on the palate. Earthy, light-bodied wines like Pinot Noir pair well with earthy food like mushrooms and earthy cheeses. It is important to consider the components of a sauce that will be served with a protein before matching the food with a wine.

Refer to the Glossary (Wine, Beer, Spirits, and Beverage Terms), which lists general descriptive wine terms, along with terms that describe wine by sight, smell, and taste.

Distilled Spirits and Cocktails

Learning Objective 12

Identify and describe popular distilled spirits and cocktails.

A distilled spirit contains ethanol and must go through the distillation process. The distillation process essentially turns a fermented beverage with relatively low alcohol into a beverage with higher alcohol. The use of fruit, grains, or vegetables is common when making a distilled spirit. Each spirit has a distinct flavor and color, and it can be consumed on its own or mixed with other ingredients. Regardless of the time period, human beings have consumed distilled spirits throughout the world. Many distilled spirits have a specific origin and a tradition within a specific country, as well as unique uses, recipes, or processes. Many spirits were first used for medicinal reasons and then later made the transition to social occasions. Spirits have a strong flavor due to the high alcohol percentage content; therefore, it became common to mix them to create cocktails. The craft of making cocktails and blending flavors became a blend of the sophisticated and the mysterious. There are famous bars with signature cocktails throughout the world, and many have lasted for generations and continue to be fashionable today, such as the Mint Julep. In addition to the traditional signature cocktails, bartenders continue to explore the endless, innovative new recipes using uniquely located liquors, high-quality flavors, and unusual ingredients. The number of small, locally owned distilleries has increased and has become a destination for customers, who have more knowledge and understand how their spirits are manufactured. Many of these establishments are creating their own juices, sodas, syrups, mixers, and flavorings and are using fresh herbs to make hand-crafted drinks. Craft cocktails with specially shaped ice cubes add to the enjoyment and appeal of a well-balanced drink. Bars with specific signature cocktails using various spirits and exotic ingredients entice consumers all across America, as shown by the popular cocktail menu in Figure 6.8.

The Gin Joint

DRINKS

SUN – WED
5 pm – 12 am

THU – FRI
5 pm – 2 am

SAT
3 pm – 2 am

– theginjoint.com –

FLIP FOR
FOOD MENU

SPRING UP

COMEBACK KID
Jasmine Gunpowder Tea Old Grand-Dad Bourbon, Aperol, Lemon, Galangal Syrup, Orange Cream Citrate, Orange Twist
$9

CHECKPOINT CHARLIE
Hibiscus Powers Irish Whiskey, Lemon, Ginger Honey, Pedro Ximénez Sherry, Grenadine, Grapefruit Bitters, Lemon Twist
$10

FLY BOY
St. George Terrior Gin, Lemon, Honey, Génépy des Alpes, Green Chartreuse, Rosebank Farm Pea Tendrils
$11

POSSUM JENKINS
Byrrh Quinquina, Pineapple, Lime, Campari, Falernum, Habanero Bitters, Blackstrap Bitters
$9

PUDDLE JUMPER
Death's Door Gin, Génépy des Alpes, Strega, Lime, Grains of Paradise Syrup, Thyme
$10

CHATTERBOX
Salers Aperitif, Lime, Simple Syrup, Manzanilla Sherry, Matcha, Basil, Louched Absinthe Float
$9

STRONG LIKE BULL

SADDLE BUM $11
Ramazzotti, Fernet Branca, Aperol, Pamplemousse Liqueur, Lime, BBQ Bitters, Peychaud's Bitters

TWEED RING
Aquavit, Nonino Grappa, Amaro Nonino, Chardonnay Tea Syrup, Grapefruit Bitters, Lemon and Grapefruit Expression, Tarragon

STUDMUFFIN
Charleston Madeira, Hoodoo Chicory Liqueur, St. George Coffee Liqueur, Amaro Sibilla, Sumac Bay Leaf Ice Cubes

COAL BITER
Monkey Shoulder Scotch, Campari, Yellow Chartreuse, Fino Sherry, Smoked Saline

---

OUT OF THE BOX

THIEVE'S TONIC $11
Pusser's Rum, Local Spade & Clover Fresh Turmeric, House Tonic, Lime, Coconut Syrup, Ginger Honey, Co2

HONEYMOONER
Chile Altos Blanco Tequila, Lime, Salted Honey, Aperol, Lime Twist

TO PIMP A BUTTERFLY
Lavender Sipsmith Gin, Pistachio Orgeat, Lime, Vanilla Syrup, Cream, Egg White, Co2

FUNNY FARM
Pelotón de la Muerte Mezcal, Roasted Poblano Honey, Lime, Giffard Banana Liqueur, Orgeat, Banana Chip

VILLAGE IDIOT
Plantation 3 Star Rum, Diplomatico Rum, Meyer Lemon Sherbet, Lemon, Arugula Cordial, Egg White, Duck Fat Powder

FOR SHARING

Punches Prepared Tableside (750 ml)

CONVICTED MELON
Altos Blanco Tequila, Watermelon Infused Dolin Dry Vermouth, Lemon, Aperol, St. Germain
$42

CHICO DUSTY
Antigua Reposado Tequila, Sotol, Celery Cordial, Lime, Hellfire Bitters
$38

THE DEBUTANTE
Ransom Old Tom Gin, Lemon, Vermut, Honey, Apricot Liqueur, Thyme
$40

WEEKEND AT FERNIE'S
Flor de Caña Extra Dry Rum, Bacardi 151 Rum, Strawberry, Orgeat, Lime, Falernum, Cointreau, Fernet, BBQ Bitters
$38

Punches are also available as single cocktails.

TOP SHELF

VIRGINIA GENTLEMAN
Reservior Rye, Demerara, Angostura Bitters, Orange Bitters

UNCLE GERALD'S MARTINI $18
St. George Rum, Botanist Gin, Local Sea Beans, Dolin Dry Vermouth
$20

ITALIAN JULEP
Stranahan's Rye, Angostura Amaro, Cynar, Tossolin, Ramazzotti, Bráulio, Mint
$20

BARTENDER'S CHOICE

CHOOSE ANY TWO WORDS $11

Refreshing	Licorice
Tart	Herbal
Savory	Vegetal
Fruit	Non-Alcoholic
Strong	Bitter
Spicy	Unusual
Sweet	Floral
Fizzy	Smoky

20% GRATUITY ADDED FOR LARGE PARTIES

FOOD

PROVISIONS

BEEF JERKY Flank with Soy & Chili
$1.50 EA

OYSTERS* Jalapeño Mignonette, Laphroaig Brine, Bulls Bay Smoked Sea Salt
$1.50 EA

PAD THAI POPCORN Palm Sugar, Lime, Fish Sauce, Chili, Peanuts
$6

SOFT PRETZELS Sriracha Cheese Sauce, Bulls Bay Sea Salt
$7

ASPARAGUS CAESAR Local Asparagus, Caesar Dressing, Shaved Parmesan, Ciabatta Croutons
$8

PICKLED SHRIMP Lemon, Caper, Onion, Toasted Ciabatta
$8

CRAB DIP Potato Mousse, House Salt and Vinegar Chips
$9

CLAMS AND CHORIZO White Wine Butter, Grilled Ciabatta
$9

CROQUE MONSIEUR Brioche, Ham, Apple Cider Mornay *(Add Fried Egg, $1.50)*
$9

RICOTTA STUFFED MEATBALL San Marzano Tomato Sauce, Ciabatta
$10

PORK BUNS Hoisin Glazed Pork, Mustard Green Kimchi, House Steam Buns
$12

CHEESE

$6 EACH With Accompaniments

BATTERY PARK BRIE Cow's Milk, Charleston Artisan Cheesehouse, South Carolina

CLEMSON BLUE CHEESE Cow's Milk, South Carolina

HOUSE PIMENTO CHEESE Tillamook Cheddar

FRESH GOAT Pink Peppercorn, Vermont

MANCHEGO Sheep's Milk, Spain

SMOKED GOUDA Cow's Milk, Illinois

DERBY SAGE Cow's Milk, England

BERGENOST Triple Cream, New York

CHEF'S SNACK BOARD
Chef's Selection of Cheeses and Meats, served with Accompaniments *Inquire with your server for daily selection.*
$32

DESSERTS

PEANUT BUTTER CHOCOLATE BAR
Pretzel, Dulce de Leche, Pop Rocks, Bulls Bay Sea Salt
$6

MILK AND HONEY Buttermilk Honey Ice Cream Sandwiched with Lemon Shortcake Cookies
$6

LAVENDER CREME BRULEE
Lavender, Vanilla Bean
$7

STRAWBERRY COBBLER
Buttermilk Ice Cream
$8

The Gin Joint
CHARLESTON, S. CAROLINA

* Contains ingredients that are raw or undercooked. Consuming raw or undercooked meats, poultry, seafood, shellfish, or eggs may increase your risk of foodborne illness.

FIGURE 6.8
Cocktail Menu
Courtesy of Gin Joint; Charleston, SC.

Style of Spirit	Color	Fermented From	Origin	Popular Cocktails
Vodka	Clear	Grain, Potatoes, Sugar Beets	Russia, Poland, Scandinavia	Martini, Cosmopolitan, Screwdriver, Moscow Mule, Bloody Mary, Vodka Tonic
Gin	Clear	Grain compounded with juniper berries	Holland, Great Britain	Martini, Dry Martini, Gibson, Gin and Tonic, Tom Collins, Gin Rickey
Rum	Clear to Brown	Sugarcane	The Caribbean	Rum and Coke, Daiquiris, Rocks, Mixers (Tonic and 7-up), Rum Martini
Tequila	Clear to Gold	Blue Agave Plant	Mexico	Margarita, straight with lemon and salt, with Sangria (a citrus juice)
Scotch Whiskey	Caramel Amber	Malted barley, Grains	Scotland	On the rocks, with soda or water, Rob Roy, Godfather
Irish Whiskey	Caramel Amber	Malted barley, Grains	Ireland	On the rocks, with soda or water, Rusty Nail, coffee
Bourbon American Whiskey	Caramel Amber	Malted barley, Grains	USA	On the rocks, with soda, ginger ale or water, Manhattan, Mint Julep, Old Fashion
Brandy	Caramel	Grapes	Anywhere	In a snifter, Brandy Alexander
Cognac	Caramel	Grapes	France	In a snifter, Sidecar
Armagnac	Caramel	Grapes	France	In a snifter

TABLE 6.4
Common Styles of Spirits

Common styles of spirits and popular cocktails are shown in Table 6.4.

Vodka

Vodka is a popular white spirit with a neutral flavor, made primarily with grains, sugar beets, or potatoes. It is either mixed with other ingredients or chilled and consumed by itself. Vodka was first distilled in Poland and Russia; it is a Slavic word meaning "little water." As the distillation process improved, vodka production became very popular and widespread in Scandinavia.

Vodka did not become mainstream in the United States until the 1950s with the Smirnoff brand, which was established in Russia. Smirnoff brand remains popular in the United States with many more vodka brands available in the United States market today. When vodka was first introduced, the American palate was in search of a lighter spirit than whiskey and the clear spirit was the perfect alternative. After World War II, vodka became a favorite of American servicemen. They added lime and ginger beer to the clear liquid, served it in a copper mug, and the Moscow Mule was born. It was a favorite drink for celebrities in the 1950s. There has been a resurgence of the Moscow Mule in recent years.

Many brands of vodka from various countries are sold in the United States, as well as premium vodkas from small producers. Premium vodkas make multiple trips through the still to increase smoothness and remove impurities. When vodka has been distilled multiple times, it is noted on the bottle and can be a measure of quality. The other factors that contribute to the quality and price of vodka include the grain used, water quality, and filtering method. Flavored vodkas are appealing and are the perfect ingredient for specialty martinis and signature cocktails. There are vodkas that are flavored with all different types of fruits and spices. Many bars will infuse their own vodka using decorative jars. When a customer sees the jars behind the bar, it is good marketing and creates a conversation between the bartender and their guests.

Whiskeys, Rye, Scotch, and Bourbon

Whiskey differs considerably from vodka. Whiskeys are brown or caramel in color and have many distinct aromas and flavors. Whiskey has a more complicated distillation process than vodka. Additional steps need to be taken to make and age whiskey. Whiskey is made all over the world but had its origins in Scotland or Ireland.

Grains such as barley corn or rye are the base for making whiskey. Whiskeys are typically aged in oak barrels, which add to the color, aroma, and flavor of the spirit. The main differences between the leading whiskey producing countries such as the United States, Canada, Scotland, and Ireland are in the type of grain used, the method of production, the method of aging, and the blending techniques.

Scotch is made in Scotland and its claim to fame is in the malted barley that gives a distinctive aftertaste. Malting is a process that converts the starch in the barley into sugar. This conversion process is important because it aids the fermentation process, which converts the sugar into alcohol. *Single malt Scotch* is produced from malted barley and exclusively comes from a single cask or barrel. The most popular Scotch is Blended Scotch, which is made by combining single malts with unmalted grain whiskeys. Another unique flavor of Scotch comes from the distinctive soft water, which is rich in minerals. The use of peat to dry the malted barley adds a smoky flavor to Scotch. The peat is cut from nearby bogs and used to stoke the fires during the drying process.

There are specific aging requirements for Scotch. Barrel aging helps to smooth the flavor of the Scotch. It is aged in oak for at least 3 years. Malt whiskeys require up to 12–15 years of aging. Grain whiskeys are best when aged for 6–8 years.

Like Scotch, *Irish* whiskey is made from a mash based on barley, with the addition of corn and rye. The difference in Ireland is that the malted barley is dried in coal-fired ovens. In Scotland, the barley is dried over peat. Irish whiskey lacks the smoky flavor common in Scotch. The Irish use a column still while a pot still is used in Scotland.

Whiskey is also made in the United States. The most popular American whiskey is Bourbon. The name *Bourbon* comes from a county in Kentucky where the classic drink was first made. For a whiskey to carry the name Bourbon, it must meet several criteria: The whiskey must be made from 51 percent corn and the rest of the mash can be made from rye, wheat, or malted barley, distilled to 80 percent alcohol, and aged in a new charred oak barrel for a minimum of two years. The use of the charred oak barrel helps smooth the flavor of the bourbon, gives it a mellow flavor, and adds color. Bourbon has become very popular recently with an increase in small-batch premium brands and can be enjoyed in a cocktail or on its own on the rocks. Bourbon is sweet because of the corn used in the mash and smoky because of the charred barrels.

Straight bourbons must be aged for at least 2 years and unblended.

Single-barrel bourbons are very popular. They are a premium style of bourbon, which command a higher price than other bourbons. They are bottled from a specific single barrel. These bourbons are not blended with any other bourbon. They are numbered, have an individually unique flavor, and come in fancy packages appealing to a premium market. *Small-batch bourbons* are similar to single barrel but may have additional years of aging, making them even more exclusive.

Tennessee whiskey is essentially straight bourbon, made in Tennessee from a mash that contains at least 51 percent corn. It is mellower than other whiskeys because it is filtered through charcoal made from Tennessee maple.

Blended whiskeys are a blend of straight whiskey and other batches of whiskey and are probably best known as coming from Canada. The lighter styles come from Canadian Club, Crown Royal, and Seagram's V.O. (Note: America and Ireland use the "e" when spelling whiskey, while Scotland and Canada spell whisky without the "e.")

Rye whiskey was popular in the northeast and Canada before prohibition. It has seen an increase in popularity in recent years. For a whiskey to be named rye, it must meet several criteria. It must be made from 51 percent rye and the rest of the mash can be made from corn, wheat, or malted barley, distilled to 80 percent alcohol, and aged in a new charred oak barrel for a minimum of 2 years. Rye is drier than bourbon and was the whiskey traditionally used in a Manhattan.

Brandy

Brandy is simply wine that has been distilled. Grapes are fermented into wine. The resulting mixture is placed in a pot still and distilled to further refine the mixture and increase the alcohol.

The two most prestigious brandies come from the Cognac and Armagnac regions of France. They have a long tradition of brandy making. In these two regions, the unique soil types, the use of varied distillation methods, and aging in specific oak barrel give the brandy distinctive flavors, aromas, and color. They are generally sipped straight from a snifter. More common varieties are mixed with other ingredients to make cocktails.

Gin

Gin is a white spirit with a unique flavor that is the result of compounding a white grain spirit with juniper berries. The Dutch originally created a tonic using juniper berries to cure various diseases. Gin became wildly popular in England, which led to production of a low-quality spirit with no regulation. When the Coffey still was introduced, gin became a better product and there were big brands that dominated the market. Soon after the introduction of the Coffey still, gin was then exported into the United States. Gin was the precursor to vodka and was used widely in cocktails before, during, and after prohibition. Martinis were, and still are, an extremely popular drink. Originally made with gin and vermouth, they are garnished with an olive and served in a stemmed glass. The martini has transformed into hundreds of drinks today, with a multitude of ingredients. Gin has a more complex flavor than vodka, which has influenced its increased popularity.

London dry gin is generally the drink of choice, while Holland's gin has a stronger taste and full body, due to its lower distillation proof, malt aroma, and flavor.

Rum

Rum is generally made from sugarcane or molasses. Because of this, it is best produced in the tropical ports of Puerto Rico and Jamaica. Early Spanish settlers in the West Indies saw that the residual molasses from their sugar factories fermented easily. Soon the rum industry was more lucrative than sugar. Each of the rum-producing countries in the Caribbean has their own style of rum that can satisfy a vast clientele. Rums can be either light (or white) or dark. Light rums are made in column stills that distill away much of the flavor and color. Dark rums are made in pot stills to retain basic ingredients and aged in oak.

Mescal, Tequila

Pulque is considered to be the first fermented beverage produced in North America. The Aztecs drank the wine-like liquid made from the blue agave plant called *pulque*. If this is true, tequila is a close descendant of this beverage.

Just as with *pulque*, the blue agave plant is the source of fine tequila. Grown near the town of Tequila in Mexico, the agave is steamed or smoked underground, fermented until a coarse wine is produced, and distilled to make tequila. Most Americans prefer the distilled, more refined tequila.

Bianco is unaged, clear tequila bottled shortly after distillation. *Joven* or gold has coloring and flavoring added or can be a blend of aged and silver tequila. *Reposado* is aged in wood for at least 2 months but no more than 1 year; this aging process imparts flavor and nuances from each producer. Aged tequilas are called *anejo* and are more expensive because they are aged in small oak barrels for at least a year. Premium tequila has become extremely popular and what was once a spirit mixed with other ingredients, is sipped, and savored on the rocks, with the popular margarita as one example.

Liqueurs (Cordials)

Liqueurs, also called cordials, were originally produced as medicinal remedies for all ailments known to man. One can argue that the original distillers were not too far off their target. After all, various roots, herbs, seeds, and flowers contain properties used today in various drugs.

When the practice of medicine took a separate path from spirits, we were left with wonderful liqueurs (or cordials). These are generally sweet after-dinner drinks. Their essential oils make them a natural aid for digestion. These begin as neutral flavored spirits and are flavored by mixing or distilling in various fruits, herbs, seeds, spices, and flowers. They are then sweetened with sugar to finish.

Liqueurs must contain at least 2½ percent sugar (with many including as much as 35 percent). This makes liqueurs popular cooking and baking liquids as well.

Liqueur Notables

- Benedictine is one of the oldest of liqueurs; developed in 1510 from many herbs and plants with a cognac brandy base.
- Chartreuse is still made by monks in France; Yellow is low proof (80–86) and Green is 110 proof, and both are spicy, aromatic, and based on brandy.
- Cointreau is an orange-flavored liqueur.
- Drambuie combines malt Scotch whiskey and heather honey.
- Grand Marnier is made from a cognac brandy base with orange peels for flavor.
- Irish Mist is a spicy Irish whiskey with a heather honey-flavoring agent.
- Kahlua is a coffee-flavored liqueur from Mexico.
- Saint Germaine is a French elderflower liqueur used to flavor wine or champagne and to make many lovely cocktails.
- Southern Comfort is a blend of Bourbon whiskey, peach liqueur, and fresh peaches.
- Tia Maria is from Jamaica and is a coffee-flavored liqueur based on rum.

Table 6.4 provides a quick reference to common styles of spirits.

Refer to the Glossary (Wine, Beer, Spirits, and Beverage Terms) for a list of some of the notable spirit brands, related cocktails, and commonly used beverage terms.

Beers, Lagers, and Ales

Learning Objective 13

Understand and explain the difference between beers, lagers, and ales.

The impact of beer on humanity has been significant. Beer making has been dated to 5000 B.C. One of the oldest recipes known to man was found in the pyramids and is a recipe for a type of beer. The religious priesthood and monasteries were central to its progression and still produce some of the most sought-after beers in the world, the Trappist Monasteries in Europe for example. However, neighborhood bakers also led the charge by combining barley and yeast to ferment and finish beer. Beer is a product we have been making in civilizations around the world for centuries.

Beer, as defined by the Rheinheitsgebot, also known as the Purity Law of 1516, is made with malt, water, hops, and yeast. Yeast was not in the original law but was added decades later after its discovery. Beer may also be made with the addition of other cereal grains, in addition to malt, including corn grits, brewers rice, unmalted barley, unmalted wheat, and oatmeal to name five. Beer should not be confused with another type of malt beverages known as malternatives, which are beverages made from malt, but do not contain hops, are clear (unless colored by the addition of natural or artificial coloring agents), and are usually flavored (most commonly by fruit extracts or flavorings) and carbonated. What many people refer to as beer is most commonly divided into two designations: lager and ale. However, a third, and rarer, product is a class of beers known as spontaneously fermented.

The primary difference between lagers, ales, and spontaneously fermented beers is the yeast added by the brewer. In lagers, the yeast settles to the bottom of the fermentation tank, while in ales the yeast floats. Spontaneously fermented beers do not have any yeast added by the brewer. Instead, after the wort (unfermented beer that has been boiled in the brew kettle) is cooled, it is then transferred into a large, shallow, open-top tank, where it is exposed to the air. Any wild yeast floating in the air will settle on the wort and begin fermenting, spontaneously. This is a very old and seldom-used practice, but is one of the original ways in which fermentation took place before we knew about yeast and how to grow and control it. The most recognized group of spontaneously fermented beers comes from Belgium, is known as Lambic, and can be fruit-flavored, like Kriek (cherry) and Peche (peach), or unflavored (Gueze). Lambics typically age 2 to 4 years before final blending and secondary fermentation.

During fermentation, lagers are fermented at cooler temperatures for longer times than ales, using yeast that settles to the bottom of the fermentation tank. Lagers take longer to make, are clear, and have a clean taste that is less complex than ales. Ales are fermented at higher temperatures than lagers, for shorter time, take much less time to make, and have more complex flavors than lagers. These differences in production result in different carbonation levels and different handling and serving practices, which will be covered later in this section.

The brewing process is quite simple but requires stringent sanitation practices to avoid problems. The following steps are used in brewing:

Malting: Allowing barley (or wheat) to begin to germinate (sprout).

Kilning: Cooking the malt by steaming (for pale malt), stewing (for caramel malt), and roasting (for dark or chocolate malt).

Mashing: Steeping the malt in hot water to extract the sugars from the malt.

Lautering/Sparging: Separating the sweet liquid from the malt.

Brewing/Boil: Boiling the sweet liquid (now called wort) in a brew kettle and adding hops at prescribed intervals for a specific flavor.

Cooling: The hops are separated from the wort, the wort is cooled through a heat exchanger, and transferred to a fermentation tank.

Fermentation: Yeast is added to the wort to begin fermentation. This is where the wort becomes an ale or lager.

Filtering/Conditioning/Maturation: After fermentation, the beer is filtered and transferred to a conditioning tank and aged. For ales, this is a short process taking days up to about two weeks; for lagers, it can be many weeks or longer.

Packaging: The beer is bottled, canned, or kegged.

Hops provide the bitterness and floral qualities in beer as well as help preserve the beer. There are many types of hops grown and each provides a different bitterness and aroma profile. A few examples of hops include Cascade, Hallertau, and Fuggle. Hops are added to the brew kettle while the wort is boiling. Hops are volatile and the flavor and aroma will cook out. The brewer controls the amount of hop flavor and aroma in beer by (a) selecting and blending different hops and (b) adding hops at different stages of the boil in the brew kettle. The earlier the hops are added in the brew kettle, the less floral and bitter and the more malty and sweeter the beer will be. As hops are added later in the boil, the beer will become more bitter and floral. The bitterness in beer is measured by its IBU (International Bittering Unit) number. The range generally runs from about 3 to 75, but some craft brewers have created beers with IBUs in excess of 115. The higher the number, the more bitter the beer; the lower the number, the more malty the beer.

Clarity in beer is measured by its SRM (Standard Reference Method). The higher the SRM number, the more cloudy the beer. Some beers are naturally cloudy, like hefeweizen, made from wheat malt, while other beers should never be cloudy, like pilsner. Knowing the characteristics of a beer can tell you if it is a good beer or has a fault.

Beer can be served with meals or by itself. The hops in beer stimulate appetites. Beer is used in various food preparations from soups to stews. It can be served with cheese and is used instead of yeast in some pancakes and fritters. The tangy quality of beer makes it popular with highly flavored or spicy dishes such as corned beef, Irish stew, sausage, cold cuts, pork dishes, fried dishes, or curry.

In judging the quality of beer, one should compare the beer with accepted standards and guidelines for the specific type or style of beer. Quality-control measures are handled at the brewery, which include the quality of the grain, hops, chemical analysis and makeup of the brewing water, and brewery sanitation, to name a few.

The American craft beer industry is small but growing at a faster rate than large brewers in both sales and volume. According to the Brewers Association, a craft brewer is small (produces less than 2 million barrels of beer per year), independent (less than 25 percent of the brewery is owned or controlled by an industry member who is not a craft brewer), and traditional (produces at least 50 percent of its volume in either all malt beers or beers that use adjuncts to enhance, not lighten flavor).

Due to the small size of craft brewers, they often find their niche by creating interesting, nonmainstream beers with unique character that attracts a small, but dedicated, following. Large brewers cannot or would not produce these unique beers due to economics (the beers are too expensive to produce for their market), or the market being too small (there are not enough consumers for the unique flavor, so it is not cost effective to produce the beer). In the United States, many craft brewers create extreme beers that can be excessively hopped; are aged in unique, small-batch containers (like bourbon barrels); are high in alcohol (high gravity beers); or have some other interesting or unique style or flavor profile. Craft beer is a good choice for those who are interested in protecting the environment. If you select a craft beer, it cuts down on the travel time and expense of large beer companies. There is less use of fossil fuels in the transportation, which helps the environment. Also, fewer preservatives are required for these beers.

The perfect temperature for most beers and lagers is 45–47°F. Ales are served a bit warmer at about 50–52°F. Dark beers should be served at a cool room temperature (but that of most European rooms, 58–68°F).

Glassware varies from pilsners, pub glasses, mugs, goblets, and specialty glasses (for those operations desiring an out-of-the-ordinary type of glass).

A clean glass is a must for the perfect head as well as the ultimate taste. Glasses should be free of oils, soaps, and fingerprints. The term "beer clean" is a description for a clean, no-residue glass that will not impart any off flavors in the beer, nor break down the head of the beer. A detergent and rinse agent specifically designed for bar glasses should always be used for the cleaning and sanitizing of beer, wine, and bar glassware.

Many bartenders pour beer by tilting the glass at an angle to prevent an overwhelming head of foam. This style has its supporters. However, the traditional

FIGURE 6.9
Beer Glasses with Foam
Courtesy of Steelite International.

serving style is to let the glass remain standing on a flat surface. The beer is poured directly into the bottom of the glass. The foam should be between ¾ and 1½ inches high depending on the type and style of beer, as shown in Figure 6.9. They do this to release excess carbon dioxide. Many American beers in particular contain more carbon dioxide than European beers, primarily because lagers are the dominant beer in America while ales dominate Europe. Beer drawn from tap should be promptly served to the guest.

Premium or imported beer is often served in the bottle to the guest. When the server is pouring beer at the table, the glass should be placed to the right of the guest. If the guest prefers to do the pouring, they will inform the server. Most often the server pours the beer. The server should carefully pour the beer directly into the center of the glass, allowing about 1½ inches of foam to appear and come to the rim of the glass, followed by a quick twist of the bottle to prevent dripping. The bottle is then placed above and to the right of the glass. It is enjoyable to have a small portion of many styles of beer to taste and compare to each other. This creates a learning experience within a social setting. In response to this, many establishments offer guests a sampling of the beer they offer and call it a "flight" and can be served as shown in Figure 6.10.

Just like wine, it can be very interesting and delightful to pair beer and food. There are over 10,000 brands of beer available to the American consumer; there is a type and brand of beer to satisfy any palate. Beer can enhance the flavor of food. Consider the flavor of the beer and the body of the beer. Serve lighter beers first and work toward heavier styles. How will the beer enhance the food you pair with it? Does the beer complement or contrast the dish you pair it with?

In terms of storage, remember that beer is extremely perishable. Odors, bacteria, air, and even artificial or natural light can destroy a beer before it reaches our palates. Beer should be stored at around 40°F. Bottled beer should be stored in a dark, cool place. Beer in cans is not affected by light, but still needs to be stored in a cool place.

Refer to the Glossary (Wine, Beer, Spirits, and Beverage Terms) for a list of the types of ales, lagers, and beers along with common brands.

FIGURE 6.10
Beer Flights Being Served
Courtesy of Steelite International.

Bottled Waters

Learning Objective 14

Know the correct procedure for serving bottled water.

Many guests enjoy bottled water as part of their everyday lives as well as with their meals. Certain guests have a preference for the mineral content or taste of a particular brand of nonsparkling water. Other guests prefer a naturally sparkling mineral water from a particular natural spring because of their traditional health benefits. Because bottled waters have become so popular, many fine-dining restaurants have a water list that will give their guests a selection of bottled waters to choose from. Some guests may even compare bottled water to wine because of its unique flavor characteristics due to the area in which it is bottled.

Bottled waters are typically opened, brought to the table, and poured by the server. The restaurant will determine the size and shape of glass to be used for bottled-water service. The server places the glass with ice on the table to the right of the guest and pours the water to about three-fourths full. Occasionally, a guest may prefer not to have ice with the water to get the full unique taste of the bottled water. The bottle is then placed above and to the right of the glass. The guest may request or the server may offer (depending upon the policy of the restaurant) a lemon or lime twist. The glass may also be served on a paper coaster.

Coffee

Learning Objective 15

Explain the different types of coffee drinks.

Ethiopia is considered to be the birthplace of coffee. Legend has it that goats or sheep ate the small red berries that contained the coffee bean seeds. They became agitated and excited. The indigenous peoples decided to partake of the same plant. Their energy and alertness were also raised. The plant was passed on to monks who created various drinks, including the current form of coffee.

Coffee quickly spread from Arabia to Syria to Constantinople. For centuries, coffee production was carefully guarded by the Arab world. The cartel was not broken until Dutch traders secured precious seeds to take to the west.

By the early 1600s, coffee was enjoyed by the French. They soon introduced the style of serving coffee after dinner. Their method of preparation (the "French Press") is still used today and has seen a comeback in recent years, particularly in fine-dining restaurants. The superb quality of the coffee produced with a French Press and upscale presentation have added to its resurgence in popularity. Near-boiling water is poured onto ground coffee, typically a courser ground than coffee, for an automatic machine. This allows for more surface area to come in contact with the grinds for better extraction of flavors. The coffee is held together by disks that act as filters, as shown in Figure 6.11a. A French Press can also create coffee for the drink

The French press coffee maker is the simplest of all brewing systems, where coarsely ground beans meet hot water right off the boil. The right temperature (92–96 °C, 195–205 °F) brings the optimal extraction power for the essential oils in the beans to develop their full flavour profile in just four minutes. An easy press on the plunger locks the grinds at the bottom of the glass carafe and stops the brewing process.

| STEP 1 | STEP 2 | STEP 3 | STEP 4 |
| Add coffee | Add water | Press | Enjoy! |

(a)

(b)

FIGURE 6.11

(a) French Press Procedure; (b) French Press
Courtesy of Steelite International.

that is unique. Prepared tableside, this visual display is tremendous, especially with the addition of a spirit cart. The press makes coffee for one or more guests (3-cup, 8-cup, or 12-cup French Press) and can be brought into any space without wires or plugs as shown in Figure 6.11b.

Over the centuries, cultivation spread from Africa to South America and then to the West Indies. Two types of coffee bushes supply most beans to the consumer. Arabica is considered the highest quality, while Robusta contains more caffeine and yields a somewhat nutty taste.

Coffee beans are roasted to bring out various flavor characteristics. Beans roasted at lower temperatures are lighter and smoother than their darker-roasted cousins. Higher temperatures during the roast produce dark, reddish-brown beans with "fiery" taste. Grinding is also a critical element in coffee making. While coffee can be ground weeks before it is brewed, the premium tastes and aromas are produced from beans that are ground directly prior to extraction, allowing time to stabilize. There is an increasing popularity in organic and fair-trade coffees. The coffee plantations are governed by organizations that control the way they are farmed. Fair-trade means that the farmer gives a portion of the money that they receive from the sale of their crop back to the community to stimulate such projects as health care and education.

With decaffeinated coffee, unroasted beans are steamed to release caffeine from the bean, and a minimum of 97 percent of the caffeine is removed during this process. A decaffeinating agent (solvent or water) is then used to remove the caffeine. Many people feel that this process, while quite sophisticated, leaves coffee a shadow of its former self.

Types of roasts commonly seen:

- Cinnamon Roast is seen in most commercial uses. The beans are roasted for 5–6 minutes and usually still have a sour taste.
- City Roast is when the beans are light brown and still high in acid. Light-bodied coffees are made from these beans.
- Full City Roast produces medium-to-chestnut brown beans and when sugars begin to develop, a balance is added to the flavor.

- Espresso Roast is deep brown with caramel and spice notes. The roast lasts at least 12 minutes.
- Italian Roast is when beans are a dark brown and oils start to be released, then a sweet flavor develops with smoky notes.
- French Roast is when beans are close to black in color, the sweetness starts to become less and smoky notes become predominant.

Darker-roasted coffees are not necessarily stronger than those that are lightly roasted. The longer the bean is roasted different flavors develop, giving unique taste characteristics.

Decaffeinated coffee starts when the beans are still green and unroasted. After roasting, they can often look darker than that of caffeinated coffee but could be the same roast. A good way to tell the difference between the two is that decaffeinated coffee beans will look darker and dry while regular beans are oily in appearance.

There are two processes to decaffeinate coffee: (1) The Swiss Water Method where the beans are passed through a high-pressure filter and soaked in water for up to 12 hours and (2) Direct Contact Method where a food-grade solvent is used to remove the caffeine during a soaking process.

Coffee service can be somewhat unique depending upon where it is served. In the United States, we now serve coffee in almost every possible way and at all times of the day. We have coffee drinks of all kinds served in "to go" paper cups, so that we can keep up with our busy schedules. Customers are looking for the best coffee experience possible, which has created some change within the industry. There has been an increase in concern for water and water quality because the coffee is a small portion of the flavor experience and water is a much larger portion of the flavor. Some specialty coffee shops will give customers a choice of more than one type of water for their coffee. Alternatives to traditional methods of coffee brewing—cold brew and pour over methods—are showing up in coffee shops. The cold brew method where coffee is steeped overnight at room temperature is less acidic, and therefore smoother in taste and easier on your stomach. In pour over brewing method, coffee is often brewed to order and you get to choose the origin of your beans; be prepared to wait longer and pay a little more. When using the pour over method, hot water is poured from a narrow spouted vessel over the coffee grinds in a continual. The hand-poured method controls the speed of the pour, giving the hot water more time to come in contact with the grounds and therefore making a richer and more flavorful brew.

Cold coffee on tap has increased in popularity, and Nitro coffee, which is cold brewed coffee infused with nitrogen gas that is flavorless and odorless, creates a creamy smooth flavor.

Baristas and Barista Training

Professionals preparing and serving coffee drinks are called baristas. The term *barista* is of Italian origin, which means bartender or a person who would typically work behind a counter, serving coffee drinks, nonalcohol beverages, and alcohol beverages. Baristas in the United States are individuals who have acquired expertise in the art of coffee making. A barista will have comprehensive knowledge of coffee origin, coffee blends, coffee varieties, type of roasts, the use of coffee-making equipment, and equipment sanitation. There are many barista schools and barista competitions worldwide where individuals learn, practice, and compete with each other to demonstrate their great coffee service and making skills needed to be a coffee professional. There are some basic guidelines for coffee served by a qualified barista. The coffee should always be of the best quality and the freshest it can be. Beans ground to order are the ultimate in freshness and will produce the best tasting coffee. Once coffee is brewed, it should be held for no more than 2 hours in an insulated coffee pot with limited exposure to oxygen. If the coffee is sitting on a burner, it should stay there for no more than 30 minutes due to evaporation and cooking as it sits. There should be a brand standard set for the coffee made in an establishment. Specific guidelines should be set forth, and then the employees should be trained and then tested on the guidelines. Coffee equipment must be cleaned thoroughly and well maintained. If any part of a coffee or espresso machine is not working, it should be immediately reported to the management. Barista service should be quick and friendly. Even when there is a line, each guest should be acknowledged within no more than 2 minutes by a friendly greeting.

One of the most important parts of a barista's job is steaming milk properly. This can be the difference between a good and great coffee experience. Always start with the freshest cold milk and a clean pitcher. Pour only what you need for the particular drink that you are making. Milk steamed more than twice can get a bitter and burnt taste. Always make sure that you are working with a calibrated thermometer; temperature is very important. Milk scorches at 160°F and then you must begin again. You can never recover milk that has been burned.

Bleed your steam wand into a towel to remove condensation. Insert it into the milk and turn on to full. Never bring the wand completely out of the milk but hold it just below the surface allowing the milk to aerate; this is what creates the foam. If you hear a high-pitched screaming, this is a sign of milk burning; check your temperature or you are not aerating the milk enough. Once the milk reaches about 100°F, fully submerge the wand to heat all the milk evenly. Remove the pitcher from the steam when the temperature reaches 140–150°F. Nonfat milk is easier to get fluffy foam because of the low fat content; soy milk can be steamed as an alternative but it is only recommended to be heated to 130°F before the taste gets bitter.

Tips for correct brewing

- Always start with a clean coffee maker.
- Use only cold, fresh, pure water for brewing. Heavily chlorinated water should be filtered, or you should use bottled water.
- Temperature for brewing should be nearly boiling.
- Grind must be right for the type of brewing equipment.
- Follow a ratio of 14–20 ounces of water to 1 ounce of coffee, adjusting to taste.
- Always use superb-quality coffee.
- Store coffee in a cool, dry place to preserve optimal freshness.

Table 6.5 provides a reference to the most common types of coffee drinks.

Spirited Coffee Drinks

For centuries, people have enjoyed wine with their meals, but what about after dinner—the twilight hours of the day?

Some say the art of spiking coffee with alcohol began even before shepherds matched wine with food. Genghis Khan was said to provide his invading soldiers with a hot drink made from pillaged wine and coffee before making forays into new lands.

Many who prefer wine as a complement to food still enjoy a properly mixed after-dinner drink utilizing coffee. It is often the perfect crowning touch to an evening. Some popular spirited coffee drinks are as follows: Spanish Coffee flambéed tableside consists of a blend of Kahlua, coffee, 151 rum, and triple sec and matched only by their showmanship and artistry. Café Diablo is prepared by flaming an orange peel into a silver chalice filled with coffee, brandy bitters, and vermouth.

Some other favorites include Café Royale (with bourbon or brandy) and Mexican Coffee (with tequila and sweetened with Kahlua); Café Pucci is an outstanding

Name	Ingredients	Appearance	Flavor	Served In
Espresso	Finely ground coffee pushed through a basket with great force.	Dark in color with a golden froth on top called "crema."	Bitter and dark.	Small demitasse cup ½ full and saucer with a twist of lemon.
Americano	A shot of espresso combined with two parts hot water.	Looks like a regular cup of black coffee.	The water lessens the strength of the espresso.	Coffee cup ¾ full and saucer.
Macchiato	A shot of espresso with steamed milk on top.	Dark in color with milk on top.	Slightly creamy.	Coffee cup ½ full and saucer.
Caffè lattes	A shot of espresso, with hot milk added and froth milk on top.	Caramel in color due to the high percentage of milk and froth.	Creamy and smooth.	Coffee cup with ¼ espresso, ½ steamed milk, and ¼ froth.
Cappuccino	A shot of espresso, steamed milk, and froth.	Similar to the robes of monks, brown.	Rich but less bitter due to the milk.	Coffee cup and saucer with equal amounts of espresso, steamed milk, and froth.
Mochas	A shot of espresso, chocolate syrup, and steamed milk.	Light brown in color.	Smooth coffee flavor with a hint of chocolate.	Coffee cup and saucer with ⅛ espresso, ⅛ chocolate syrup, and ¾ steamed milk.
Café au Lait	Half drip coffee and half steamed milk.	Light brown in color.	Creamy and smooth.	Coffee cup and saucer with ½ coffee and ½ steamed milk.
Flavored Café au Lait	Half drip coffee and half steamed milk flavored with 1 ounce of Italian syrup such as almond, raspberry, chocolate, vanilla.	Light brown in color.	Creamy and smooth with a sweet flavor.	Coffee cup and saucer with ½ coffee and ½ steamed milk with 1 ounce of syrup.
Café Coretta	Espresso with liquor, usually brandy added.	Dark brown.	Bitter and rich with the flavor of the alcohol.	Coffee cup and saucer with a shot of espresso and liquor.

TABLE 6.5

Type of Coffee Drinks

drink made with Trinidad rum and Amaretto; Kioki (or Keoke) Coffee tastes wonderful with brandy; and Royal Street Coffee is exceptional with Amaretto, Kahlua, and nutmeg, served dry (no sugar).

Tea

Learning Objective 16

Describe how tea is prepared and served.

Learning Objective 17

Understand the various food and tea pairings.

People around the world have enjoyed tea for over 5,000 years. Next to water, tea is the most commonly consumed beverage in the world, with an estimated one billion cups consumed daily worldwide. Tea leaves come from the *Camellia sinensis* plant that grows throughout the world, including the United States. There are five categories of tea that come from the *Camellia sinensis* plant: white, green, oolong, black, and pu-erh. Although the same plant is used for the different types of tea, each tea has a unique quality.

White teas are made from the most tender of the tea leaves, which are picked first usually a few days in the spring. White tea is not processed in any way, so it maintains maximum nutrients from the bud at the tip of the plant. White tea is popular for its antioxidant healthy qualities. White tea has the lowest caffeine content of all the teas made from the *Camellia sinensis* plant. White teas have delicate flavors and aromas that are light, sweet, fresh, and floral. Examples of white teas are Silver

Needle, Bai Mudan, and Yin Zhen from China. White teas can pair well with light foods such as salad, vegetables, and fruit such as peaches and bananas.

Green teas are not allowed to oxidize. The leaves are dried and then stemmed or roasted to inhibit a reaction with oxygen. The leaves therefore maintain their green color and natural antioxidant qualities. The flavor of green teas can range from grassy, vegetable-like astringency, seaweed like, earthy, buttery, toasty, to nutty. Examples of green tea are Dragonwell, Gunpowder, and Matcha. Matcha is a powdered green tea traditionally used in the Japanese tea ceremony; it has become popular because it is concentrated and has more nutrients and caffeine. Matcha is very versatile and can be used in desserts, cocktails or served hot or as a latte. Green teas pair well with brie and camembert cheeses, milk and white chocolate, and carrot desserts and fruit desserts. Savory options are quiches and seafood.

Oolong is partially oxidized and therefore has characteristics of green and black tea leaves. Leaves are tossed to bruise the edges; this allows partial oxidation. The oxidized part of the outer leaf turns dark, almost black, while the unbruised portion of the inner leave remains green. The flavor of oolong is complex because of the oxidized and unoxidized leaves. The common flavors are soft astringency, very smooth, and rich in floral or fruity taste with a long, sweet finish. Oolong teas can complement cheddar, edam and muenster cheeses, dark and milk chocolate, and nut pies and fruit pies.

Black tea is fully oxidized, which is responsible for the dark color. Leaves are picked, dried and rolled, and then spread out so that the inner enzymes can react fully with oxygen. After they react with the oxygen and turn brown, they are fired to prevent any other changes. Examples of black teas include Lapsang Souchang, Darjeeling, Ceylon, and Assam. Most black teas have pronounced tannin that can be paired well with full-flavored food such as aged cheeses, creamy dessert, dark chocolate, smoked salmon, meat dishes, and spicy foods.

Pu-erh is fermented then aged; the aging process is linked to increased health benefits and creates unique flavor profiles such as earthy, woody, mushrooms, herbs, leather, hay, tobacco, and barnyard. It pairs well with dark chocolate and coffee flavored desserts. Pu-erh is primarily produced in china and is rare and expensive.

There are numerous varieties of tea found throughout the world. Some teas are named after their places of origin, such as Ceylon from Sri Lanka (formerly Ceylon), and Yunnan and Darjeeling from the Himalayas. The first established tea plantation in the United States growing the Camellia Sinensis plant is located on Wadmalaw Island in South Carolina. The plantation has 127 planted acres and a working tea factory on site. It produces a popular brand of tea named American Classic Tea.

Each tea has its own unique flavor, color, and aroma. Teas can be compared to wine with similar influences on their flavor, which can come from where the plants are grown, the time the leaves are picked, the soil, the climate, and elevation. Often different teas are blended to create a new flavor. Earl Grey, English breakfast, and orange spice are examples of teas that are blends of different varieties. Decaffeinated teas are available, and herbal teas are 100 percent caffeine free. The herbal teas are not made from the *Camellia sinensis* plant, instead they are made from dried leaves, fruit, spices, and flowers that are steeped in boiling water. Herbal teas such as Chamomile, rooibos, and yerba mate are very popular because of their smoothing and healing qualities. One of the most prized herbal teas is Chamomile that is made from a daisy-like flower grown in western Europe, India, and western Asia. It is prized for its therapeutic and calming attributes. Chamomile is used for easing stress and to encourage a restful night's sleep. Chamomile is typically served with honey and lemon. Rooibos or red bush tea is made from a South African bush, is caffeine-free, has antioxidants, and has antiaging benefits. Yerba mate is an herbal tea made from a tree grown in the Amazon. Yerba mate provides a natural energy boost, can improve mood, and has antioxidant properties. The United States is one of the largest markets for organic tea. The demand is from young people who are concerned about health and sustainability when buying consumer products.

FIGURE 6.12

Tea Control Range (Infuser) A turn of the lid can slow the brewing process to maintain flavor.
Courtesy of Service Ideas, Inc.

The popularity of tea is increasing; therefore, guests can find tea in their cocktails used to smoke their food, or fermented Kombucha tea in the health food store. Specialty flavored iced teas and coffee-inspired tea drinks such as tea lattes are becoming mainstream.

Tea service is an important part of service for the professional server who should understand the basics of teas and its service to better accommodate their guests. Tea can be served with a cup of hot (near-boiling) water and a tea bag placed on the saucer, with a teapot of hot water and the tea bag placed next to the teapot when served, or with a teapot with infuser that retains the leaves when pouring into teacups as shown in Figure 6.12. The teapot should be placed to the right of the cup with the handle turned at 4 o'clock. This allows the guest to open the package containing the fresh tea bag and place it in the hot water to steep to the desired strength. The tea infuser should also be placed to the right of the cup. The tea infuser is used in fine-dining restaurants that offer premium loose-leaf teas for guest selection. If the guest desires a lemon wedge and/or milk (or cream), it should be placed on a small plate lined with a doily. The plate is placed above and to the right of the cup. Classic tea service is typically served in three courses: tea, finger sandwiches, and sweets and sconces with accompaniments as shown in Figure 6.13.

Iced tea, which is popular in the southern United States, is served in a large glass with ice, a lemon wedge, and a long-drink spoon. The glass is typically placed on top of a small plate with a paper doily or coaster. Sugar and/or artificial sweetener

FIGURE 6.13

Classic Tea Service
Courtesy of Steelite International.

Style of Tea	Common Characteristics	Flavor and Food Pairing
White Silver Needle, Bai Mudan, and Yin Zhen	The delicate top leaves or bud of the Camellia Sinensis plant picked first, not oxidized, most natural, high antioxidants, lowest caffeine, brew temperature 175°F for 1–3 minutes.	Flavor: light, sweet, fresh, and floral. Pairs with light foods such as salad, vegetables, and fruit such as peaches and bananas.
Green Dragonwell, Gunpowder, and Matcha	Leaves picked early, not oxidized, dried, rolled then steamed or roasted, most natural, maintains its natural green color, high antioxidants, low caffeine, lowest brew temperature 145–185°F for 1–3 minutes.	Flavor ranges from grassy, vegetable-like astringency, seaweed like, earthy, buttery, toasty to nutty. Pairs with brie and camembert cheeses, milk and white chocolate, and carrot desserts and fruit desserts. Savory options are quiches and seafood.
Oolong Dan Cong, Da Hong Pao, and Wu-Yi Wulong	Partially oxidized, both green unoxidized and black leaves fully oxidized, brew temperature 185–195°F for 2–3 minutes.	Flavors are soft astringency, very smooth, and rich in floral or fruity taste with a long, sweet finish. Pairs with cheddar, edam and muenster cheeses, dark and milk chocolate, and nut pies and fruit pies.
Black Lapsang Souchang, Darjeeling, Ceylon, and Assam	Fully oxidized creates the dark color, leaves are picked, dried and rolled then react fully with oxygen, brew temperature 212°F for 3–4 minutes.	Flavors are pronounced tannin. Pairs with full-flavored food such as aged cheeses, creamy dessert, dark chocolate, smoked salmon, meat dishes, and spicy foods.
Black Pu-erh Sheng	Oxidized then aged, the aging process is linked to increased health benefits, brew temperature 212°F for 1 minute.	Flavor profiles such as earthy, woody, mushrooms, herbs, leather, hay, tobacco, and barnyard. Pairs with dark chocolate and coffee flavored desserts.
Herbal	Not made from the Camellia Sinensis plant, instead made from other plants, brew temperature 212°F for 3–4 minutes. Chamomile, Rooibos or Red Bush, and Yerba Mate.	Flavors vary. Pairs with various foods.

TABLE 6.6

Common Types of Tea

Learning Objective 18

Recognize the popularity of specialty and customized cocktails.

are also brought to the table. When served, the iced tea is placed to the right of the guest. Iced teas flavored with syrup have become popular.

Table 6.6 provides a comparative reference to the common types of tea according to style of tea, common characteristics, flavor, and food pairing.

RESTAURANT REALITY: A FEELING OF BEING WELCOMED HOME WITH HOSPITALITY AND SPECIALIZED DRINKS

While attending a business technology conference and product trade show in an historic southern city, three friends and coworkers from the Midwest discovered a very different type of experience when ordering cocktails during a local bar's happy hour.

Stephanie, Paul, and Sara decided to explore the city following the second day of the conference. They enjoyed browsing several antique shops and made a few purchases among the many unique stores filled with out-of-the-ordinary type items. As they were leaving one of the shops, they noticed a small bar across the street where people were waiting in line for the bar to open at 5 P.M. Since their dinner reservation was not until 7 P.M., they agreed that having a cocktail with time to relax for a while would be a good idea. Stephanie commented that the bar must be offering something special as they joined a line of about 20 people waiting for the bar's doors to open. The doors snapped opened at exactly 5 P.M. and the guests in line were greeted with a huge smile from the bar's manager and an instant shout-out when he said, "Welcome home my friends— yaw'll thirsty for the best drinks in the city!" To which the people in line shouted back, "Yes, we're thirsty!" At that very moment, Stephanie, Paul, and Sara felt like family friends of the bar being welcomed home after a hard day's work. They followed the line into the bar filled with southern charm and gracious hospitality. The center of the room was dominated by a circular mahogany bar where guests could sit at the bar or be seated at surrounding tables. Guests quickly found seats and Stephanie, Paul, and Sara were invited to sit at the bar by a bartender's welcoming hand waving at them to come join her. She introduced herself while inquiring if they had been home at the bar before or if this was their first time home. Since this was their first time, the bartender handed a menu to each of them. There were many drinks on the menu with clever names, so that the choice for first-timers could be difficult. Then there was also the option of choosing two flavors and getting a custom drink. Paul was so intrigued he did not know what to order, Sara asked for a recommendation, while Stephanie was reading every word on the menu. As they sat there, they looked around at all the bottles of liquor, variety of glassware, the drink-making gadgets on the back-bar, the jars of fresh herbs, and the rainbow of different flavorings. This was a place that indeed felt like home. The bartender moved with ease selecting the right glass, adding ingredients to a shaker, pinching fresh herbs, and carefully adding flavors with an eye dropper. She created ice cube spheres with a special tool and skillfully sliced citrus. Stephanie, Paul, and Sara were thoroughly entertained and amused.

Stephanie and Sara selected a drink from the menu; Paul wanted a customized drink. He picked his two flavors that were sour and herbal. The bartender smiled and began to mix a custom cocktail for Paul. She started with some freshly squeezed grapefruit juice, added a dash of honey then tequila and a garnish of orange and a cilantro sprig. She placed the drink in front of Paul and watched for his reaction. Paul took a sip and then with a big smile said, "Yaw'll make one heck of a customized cocktail." He loved the combination of flavors and the balance of the drink combination. Stephanie and Sara also loved their cocktails, and when finished, the three ordered a second round of drinks. Discovering this new experience added to the fun and enjoyment of their visit to this old southern city along with the new information they had learned from attending the conference. This made for a memorable experience that they would often talk about and truly felt welcomed home by the hospitality and specialized drinks.

Summary

Servers should always be conscious of taking good care of their guests and should protect them from the effects of misusing alcohol. Along with being a legal obligation, it constitutes good business, and is the morally correct thing to do. Many states have a mandatory server education program for owners and employees of licensed businesses that serve alcohol. These states require alcohol servers to have a service permit, which is obtained by taking a class in responsible alcohol service.

Wine service begins with the knowledge of serving temperatures and the correct use of an ice bucket during the service of wine. The importance of properly presenting a bottle of wine or Champagne to a guest along with being able to open and serve it is a measure of a server's professionalism.

Occasionally, wine will need to be decanted. The server should be able to recognize when this occurs and what the procedure is to decant a bottle of wine. Servers should be trained in the fundamentals of wine varieties and other alcohol beverages such as vodka, Scotch, bourbon, blended whiskeys, brandy, gin, rum, tequila, and liqueurs (cordials). Also, the server should know what to look for in recommending beer along with the best serving temperatures of beers, and to be able to explain the differences between beers, lagers, ales, bock beer, pilsner, malt liquor, stout, and porter. Ultimately, if the server can describe the qualities of the various alcohol beverages, the guests will appreciate the server's expertise and the selection.

The server should know how to serve coffee, as well as espresso and espresso drinks, such as caffé lattes, cappuccinos, and mochas. In addition, they should understand the different types of teas and tea service.

Discussion Questions and Exercises

1. What is the server's legal responsibility when serving an alcohol beverage, and when should an incident report be used?
2. Why is it important for the server to understand the restaurant's wine list?
3. What is the recommended temperature for serving each of the following wines: white wine, red wine, and dessert wine?
4. Explain how to prepare an ice bucket for use and when salt should be added.
5. What is the correct way to present a bottle of wine to a guest?
6. Explain the procedure for removing a cork from a bottle of wine.
7. When a bottle of wine is opened, what should be done with the cork?
8. Explain the procedure for pouring wine once the cork has been removed.
9. How full should wine glasses be filled?
10. Explain the procedure for opening a bottle of champagne.
11. Describe the process of decanting wine.
12. Name the basic styles of wine.
13. How does climate affect the grapes that produce wines?
14. When would fortified wines be served and how else could they be used?
15. List three examples of food and wine pairing.
16. Explain how vodka is made and name two popular vodka drinks.
17. Explain the origin and production process of both Scotch and bourbon.
18. What distinguishes Tennessee whiskey from other whiskeys?
19. Name two popular brands of Canadian blended whiskeys.
20. What is the difference between Irish whiskey and Scotch?
21. What is brandy?
22. What are two popular drinks made from gin?
23. What is rum generally made from?
24. Name three popular drinks that are made from rum.
25. Explain the process of producing tequila and name two popular tequila drinks.
26. What are liqueurs?
27. Identify three different liqueurs and explain the characteristics of each one.
28. What are light-style beers generally known as?
29. What is the primary difference between lagers and ales?
30. Describe the traditional serving style when pouring beer.
31. What is the recommended temperature for beers, lagers, ales, and dark beers?
32. Describe the procedure for serving bottled water to a guest.
33. Name and describe five types of coffee roasts.
34. How is a French Press used to make coffee?
35. Explain the process of making espresso.
36. Name the ingredients and their approximate percentage in the following espresso drinks: caffé lattes, cappuccinos, and mochas.
37. Discuss several coffee and alcohol combinations.
38. How are herbal teas made?
39. Explain two ways of serving hot tea.
40. How is iced tea served?

CHAPTER 7

Guest Communication

INTRODUCTION

Exceptional guest service can be described as exceeding guest expectations in a professional, friendly, competent, and timely manner. To do an effective job, the server must establish emotional connection with guests, use the techniques of a salesperson, and maintain a professional attitude, which should be accompanied by charm and grace. Guests often want to feel pampered and special, which requires the server to be able to effectively meet and exceed the individual expectations of every guest.

All guests bring a personal expectation about service to each restaurant experience. These expectations may change depending on the style of the restaurant. As the dining level, along with the price of the meal increases, a guest's expectations will also increase. Some guests like to eat quickly and expect the server to respond in a prompt, efficient manner, which keeps pace with the speed of their eating habits. They may simply be hungry and want their food as fast as possible: The server must feed the need. Other guests may want to relax over a leisurely meal and savor the dining-out experience. Dining out has become a social event, which many people look forward to as they enjoy a fabulous meal in a special setting accompanied by excellent service. The server must read the need. The server must read all of the guests' cues. The guests who are dining in

a leisurely manner want more than just food. Not only are they hungry, but they also want to enjoy the experience of dining and savor the atmosphere.

Servers become the "personality" of a restaurant. They are the familiar faces to regular guests and new acquaintances to first-time customers. The servers are the providers and the salespeople, selling food and beverages, and providing service. The server's job consists of the following:

1. Represent the restaurant and the management in a positive way.
2. Serve guests to their complete satisfaction by positively managing the guest experience.
3. Perform within the restaurant's established standards of quality and service or protocol.
4. Earn the privilege of receiving maximum tips.

Many people seem to believe that there is a "secret" to being a successful server. There are no hidden secrets, and the required techniques can be easily learned. The learning process begins with the self-discipline and commitment needed to acquire new skills, accompanied by the dedication to providing the best in customer service, which is rewarded with a feeling of personal satisfaction as well as financial remuneration.

CHAPTER 7 LEARNING OBJECTIVES

As a result of successfully completing this chapter, readers will be able to:

1. Identify how to make a personal connection with guests.
2. Explain the procedure to follow when taking a guest's order.
3. Understand how to develop server enthusiasm.
4. Describe several different types of guests.
5. Explain how to serve guests with special needs.
6. Describe how to anticipate the guest's needs.
7. Understand how nonverbal cues and prompts can help the server anticipate the guest's needs.
8. Demonstrate suggestive selling.
9. Explain the basic guidelines for suggestive selling.

10. Give examples of suggestive selling with the use of dining room showmanship.

11. Identify the procedures that can help a server to conserve steps and improve service timing during rush periods.

12. Explain what the server should do in an emergency situation.

13. Recognize that a warm greeting and personalized service can result in loyal guests.

CHAPTER 7 OUTLINE

Getting to Know Your Guests

Taking the Guest's Order

Server Enthusiasm

Different Types of Guests

Guests with Special Needs

Anticipating the Guest's Needs

Nonverbal Cues and Prompts

Suggestive Selling
    Upselling
    Suggesting "Related" Menu Items
    Suggesting New Menu Items or the "Chef's
        Specialties"

    Suggesting Items for Special Occasions
    Suggesting "Take Home" Items

Guidelines for Suggestive Selling
    Beverages
    Appetizers
    Entrées
    Desserts
    After-Dinner Drinks

Server Incentives

Showmanship Sells Suggestively

Service Timing

Emergency Situations

Getting to Know Your Guests

Learning Objective 1

Identify how to make a personal connection with guests.

A server's task is more than taking an order. If a server is interested only in order taking, they do not live up to their full potential as a professional server. The server must have the desire to become knowledgeable about all of the food and beverage menu offerings, have the ability to recognize and greet repeat customers by their names, and enthusiastically help guests with menu selections. The initial server approach to the table has become more challenging as guests embrace their electronic devices. The server must compete with the technology and learn new ways to engage the guest. The server must approach the table at the precise moment that the guest is finishing on their device so that the server has the guest's full attention and can make a positive first approach and impression making a personal connection.

First and foremost is the server's attitude toward the guest. At times, the server's enthusiasm is more important than the technical aspects of service. Every restaurant has established rules in order to have smooth, consistent operations. However, it is important for the server to put their personality on display in a manner that will have a positive effect on guests, resulting in an enjoyable dining experience.

Promptly acknowledging guests after they are seated displays an important sense of urgency on the server's part. The first impression can set the tone for the remainder of the meal. A positive first encounter can be accomplished with a smile and a nod, a small wave, or brief eye contact, while still serving another table.

Often, a server wears a name tag that is clearly visible to guests. Typically, the server greets guests by introducing themselves. If the server learns the guest's name through a reservation or was introduced to the guest by the host, it is then appropriate to address the guest by name, Mrs. Smith or Mr. Jones.

The server's introductory greeting must be genuine and original to each guest and table. Other guests seated at nearby tables will certainly hear the server's greeting for each arriving guest or group. The greeting should be different for each table;

Good	Better
"Hello"	"Good evening, my name is Maria"
"Welcome to (restaurant's name)"	"Welcome to (the name of the restaurant) My name is Maria, how may I accommodate your needs this evening?"
"Hello, is this your first visit to our restaurant?"	"Good evening, are you new to the area? I will be happy to help you with the menu and bring you a beverage while you are deciding."
"Welcome to (restaurant's name), would you care for some water?"	"Good evening, welcome to (restaurant's name), I will bring some water while you decide on one of our famous specialty drinks."
"Good evening, Mr. Alden"	"Good evening, Mr. Alden, it's good to see you again. Would you like me to bring the usual or would you like to try something new?" I highly recommend our new cocktail and chef's special this evening.

TABLE 7.1
Appropriate Greeting

otherwise, the server may appear to be robotic, using the same script over and over. It is important to remember to find a personal greeting you are comfortable with that reflects your unique personality. Table 7.1 offers some appropriate greetings.

Remembering names, what the guests ordered at their last visit, their preferred beverage, and the memorable event of their last dining experience with the server are several factors that enhance the personal connection between server and guests. It is important to show guests that you are able to remember their name and it reflects positively on the restaurant. The guest will have a personal connection to you and will request your service in the future. The food may be equally as good in a competitor's restaurant, but the server's connection to their guest ultimately may be the deciding factor when they make a restaurant choice. Customer service studies have revealed that among the many things that a restaurant can do to make a guest feel welcome is to greet the guest by name.

When guests trust the server, they are inclined to respond favorably to appetizer, entrée, dessert, and beverage suggestions. This will affect sales and tips, and it provides the spark that encourages guests to return again and again.

Taking the Guest's Order

Learning Objective 2

Explain the Procedure to follow when taking a guest's order.

Knowing when to approach guests to take their order can be a challenge to the server, because guests vary in their likes and dislikes in terms of service. However, the best practice is to approach the table with a welcoming smile as soon as guests are seated. First impressions are important; the server should be prompt, organized, and professional. Courtesy is essential in every detail, beginning with "please" and followed by "thank you" as part of the conversation while taking guests' orders. The server could ask the guests if they would like to dine leisurely or if they prefer a faster service. Many people want to have a casual dining experience, have one or more cocktails, and enjoy the process. On the other hand, other guests may have a limited amount of time and expect to be served quickly. This could be the situation if the restaurant were located near a theater where guests would be dining before theater time and would need prompt service. Conversely, after the theater they would perhaps enjoy the pleasure of leisurely dining.

When taking a guest's order, the following procedure should be followed:

- Stand straight, at the left of the table if possible, and close enough to hear the guest's voice.
- Listen carefully and lean forward slightly to hear if necessary.

Table diagrams assist in taking orders
and serving correct meal to each guest.

Service is further
personalized when
the server can refer
to the guest by name.

Upselling prompts
remind servers to
suggestively sell
menu items.

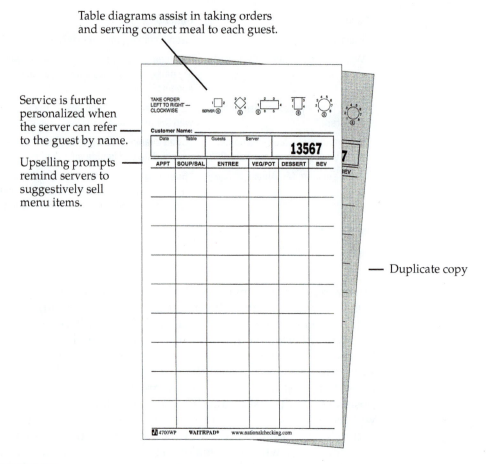

— Duplicate copy

FIGURE 7.1

WaitRpad®. Courtesy of National Checking Company.

- Some guests may need assistance in reading the menu.
- Be prepared to explain the menu and answer the guests' questions.
- Utilize suggestive selling techniques.
- Write the guests' orders using a WaitRpad® as shown in Figure 7.1 or a hand-held tablet as shown in Figure 7.2.
- Read the order back to the guests in order to prevent any possible misunderstanding.
- Thank the guests for their order.
- Immediately place the order with the bar and/or with the kitchen if using handwritten guest checks or just press "send" at the POS or if using a tablet.
- Begin the service at the table as soon as possible.
- While all of this is happening, be enthusiastic, smiling, courteous, and efficient.

When taking guests' orders, a system needs to be followed; most restaurants have such a system. The purpose of the system is to help the server remember who is served what dish, so when the meal is served it is done in a fast, efficient manner. A tool to assist servers in accurate order taking is WaitRpad® as shown in Figure 7.1. This pad helps the server to remember what each guest orders and even prompts them to suggestively sell. This system of writing things down can also help when the restaurant is busy. The server can take the order and then input it into a POS

FIGURE 7.2

Tablet with Interactive Screen for Servers and Guests is Quickly Replacing Paper Guest Checks. Courtesy of Oracle.

or deliver the paper guest check order to the kitchen. Chapter 5, Serving Food and Beverages, discusses a pivot point service system with a designated starting position with all orders served clockwise from that point.

Server Enthusiasm

Learning Objective 3

Understand how to develop server enthusiasm.

The server with enthusiasm demonstrates the following attributes:

- Smiles often
- Always well groomed
- Walks quickly and has good posture
- Alert and attentive to guests
- Friendly, tactful, and tolerant
- Poised and composed
- Speaks clearly and distinctly—voice carries conviction with proper inflections
- Knows what they are doing and why

Enthusiasm comes naturally to some people, but for most it takes a concentrated effort to develop the traits that evolve into an enthusiastic personality. It begins with identifying where you are now and where you want to go. You have to visualize what you want to accomplish. This begins with asking, "How will enthusiastic behavior help me in becoming more professional as a server?" The answer of course lies within the fact that servers work for tips. A good server truly is a good salesperson who truly believes in the product they are selling. It is easy to be motivated by an increase in salary each and every night. Most other professions rely on a boss who controls their yearly increase in salary. There is a direct link to the amount of enthusiasm a server has for their job, the products they sell, and an increase in their tips. Guests can see this excitement and undoubtedly they are more generous when the time comes to tip.

The act of smiling is the first step toward developing enthusiasm. What a difference it makes in your appearance! A smile communicates to the guest, "I am glad to see you." It is essential to start guests off right when they come to dine, so smile and greet them enthusiastically with your own personalized greeting. Many servers may not be aware that they are smiling, because they usually do it as a natural reflex. If necessary, the server should become conscious of when they are smiling and work at enhancing those smiles.

The server who develops vitality fueled by positive energy will be able to generate an enthusiastic atmosphere for guests. When a server is sincerely enthusiastic, the server's face lights up, eyes shine, and the voice is vibrant. The server compels the guests' attention, and every word carries conviction. Enthusiasm is the key that unlocks the minds of your guests, causing them to like you. It is also important to remember that it does not overshadow poor service and/or poor quality food. Remember, to be enthusiastic, you must act enthusiastic!

A server should always approach guests with the feeling that they are nice people who will be enjoyable to serve. To be able to realize this full potential, a server needs to display an ability to generate sincere enthusiasm. If enthusiasm is not sincere, it may be seen as patronizing, which can generate negative feelings from guests. Genuine enthusiasm is contagious and a server who displays it in personal performance will achieve positive results.

Different Types of Guests

Learning Objective 4

Describe several different types of guests.

The server needs to be prepared to serve all types of guests. There are certain situations that require a great deal of patience and tact on the part of the server, especially when a guest is difficult. However, the guest is there and the server has to take care of that guest, and not allow them to disturb other guests. The following are some examples and approaches to handling different types of guests.

The child may think that they are old enough not to need a booster seat, so always ask the parents whether they want a booster seat or high chair for the child. If the restaurant has bibs for children, special place mats, or games of any type, promptly bring them to the table. If appropriate, ask the parents if they would like you to bring some crackers for a small child or baby. This would help pacify the child until the meal is served. Furthermore, look to the parents for the lead in ordering for the child. If the restaurant has a special child's menu, make sure that it is available. If a child orders an expensive menu item, always check with a parent for final approval, and be prepared to suggest another item or two from which the child can choose. Be patient with children, be alert for spills, and be prepared to provide extra napkins if needed.

The procrastinator is a guest who just cannot make up their mind. This is where you have the opportunity to practice suggestive selling skills. The procrastinator would probably appreciate you helping in the decision-making process. You can do this very skillfully by suggesting two or three menu items. If that does not work, allow the guest to have a little more time, mentioning that you will check back in a few minutes. Then check back every few minutes to see if the guest is ready to order.

The skeptic may be doubtful about the quality of food or the way it is prepared. The guest is often very fussy and wants it exactly a certain way. In this situation, your knowledge of menu item ingredients, cooking times, preparation, and serving methods will help you to solve the problem. Furthermore, you need to be very positive with a guest like this, speaking with assuredness and in a professional manner.

The fussy eater will send items back because they know exactly what they want. Therefore, it is important that you thoroughly understand the guest's complaint. Also, you must give this guest exactly what they want and demonstrate that you genuinely desire to please with every detail. Most restaurants have a policy of allowing the guest to order something else. If something else is ordered, be very specific and ask the necessary questions to ensure that the guest's order is cooked and prepared exactly as desired.

The older guest often requires a little extra care. Occasionally, help may be needed in seating the guest, reading the menu, or speaking a little louder. Some restaurants may have an early-bird menu from 3:00 to 5:00 P.M. that offers smaller portions that attract older guests. Your knowledge of menu item ingredients, cooking times, preparation, serving methods, and the nutritional information will be very helpful. The older guest will appreciate patience and not being rushed.

The rude guest is a person seeking attention and as a result can be somewhat irritating to you and other guests. The person may pass a degrading remark, tell a crude joke, or ask the server for a date. The server should be polite and not engage with this guest's comments. If the person continues, respond by stating that you will have to inform the manager.

The talkative guest wants to visit and impress you with their knowledge, which can be frustrating. This type of guest wants to dominate your time and get all of your attention. Answer their questions, keep a pleasant smile, and engage with your other work.

The silent guest is a shy and soft-spoken individual, so listen with care. Smile and do everything you can to make this guest feel as comfortable as possible, as they will appreciate it.

The diet conscious guest has diet restrictions and will expect the server to be knowledgeable in answering questions and in making appropriate menu suggestions. The server should be competent in answering specific questions regarding menu item ingredients, cooking times, portion sizes, preparation and serving methods, and sugar or salt substitutes, etc. If it is impossible to fulfill the request, the server should be quick to explain that fact and suggest something else for the guest's consideration.

The coffee drinker who only orders coffee, reads a newspaper or from a device, or visits with a friend and sits at a table for an hour or more is using productive space without spending much money. The server can suggest a piece of pie or dessert to accompany the coffee. If the guest declines, after the second refill, the guest could be charged for a second cup of coffee, depending upon the policy of the restaurant. If the dining room is busy and other guests are waiting to be seated, then the manager, host, or server, using good judgment, may need to inform the guest politely that the table is needed for lunch or dinner guests.

The budget conscious guest has a serious concern about the price of menu items. An experienced server will quickly recognize when price is a factor, and will suggest medium and lower priced entrées. The important thing is that the guests do not feel ill at ease and that they enjoy dinner and feel that they received a good value for the price of the meal.

The bad tipper is a guest who frequents a restaurant and is recognized as someone who does not leave a tip or tips only a small amount; that guest should be served in the same professional manner as any other guest. Not every guest will leave the traditional 15–20 percent or higher tip. A guest may not understand how to tip correctly. Also, there are some guests who do not tip for any reason, even when they receive excellent service. It is important for the server to remember that not receiving a tip should not affect their actions and service to other guests. The best way to react is to double the efforts in providing the best service.

Guests with Special Needs

Learning Objective 5

Explain how to serve guests with special needs.

It is very important for a server to understand how to serve a guest with special needs. The ADA (American Disabilities Act) requires reasonable accommodations for people with disabilities. The reasonable accommodations are easily applied when a service establishment is aware of them.

A guest with a hearing impairment may require a server to incorporate several techniques into their service. A server must be attentive to the order-taking process to correctly execute the order. The first thing a server should be aware of is that this type of guest may have a service dog to assist them and is legally allowed in the restaurant. In addition, the server should look directly at the guest when speaking; the guest may read lips. If not, extra care can be taken to complete the guest's order. A pen and paper is helpful or a guest can point to the desired items on the menu.

A guest with a visual impairment may or may not be accompanied by a sighted person; the server should not hesitate to offer services if needed, such as helping the person to be seated at a table or booth. This type of guest may also have a service dog to assist them and, as stated earlier, the dog is legally allowed in the restaurant. Service animals generally lay under the table on the guest's left side. A server should refrain from petting or feeding the animal. Many restaurants have a menu available in Braille. When this is the case, it should be offered to the guest. The guest may prefer the server to read several menu items along with the prices. The server should do everything in a normal way, the only difference being that when something is set on a table, the server should say the name of the item, such as, "Your salad, Sir/Ms." If the guest needs assistance in any way, the server should be available to promptly accommodate the guest. When the guest check is brought to the table, the server should offer to read the menu item and price, the sales tax amount (if applicable), and the check total. In addition, the server should inquire if the guest would like to have the check and payment taken to the cashier.

A guest in a wheelchair or a guest requiring the use of a walker or cane will appreciate being seated away from the traffic flow, if possible.

A guest with a hand or arm injury that would make it difficult to eat will appreciate menu suggestions for easy-to-handle entrées and perhaps one that you could offer to cut up, if this seems appropriate. Be prompt and willing to help the guest in any way needed. Also, the guest may appreciate the server offering to take the guest check and payment to the cashier for them.

Anticipating the Guest's Needs

Learning Objective 6

Describe how to anticipate the guest's needs.

A professional server will always anticipate the needs of guests by keeping an alert eye on guests and by promptly attending to their needs before they occur. Anticipating guest needs is a combination of close observation and being able to interpret nonverbal communication from the guest. This is also referred to as "reading the need," which involves determining the guest's priorities. For example, during lunch a guest may have time restraints that necessitate fast service. The nonverbal message from the guest might be frequently looking at their watch. By reading the nonverbal cue, the server may present the check right after delivering the entrée, at the same time suggesting dessert and coffee. Another example is when guests have business papers spread on the table and are engaged in conversation. The server should avoid interrupting the guests and wait for the proper moment (the same as if guests were engaged in social conversation) to become available to serve guests. Bringing glasses of water to the table and presenting menus could accomplish this.

The server must develop an expertise for "reading (observing and listening to) the guest" in order to build a comfortable personal connection. Servers with an anticipatory understanding of guest needs are perceived as providing exceptional service. "Reading the needs of guests" correctly allows the server to be proactive with responses that not only meet but also exceed guest expectations. When service surpasses the guest's expectations, the guest may feel that the server has gone "beyond the call of duty," which is rewarded by a generous tip and the desire to return often. The reality is that often this perception is achieved via the simplest levels of "reading the need" correctly. Some helpful suggestions are as follows:

- Always remove extra place settings as soon as the guests have been seated, to allow extra room on the table.
- If guests are seated in an area that may be drafty, or if the sun is shining in their eyes, the server should offer to seat the guests at another table or adjust the blinds.
- Salt, pepper, and sugar should be moved within easy reach of guests, particularly when guests are seated at counters.
- Never break into a guest's conversation, and time questions so that the guest will not have to try to answer with a mouth full of food.

- Check each food plate from the kitchen to ensure completeness and for the best plate presentation prior to serving.
- Be alert and notice when a napkin or piece of flatware has been dropped on the floor. Pick it up and immediately replace it with a clean item.
- Recognize when guests are not in any special hurry, such as after a movie, date, or ball game, allowing for additional suggestive selling opportunities.

Nonverbal Cues and Prompts

Learning Objective 7

Understand how nonverbal cues and prompts can help the server anticipate the guest's needs.

Nonverbal cues and prompts from the guest can assist the server in anticipating the guest's needs. They appear in common body language displays and facial expressions that are used every day in normal communications. There are also some behaviors unique to the dining experience, such as the following:

Menus: Guests do things with menus that communicate their level of urgency. They will close the menus, and as the urgency increases they will stack them, move them to the edge of the table, or even push the stack out over the edge of the table to get the server's attention.

Napkins: Guests will unfold napkins and place them on their laps when ready to order. As the meal is completed, they may lay the napkin back on the table or place the napkin on top of their empty plate. They may also push the plate to the side or center of the table when they are finished eating.

Looking Around: When a guest is looking around, it generally means something may be wrong or the guest may need something else.

Suggestive Selling

Learning Objective 8

Demonstrate suggestive selling.

When a server uses suggestive selling, they are helping guests discover what is on the menu, and furthermore preparing the way for the guests' desire to return again, along with increasing sales for the restaurant. Suggestive selling helps the server to engage in conversation with the guest instead of just taking an order. Guests generally appreciate it when a server takes a personal interest in helping them get better acquainted with the menu choices, and to further enjoy their meal by having items suggested that would complement their selection. This is a specific responsibility of the server and the more skillful the server becomes, the greater the opportunity to earn increased tips. The server's skill begins to develop with increased self-confidence, believing that the guest will have a more enjoyable dining experience, and the enthusiasm reflects in the server's voice and facial expressions.

To be successful at suggestive selling, it is absolutely essential to know the menu, as presented in Chapter 4, Service Readiness. The server should be prepared to answer any questions the guest may have about any menu item; for example, the quality and ingredients used, the method of cooking, the portion size, the way it is served, the flavor and taste, and the cooking time. Guest satisfaction should always be the first consideration.

There are several types of suggestive selling, and each is geared toward helping the guest enjoy the meal more and have a better dining experience. The different types of suggestive selling are as follows:

Upselling

This type of suggestive selling entices the guest to spend more money and is a real service. Many times, the guest is not aware that they can get more value and enjoy the meal more by spending a little more money—for example, by ordering the complete dinner instead of à la carte, or by ordering an appetizer, Caesar salad, or a bottle of wine with dinner. Also, larger drink sizes are typically a better value than the regular drink size.

Suggesting "Related" Menu Items

Related menu items refer to items that "naturally" seem to go with other items, such as soup or salad with sandwiches, cheese on a sandwich, French fries along with a hamburger, or a scoop of vanilla ice cream with apple pie.

Suggesting New Menu Items or the "Chef's Specialties"

Most guests appreciate it when the server tells them about new menu items or "specialties" for which the restaurant may be famous for.

Suggesting Items for Special Occasions

On birthdays or anniversaries, and during holidays such as Mother's Day, Father's Day, Valentine's Day, and St. Patrick's Day, and during the Christmas and New Year's season, people are interested in enjoying a fine meal and creating a memorable occasion. Most restaurants offer special menu items that should be suggested to the customer for these special occasions.

Suggesting "Take Home" Items

Many restaurants have items available for "take home," such as pies, cakes, cinnamon rolls, and salad dressings. These items may be listed on the restaurant's menu, but still the server should always take the opportunity to mention those items to guests. If the guest does not have a dessert with the meal, the server may suggest taking a dessert home. Also, some restaurants offer curbside pickup for guests ordering "take-out" meals.

Guidelines for Suggestive Selling

Learning Objective 9

Explain the basic guidelines for suggestive selling.

Some guests welcome suggestions and others resent them. The experienced server will recognize the signs when suggestions are appreciated. It is also important for the server to recognize the importance of professionalism that supports suggestive selling versus high-pressure selling that annoys guests. Successful suggestive selling depends on the interest and enthusiasm of the server who has a thorough knowledge of the menu, as well as knowledge of the different types of guests.

A server can quickly qualify guests by inquiring if they have eaten in the restaurant previously. If they are return guests, they already have a feel for the menu items and staff and may not require the full menu introduction given to first-time guests. But if it is their first visit, the server should be prepared to provide all the information necessary to make their dining experience complete.

The following example situation is given to demonstrate the importance of "reading the need" prior to any suggestive selling.

After having quickly looked at the menu, the guest asks the server, "What do you recommend?" The server eagerly describes, in delicious detail, "Our house favorite is fresh salmon filet with blackened spices pan seared, then baked and served with a tequila-lime-sour cream sauce." With furrowed brow and pursed lips the customer replies, "I hate fish!"

The server made a mistake by not asking about the guest's interests before launching into a recommendation. The server has been placed in an awkward position and possibly annoyed the guest.

The server should have responded with the following inquiry: "Do you have a preference this evening? Are you looking for beef, chicken, seafood, or pasta?"

When narrowing the guest's interests, the server can then make the appropriate suggestions from the menu. By asking the right question(s), listening to the answers, and being alert to nonverbal cues, the server can guide the guest to the appropriate choices. This illustrates the importance of first "reading the need" and effectively anticipating guest's needs and expectations.

The effect of suggestive selling is to let the guest know what is available and to suggest items that "go with" the ordered menu item, because they fit into and create the guest's "needs." If the guest does not "need" the suggested item, they will reject the suggestion. The server's experience will help develop an intuitive understanding of what the guest's needs are, then guide the guest into making decisions through suggestive selling.

The server should know what to suggest and understand the relationships between food items. The server should be specific in naming food and beverage items, not categories. Say, "Would you like a slice of our popular blueberry peach or chocolate pecan pie for dessert?" and not "Do you care for dessert?" Say, "Would you like strawberry lemonade or lemon–ginger iced tea?" and not "Do you want a beverage?" Dessert and beverage are not descriptive words. They do not taste like anything to the guest. When you suggest and describe specific items, a picture develops in the guest's mind, which may make it difficult for the guest to refuse. Furthermore, while the server is creating this mental picture, if they smile and approvingly nod "yes," the guest quite often will be inclined to smile and nod "yes" back, agreeing that the server's suggestion is a good one.

The server should typically suggest two of the possible choices within each food and beverage category, so that the guest's choice will be made easier, as compared to five or six choices. Following are a number of examples showing how suggestive selling works.

Beverages

The server should always suggest one alcohol and one nonalcohol beverage choice. Furthermore, the server should note whether the guest's eyes are scanning the beer or wine list, or looking at table tents. These are nonverbal cues to what may interest a guest. If it is beer, ask the guest if they prefer light or dark beer, imported or domestic. If it is wine, ask the guest if they prefer red or white wine, dry or sweet. These are excellent opportunities to suggest regional wines or local microbrews. When a guest asks, "What do you recommend?" the server should respond with questions like, "What do you drink at home?" or "What is your favorite type of beer or wine?" The answers will indicate the guest's flavor and taste preferences. Many wine menus have suggested pairings of wine and food. Some restaurants offer samplings of wine as well. This affords the more sophisticated guest the opportunity to have a small taste of various wines so that they can choose which wine matches their entrée best. Once a selection is made, the wine is served immediately. Restaurants that are promoting certain house brands may even offer sample tasting to guests.

For spirits, again inquire what type the guest may like. Then suggest common brand names that are easily recognizable. For example, if the guest likes Scotch, suggest Chivas Regal, JB, or Cutty Sark. These three scotch brands are internationally recognized and offer three levels of quality and price. If the guest says, "I'll just have water," ask if they prefer bottled or tap. Refer to Chapter 6, Beverages and Beverage Service, for additional information.

Appetizers

Appetizers should be suggested in pairs when a menu offers a variety of appetizers and salads; the server could suggest two of them as follows: "We pride ourselves on our Warm Goat cheese salad, and among our most popular appetizers is the Calamari." On the salad, there are additional items to be added. The suggestion of an addition of shrimp or chicken is very important. This will increase the total of the check and enhance the guest's experience. The server must also be prepared to promptly provide additional information, when asked, about any of the menu items. What is an Aioli (a garlic mayonnaise), or the portion size of the additional shrimp? When guests want to split an appetizer, the server should know what the additional charge would be, if there is one.

Entrées

Suggesting entrée selections should begin with finding out the guest's preferences. Many dinner menus have a variety of meats, chicken, pasta, seafood, and shellfish selections, along with a vegetarian choice. Ask what the guest enjoys from those categories, and then offer two suggestions, being ready to follow up with additional information in response to questions regarding cooking methods, sauces, portion sizes, accompaniments, etc. For example, if the guest orders a Signature Steak Dinner, which includes the cooking technique of char-broiled, deglazed with Madeira, and served with béarnaise sauce, the following questions could arise: "What is char-broiled?" (quick cooking by open flame and/or direct heat); "What is Madeira?" (a rich brandy-based wine from Spain); and "What is in a béarnaise sauce?" (eggs, butter, shallots, tarragon, and lemon).

When an order has been placed à la carte, read back the order and suggest items that will "go with" the item ordered, like "Would you like a bowl of French onion soup or a hearts of romaine salad?" or "May I recommend either creamed spinach or Brussels sprouts?"

Desserts

Desserts can be suggested with a menu, as discussed in Chapter 4, Service Readiness, or by a presentation tray as discussed in table service section of Chapter 3, Table Service, Table Settings, and Napkin Presentations. In either case, the words used to offer the suggestions are important; for example, say something like, "Our home-made caramel sea-salted chocolate cake with seasonal berries and whipped cream is sensational, can I bring you one?" While presenting a dessert tray, the server could say, "The classic crème brûlée is my favorite." Another approach if a dessert menu is used is to place the menu on the table for the guest to pick up and review followed by some server suggestions. Many desserts can also be sold to take home as a treat for later.

After-Dinner Drinks

If the guest wants coffee, suggest the choices that may be available, such as espresso, latte, cappuccino, mocha, and decaffeinated, along with any specialty blends that the restaurant may have; also suggest traditional and herbal teas, alcohol beverages, spirited coffees, and house specialty drinks. Again the key is to suggest two items every time, such as, "May I bring you an Irish or Spanish coffee?"

Server Incentives

Incentives are an excellent way to reward the servers who sell on a regular basis and to motivate servers who need to hone their selling skills. Most often, servers know the relationship between suggestive selling and an increase in their tips. Management, however, could encourage the servers to sell as much as they can to their guests by using incentives. A good incentive should be well defined and easy for management

FIGURE 7.3

Welsh Slate Pig Charcuterie Board. Courtesy of Steelite International.

to track. It is popular to pick one particular item for the server to sell. Define a specific length of time the incentive program will run and offer a desirable prize. A good example of an incentive program could be selling a specific wine by the bottle. The wine would be presented to servers for tasting followed by a discussion about the characteristics of the wine and menu items that could be paired with the wine. The time the incentive program is running should be identified; for example, one month. The server who sells the most bottles of that wine would be awarded a prize that is determined by the manager. It could be a cash prize or even a bottle of the wine that is featured in the incentive. This can create excitement, friendly competition, as well as an increase in the restaurant's wine sales.

Showmanship Sells Suggestively

Learning Objective 10

Give examples of suggestive selling with the use of dining room showmanship.

Certain food items can be served with flair, excitement, and showmanship by displaying a special technique or method of presentation. When these items are served, they have a visible presence in the dining room that attracts guests' attention, and creates interest and curiosity. The result is that other guests will be tempted to order the same items. Also, the server has the opportunity to point these items out, as they are being served and/or enjoyed by other guests, while suggestively selling. For example, the server could say, "Our Welsh Slate Pig Charcuterie Board (as shown in Figure 7.3) is being served to the guests seated at the nearby table."

Foods that can be fun and exciting for guests are flamed dishes and sizzling platters. Examples of flaming dishes include flaming salads, shish-kabobs, desserts, and the famous crepes Suzettes. Certain techniques are used to light the different foods, to display them, and to skillfully put them out at serving time. Cognac, fruit liqueurs, and rum are generally used in flaming desserts. Flaming requires time and special equipment and is suitable only for certain dishes. Flaming does not actually cook the food but adds to the flavor. Restaurants that offer flamed dishes typically have one or two people trained to provide the service competently, such as the maître d' or dining room manager.

Service Timing

During a normal shift, an adequate amount of time can be allotted to serve each guest. However, during a Friday night dinner rush, the server's speed and efficiency are critical to giving proper attention to all the tables without seeming to "rush" the guests. During these rush times, the server may constantly have to change speed and direction. Therefore, reading each table and anticipating its needs is critical in controlling

Learning Objective 11

Identify the procedures that can help a server to conserve steps and improve service timing during rush periods.

the service timing for all tables in the server's station. The server must observe them carefully and plan steps in advance of guest requests. This will save the server time and stress, and ensure good tips because the guests did not have to wait or ask for service.

The following procedures can help to consolidate steps:

- When two or three tables are seated at the same time, the server should take the orders from each table, one right after the other, using good judgment and considering how many people are seated. Then submit the orders to the kitchen and/or bar at the same time.

- If one person orders a second beverage, invite the other guests at the table to have a second beverage.

- When returning to the station, take several seconds to size up each table. What is each table going to need next? That is, beverage refills, pre-bussing, desserts, entrée orders, guest check, initial greeting, appetizer plates, etc. It is critical to always stay focused.

- When leaving the station follow the same procedure. Look to see what needs to be brought back out to the tables when returning to the station. Never leave or go to the dining room empty-handed.

Emergency Situations

Learning Objective 12

Explain what the server should do in an emergency situation.

There has been an increase in the incidences of food allergy reactions within the restaurant industry. A food allergy can be mild or, on the contrast, fatal. Therefore, a server must be attentive to guests who are communicating their food allergies to them. The server must double-check that the allergy issue from the guest is communicated properly to the kitchen. If not, an emergency situation can occur. If a guest becomes ill during the meal, or is choking, notify the manager immediately so that action can be taken. The server should try to remain with the guest as much as possible to attend to any needs such as bringing a drink of water or a cold towel. If a guest has fallen, do not try to move the guest. Also, do not attempt to administer first-aid, except to ensure the guest's comfort. The manager or a designated person on the staff should be certified in first-aid training and qualified to provide immediate care. Ask the guest or those accompanying them if you should call 911 for emergency help. The restaurant should have standard guidelines for all employees to follow during any type of emergency situation.

CONNECTING TO THE GUEST TO CREATE GUEST LOYALTY

John L. Avella, Ed.D, has 45 years of human resource development and operations experience in the hospitality industry. He has been vice president of human resources for Marriott Corporation, The Rainbow Room, and Windows on the World. As a consultant, some of his clients included: Marriott Corporation, Restaurant Associates, Hilton Hotels, The Culinary Institute of America, Holiday Inns, American Red Cross, Compass Group, Coca Cola, and Port Authority of New York and New Jersey. In 2001–2002, Dr. Avella was the Human Resource Director at the Winter Olympics in Salt Lake City for the food services facilities, serving 125,000 meals per day. He has also managed several large projects, including the opening of the new Cleveland Brown's stadium (1999) and the US Tennis Open (2002). He is currently Executive Director of the Sustainable Hospitality Management Program at California State University, Monterey Bay, and President of EQ International Perspectives. As a distinguished speaker/trainer/consultant, Dr. Avella offers the following:

Connecting emotionally to the guest is the most critical part of a successful guest interaction. A good definition of guest service is: "creating a unique emotional experience for the guest." When you think of it, it is a relatively simple process—connect emotionally to the guest, develop a relationship, and create loyal guests.

Positive service is all about the interaction with the guest; as a matter of fact, research tells us that servers who connect emotionally to the guest make 127 percent more in tips than servers who do not connect. When you think about it, the server's section is their own little business, and they have to treat it like they own it. They benefit from the sales from that section; the higher the sales, the bigger the tips. Their percentage is higher than the restaurant owner. Note: The server makes 10–20 percent of sales, whereas the owner makes 4–6 percent on sales. An important thing to remember is that when building sales, guests buy from people they trust and like—there is that emotional influence again. To piggyback on the emotional influence, the Gallup organization, based on their research (2003), found, "Regardless of how high a company's satisfaction levels may appear to be, satisfying guests without creating an emotional connection with them has no real value."

It would seem obvious that we would want loyal guests, but there are economic benefits from creating guest loyalty. Frederick F. Reichheld, author of **The Loyalty Effect,** lists some of these benefits:

- Raising guest retention rates by 5 percent could increase the value of an average guest by 25–100 percent.
- Loyal guests always return and become a dependable lifetime sales stream.
- Loyal guests brag about your organization and create the most effective advertising strategy—word of mouth and it is free of cost.
- It costs five times more to acquire a new guest than to keep an existing one.
- Referred guests tend to be of higher quality—that is, their business is more profitable and they stay with the business longer, creating more revenue and profits.
- Loyal guests are willing to pay more for your product or service.
- Loyal guests are more forgiving when you make a mistake.

Therefore, the "loyalty effect" means more sales and profit for the organization and more business and tips for the server.

Let's explore a recent experience where you were the customer or guest. What was memorable about it? Was it positive or negative? What made it such? How did you feel about it? What emotions were involved? How important were the emotions in this experience? Are emotions important in the guest experience? Think about the answers to these questions: Would you rather deal with a restaurant you like or dislike? How many purchasing decisions are based on emotion, instead of need? Would you rather deal with a restaurant that was highly recommended by someone you know or a restaurant you saw in an advertisement? The answer seems obvious but do we think in these terms?

Emotions matter in the guest experience because guests and staff are always emotional. In the service industry, the emotions of the guest and staff can be more intense. So, let's look at what emotions tell us about guests. The more concerned a guest is about an experience, the stronger the emotional response. Many times, the intensity of a guest's emotion has nothing to do with the present situation; those guest emotions can be influenced by memories, life circumstances, and the guests' and staff's emotional state at the time.

So, as a guest service provider how do I know what emotions the guest is feeling? Well, there are many verbal and nonverbal cues that the guest displays if you are watching for those cues. Properly reading those cues could turn a negative guest experience into a positive one. By reading the cues you can control the interaction. Again, your job is to manage the guest experience and make sure it turns out to be a positive one. Reading the guest starts with observing the guest as they enter the dining room. How fast is the guest walking, head down what is the expression on their face? Based on that observation, you can determine how you will approach that table. For example, if the guest seems to be in a hurry, make sure you take that into account when you recommend drink and food. Do not suggest a five-course tasting menu. If the guests are involved in a conversation, wait for an opportunity to speak, always leaning forward toward the guest and at the same time trying to make eye contact with one of the guests. Do not interrupt by saying, "excuse me"; you need to work on their agenda, not yours.

If a guest leans toward you as if looking for help or reassurance, lean toward them using a reassuring tone of voice. If the guest's facial expression seems sad or depressed, be ready to help in a sympathetic way. If the guests seem joyful and celebratory, that is easy. Keep the positive emotions rolling, but do not get too familiar. Remember the occasion is about them, not you. If guests seem embarrassed or reluctant, perhaps with heads slightly bowed and not making eye contact, be positive and reassure them you are there to help and make the experience a great one. If there is anger or tension, guests are likely to have arms crossed, be leaning back, and have a scowl. Be just the opposite with your best "happy to see you" expression and positive body language. Show interest, listen carefully, and pick up on cues that might change the mood. You can have a dramatic influence on each interaction by setting a positive tone. Use your smile and body language to create the right atmosphere for a great guest experience. If their emotions are negative, your positive emotions can change them to positive or neutral. If guests are in a positive mood, you can reinforce and enhance their pleasure. Remember, a healthy way to view emotions is not as a problem to be solved BUT as the basis for forming relationships—this is how you create loyalty. An even bigger opportunity to form a relationship with the guest is if they have a problem that you solve.

To create a positive relationship with the guest, you need to start with yourself. Remember, you cannot change the guest but you can change yourself. Research tells us that if you do not know yourself physically and emotionally, your system reverts to "hostility" in stressful situations. Remember, self-awareness is the emotional foundation of service. So, we start by taking a look at your body language. There is an old expression that states, "I can't hear you because your body language is drowning out your spoken word." What nonverbal messages are you sending to the guest? Have a friend look at your body language and give you some feedback. What are your posture, eyes, and expression saying?

- Welcome, I value you.
- Talk fast, I have other guests.
- Do not ask such dumb questions.
- I want to help you have a great dining experience.

With every guest you should be conscious of:

- Your facial expressions and attitudes as you approach the guest; be sure you are focusing on those guests and no one else.
- Make eye contact; avoid slouching or leaning on the table or counter.
- Be welcoming, warm, and engaging.
- Avoid behavior that suggests you are preoccupied or hurried.
- Communicate delight at having the opportunity to serve them.

The last thing to discuss is developing trust. Why? Because people naturally gravitate toward those they trust. When you have established trust, the guest will be interested in your suggestions and make a point of seeking to be helped by you. The keys to trust are:

- Be yourself.
- Give the guest your full attention.
- Put the guests' interests ahead of yours.
- Be knowledgeable and honest about quality and costs.
- How would you serve this person if they were a family member or friend?

Learning Objective 13

Recognize that a warm greeting and personalized service can result in loyal guests.

Since your job is 80 percent emotional and 20 percent technical, make sure you focus on that 80 percent. The bottom line in a successful guest experience is to connect emotionally to that guest, and create a relationship that will create guest loyalty—the ultimate guest outcome.

RESTAURANT REALITY: A WELCOMING GREETING AND PERSONALIZED SERVICE CREATES LOYAL GUESTS

There is a small, privately owned restaurant in an average-sized city, named "The Corner Place." Jennifer, a mom with a busy schedule, and two small children were out at lunch time when the children needed to use a restroom. She entered "The Corner Place" and was enthusiastically greeted by Barbara, who worked there for many years. Jennifer immediately felt welcome and asked for a table for three, but first took the children to the restroom and then got them settled at the table. Barbara had a big smile when she approached the table with two small covered cups with crayons along with two paper place mats for the children to color. Jennifer happily responded by saying, "Thanks so much." The children's initial needs were kindly taken care of and then Barbara suggested a lemon–ginger herbal iced tea for Jennifer. She returned with the tea and then helped Jennifer navigate the menu.

Jennifer's youngest child was gluten intolerant, therefore, having special dietary needs. Barbara patiently helped with menu suggestions and then placed their lunch order with the kitchen. After about 5 minutes, Barbara returned to the table to check on her guests and briefly chatted with Jennifer. Shortly after Barbara served the food with extra napkins for the children, she checked back again after a few minutes to make sure that all was well. Jennifer thanked her for the excellent service as they all enjoyed their lunch. When finished, the plates were quickly cleared. Then Barbara served two small scoops of ice cream to the children and asked if Jennifer would like anything else. The guest check was presented with a big smile and thank you. Jennifer was so impressed with Barbara's ability to read her family's needs and felt so good about her lunch experience that afternoon.

The following Saturday Jennifer returned to "The Corner Place" with her husband and children and was warmly greeted by Barbara who remembered her name and gave them the same friendly and efficient service. "The Corner Place" became this family's special lunch spot for many years to come because Barbara made them feel so welcomed.

Summary

A server's task is more than just taking an order; it begins with the server's ability to gain the guest's confidence, and provides the best in food and beverage service. A server who generates an enthusiastic atmosphere for guests, coupled with personal enthusiasm, can produce a positive dining experience that will result in repeat business for the restaurant and increased tips for the server.

The server needs to be prepared to serve all types of guests, particularly those who may need special attention, such as the following: The *procrastinator* needs suggestions to help with a decision; the *skeptic* needs reassurance; the *fussy guest* knows what they want and the server must understand those needs; the *older guest* may need some special consideration and help; the *child* may need patience and understanding and a parent's approval for menu selection; the *rude guest* needs to be handled with tact, but very firmly; the *talkative guest* needs to be given short answers and quick service; the *silent guest* appreciates understanding; the *diet conscious guest* wants knowledgeable answers regarding ingredients and cooking methods; the *coffee drinker* should be handled according to house policy; the *budget conscious guest* will need to know the less expensive items on the menu; and the *bad tipper* should be treated with the same attention and service as everyone else. In addition, the server must apply the necessary skills to accommodate guests with special needs, such as those with hearing or visual impairment, or those using a wheelchair.

A professional server will always anticipate the needs of guests by keeping an alert eye on guests and promptly attending to their needs. The server should also be aware of nonverbal cues and prompts from the guests, such as menu and napkin positioning, body language displays, and physical expressions.

Suggestive selling needs to be done with tact. It requires the server to have self-confidence and a positive attitude. It takes complete knowledge of the menu and of the combinations that go well with the item selected by the guest. Suggestions should be made with enthusiasm and by using the menu descriptions to create an appetizing image. The server who successfully uses suggestive selling will increase guest check averages and tips. The larger the guest check, the larger the tip. Also, suggestive selling provides a definite service to the guest with the opportunity to have a better meal and a better value. The different types of suggestive selling include "upselling," suggesting "related" menu items, suggesting new menu items or the "chef's specialties," suggesting items for special occasions, and suggesting "take home" items. Also, showmanship in the dining room with specially served food items can effectively enhance sales to other guests.

The proper procedure for taking the guest's order needs to follow a system, and most restaurants will have a designated system for servers to follow. Finally, all emergency situations should be handled according to the policy set forth by the restaurant.

Discussion Questions and Exercises

1. What is involved when a server makes a personal connection with a guest?
2. Give three examples of a server introductory greeting to guests.
3. How can a server measure the effects of their service enthusiasm?
4. What is the first step in developing server enthusiasm?
5. List and describe the characteristics of 10 different types of guests.
6. How should a server react if a rude guest looks at the server and loudly says, "Hey shorty, I need more bread"?
7. When anticipating guest needs, what does "reading the need" mean?
8. Give five examples of when a server can be proactive in anticipating guest needs.
9. List and describe two nonverbal cues and prompts from guests that can assist the server in anticipating guests' needs.
10. What is suggestive selling?
11. Explain the five different types of suggestive selling.
12. Which offers a greater opportunity for suggestive selling, a dinner or an à la carte menu? Explain your answer.
13. Why should the server always include menu descriptions when describing menu items to guests?
14. What is the effect of suggestive selling?
15. When practicing suggestive selling, how many choices within each food and beverage category should the server suggest to the guest?
16. List the basic guidelines to follow for suggestive selling.
17. Give an example of when dining room showmanship suggestively sells.
18. Describe the procedure to follow when taking a guest's order.
19. Since timing can be critical during rush periods, identify three procedures that could help a server conserve steps.
20. What should a server do in an emergency situation when a guest becomes ill?
21. Describe how servers can emotionally connect with guests in a way that can earn trust and the desire to become loyal to the restaurant.

CHAPTER 8

The Technology of Service

INTRODUCTION

Point-of-sale (POS) systems are widely available and benefit both restaurants and consumers worldwide. POS touch screen and tablet/cloud POS technology have simplified the efforts in efficiency and speed with the end results being improved customer satisfaction.

Every restaurant operation relies on technology in one form or another and in varying degrees, from the small deli that may use a limited function POS to a large hotel or massive resort with many POS screens that have multiple functions and hundreds of employees for food, beverage, and merchandise sales. Technology is used to increase productivity and satisfy busy customers whose time is very valuable. It is fortunate that many forms of technology are now mainstream and employees feel comfortable with the technology, which is easily used in the restaurant environment. Additionally, as technology advances, restaurants can facilitate integration with the guest's devices for menu ordering and guest check payment.

POS systems have the capacity to strengthen every level of service in a restaurant operation, with the emphasis toward maximizing guest service and optimizing server productivity and selling time. Common POS functionality includes:

- Credit and debit cards authorization.
- Speed tendering for a server, cashier, or bartender when taking various denominations of dollar bills. In one step, the system can tender and compute exact change due back to the guest. For example, a customer paying a guest check total of $16.48 with $20 would have the system compute the exact change due back of $3.52, which speeds up the tendering process.
- Integrated Gift card and Loyalty program, which allows for gift card tendering and tracking of guest purchasing history.
- Multiple price levels that allow the restaurant to offer any happy hour or early bird menu pricing that may be needed. Prices can change by time of day and day of the week automatically.
- Separate or split guest check by item, person, and group of seats or persons. This feature gives guests any format of guest check presentation they request.
- Gratuities automatically added to group guest checks. Large groups typically expect to pay a gratuity and it becomes easy to add it to the guest check.
- A "send" order that allows the server to give appetizers or drinks from the bar a head start during the order process. The "send" order allows all the items entered at any given point to go immediately to their appropriate display screens, such as in the kitchen (salad prep area) and in the bar.
- "Hold and Fire" coursing. This facilitates the server taking the guests' entire order but to "Fire" individual courses to the kitchen as the guest's pace of dining dictates. The POS system "holds" subsequent courses and prompts the server to "hold or fire" each time they access the POS system.
- A training mode (tutorial) for new servers, bartenders, cashiers, etc., that can be turned on or off and will not affect daily reports, but will guide the new employee through the training process.
- Menu item modifiers (instruction for food preparation) that prompt the server in the exact way they want to inform the kitchen, salad prep, or bar in specific preparation choices of the guest as shown in Figure 8.1. If the modifier has not been programmed into the POS, a server can type what they want to type and it will be relayed to the appropriate kitchen display station. This can eliminate confusion over illegible handwriting and differences in abbreviations or terminology; it reduces the server's trips to kitchen and/or bar.
- Management reports that include the following functions:

1. Labor management with labor scheduling
2. Employee time and attendance reporting
3. Transaction analysis of sales activities, employee activities, etc.
4. Product management with inventory control, ordering, receiving, and supplier bids
5. Financial management

FIGURE 8.1

Menu Item Modifiers on a Handheld Tablet/Cloud POS System. Courtesy of Action Systems, Inc.

CHAPTER 8 LEARNING OBJECTIVES

As a result of successfully completing this chapter, readers will be able to:

1. Recognize the benefits of technology in the restaurant industry.

2. Understand and explain the areas of improved guest service when technology is properly implemented.

3. Know the functions of handheld touch-screen tablets.

4. Discuss the advantages of product management applications.

5. Recognize the rapid acceptance of tabletop tablets.

6. Describe the purpose of a kitchen production screen and explain how it works.

7. Know how a handheld pay-at-the-table device functions.

8. Describe the benefits of an alert manager application.

9. Understand the value of a customer relationship management application.

10. Know the functions of employee scheduling and communication.

11. Recognize the effectiveness of training with technology.

12. Understand online table reservation applications.

13. Describe how table service management applications function.

14. Describe the functions of a restaurant website.

CHAPTER 8 OUTLINE

Benefits of Technology

Technology Applications

Handheld Touch-Screen Tablet

Product Management Applications

Tabletop Tablets

Kitchen Production Screen

Handheld Pay-at-the-Table Devices

Alert Manager Application

CRM (Customer Relationship Management) Application

Employee Scheduling and Communication

Training with Technology

Online Table Reservation Applications

Table Management Applications

Web Presence

Benefits of Technology

Learning Objective 1

Recognize the benefits of technology in the restaurant industry.

A POS system can provide a platform for a complete restaurant management system. The POS system can give the restaurant's operator a solid foundation for all of the restaurant's information requirements and application needs. It begins with eliminating errors between servers and the kitchen. It tracks everything being served and charged to the guest. Guest checks are fully accounted for according to each server. Guest orders instantaneously go directly to the kitchen's display screen, with no chance of misplacement. This speeds up production and service, allowing the server to spend more time with guests for personalized service and merchandising.

Pre-check features allow the server to look up menu recipes to correctly advise guests with special requests about ingredients (no salt, diabetics, allergy related, etc.). It can also highlight features and promotions or alert the server of items no longer available. Additionally, the server can see the guests' order history and number of visits. The post-check ensures a clean, clear check presentation for the guest. Additionally, some features enhance the speed and accuracy of producing separate checks, transfers between departments (bar tab transferred to the dining room), discounts, coupons, promotions, and adjustments to the bill.

Credit card transactions can be processed on multiple POS workstations or at pay-at-the-table devices, reducing waiting time. Tips are automatically calculated and tallied, providing tip records for each server and the restaurant owner for tax reporting.

Server productivity, sales analysis, menu tracking (appetizers, wine, desserts, etc.), ticket times, guest waiting times, and labor can be tracked. This is useful for forecasting service and menu focus, performance reviews, scheduling, contests, and seasonal adjustments. Promotions and discounts can be printed on guest checks (happy hour, holiday dinner special, etc.). Some features include the ability for the server to create a personal message on the guest check, such as "Happy 25th Anniversary, Mr. & Mrs. Jones" or any other message with a total of 32 letters.

Handheld devices with pay-at-the-table capability and alert manager allow the server to provide enhanced tableside service. These are ideal for restaurants of all sizes, ranging from casual table service to large properties such as resorts, hotels, convention centers, casinos, stadiums, theme parks, cruise ships, or caterers with multiple remote outlets. The speed of service is increased and the number of server trips is reduced.

A POS system can automatically record and report all time and attendance information as employees sign in at the start of a scheduled shift and sign out at the end of the shift, and it can also integrate with a payroll service. POS workstations, host displays, and kitchen order displays can access and display training materials and videos, allowing new employees to become productive in a short time. There are applications for direct automated purchasing, receiving, and inventory to control waste, theft, and stock levels. These can be programmed for simultaneous access to multiple products and suppliers.

Technology can manage and control all aspects of a restaurant operation if properly used. A POS system as shown in Figure 8.2 can be designed to simplify the difficult task of maintaining tight financial control. It can eliminate costly errors, save time, and be the vehicle that allows the servers to provide the best in customer service.

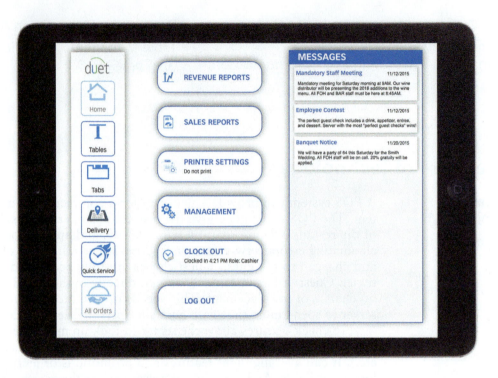

FIGURE 8.2

A Handheld Tablet/Cloud POS System that Provides Real-Time Mobile Operational Information, Reports, and Alerts—Anytime, Anywhere. Courtesy of Action Systems, Inc.

Technology Applications

Learning Objective 2

Understand and explain the areas of improved guest service when technology is properly implemented.

It is important for a restaurant to define its goals, both short- and long-term, before purchasing a POS system. The systems of today are innovative and expensive, and they can change quickly so upgrade potential should be considered. POS systems can meet the demands of a wide variety of businesses in the hospitality industry. There are many systems to choose from; therefore, all options should be considered before a system is selected and implemented into a restaurant. Restaurants are looking for ways to stay competitive in a demanding industry, with creating excellent guest relations and satisfaction top priorities. When technology is properly implemented, the results are reflected in employee success and improved guest service. This can begin with efficiently taking reservations, reducing wait times for seating, and increasing the speed of service. A POS system is fast and easy to use, as shown in Figure 8.3, and is designed to accomplish the following:

- Seat guests more quickly and accommodate any requests.
- Increase the speed of guest service by reducing order turnaround time.
- Increase the accuracy of food and beverage preparation and pricing.
- Accommodate guests who need separate checks, particularly when seated in large parties.
- Eliminate common mathematical errors.
- Provide prompt, accurate guest check presentation when guests are ready to leave.
- Reduce cash-handling problems and/or errors.
- Provide secure and efficient credit card authorization.

FIGURE 8.3

Tablet- /Cloud-Based POS System Workstation/Order Stand. Courtesy of Action Systems, Inc.

Handheld Touch-Screen Tablet

Learning Objective 3

Know the functions of handheld touch-screen tablets.

The handheld touch-screen tablet speeds up service and allows the server to take orders directly at the table. There are many benefits to the handheld system. This system eliminates frequent unnecessary trips to the kitchen, allowing servers to remain in the dining area to better meet their guests' expectations. It provides flexibility and portability in remote locations like patios and in large facilities such as stadiums, casinos, and resorts where the server must go some distance to serve guests. The handheld tablet provides accurate, up-to-date information if a menu item is out of stock, which eliminates guest disappointment before they place an order. Handheld touch-screen tablets can also allow the manager to perform functions that require authorization on the go, such as promotional comps (complimentary food or beverages), adjusting menu item availability, and transferring tables between servers.

Product Management Applications

Learning Objective 4

Discuss the advantages of product management applications.

When product management applications are implemented into a POS system that is designed to handle it, guest service is brought to a higher level by having important information available for servers. At the touch on a screen, the server can view a menu item picture, list of recipe ingredients, nutritional information, serving instructions, preparation instructions, or even a video clip on how to serve or prepare the item. The information is displayed on a handheld touch-screen tablet (iPad) or can even be printed on the POS printer for the server or the guest. This greatly aids in helping a guest avoid any possibility of an allergic reaction to a certain food item or recipe ingredient. Along with menu item descriptions, appropriate wine suggestions and tasting notes may also be included.

Tabletop Tablets

Tabletop tablets as shown in Figure 8.4 are increasingly being used by casual table service restaurants with overwhelming acceptance. When tabletop tablets are in use, the following occurs:

- An increase in drink and dessert orders; see Figure 8.5.
- Servers earn more in tip income; see Figure 8.6.
- Guests are able to order and pay at the table allowing them to dine in less time, which increases seat/table turnover.
- Guests have a choice of printing a receipt or having it e-mailed to them; see Figure 8.7.

FIGURE 8.4

Tabletop Tablets Allow Guests to Quickly Browse through the Menu, which Provides Graphic Descriptions Accompanied by Photos that Further Enhance the Dining Experience. Courtesy of Ziosk.

FIGURE 8.5

The Tabletop Tablet Gives Guests Greater Control over their Beverage and Dessert Choices. Courtesy of Ziosk.

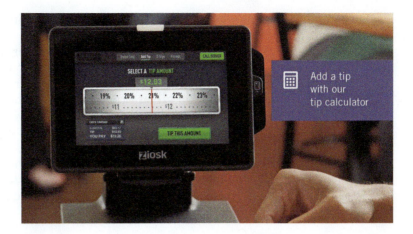

FIGURE 8.6

Tabletop Tablet Select-A-Tip Makes it Easy for Guests to Determine the Server Tip Amount. Courtesy of Ziosk.

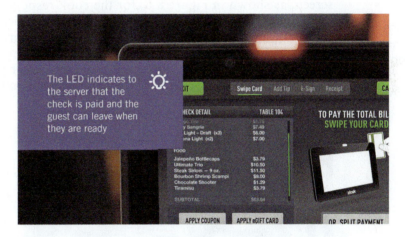

FIGURE 8.7

Guests Can View their Itemized Check, Add a Server Tip, Pay at the Table by Swiping their Credit Card, and Have the Receipt Printed or Sent to their E-mail Address. Courtesy of Ziosk.

- Restaurants offering customer loyalty programs register an increase in loyalty club enrollment.
- Guests are able to give real-time feedback about their dining and service experience.
- Games offered for a small fee serve to keep children amused or may act as ice-breakers for adults.

Malika Ikramova, a hospitality management honors scholar at New York City College of Technology, reported the following from a research report entitled *Measuring the Cost Effectiveness of Restaurant Tabletop Tablets* (December 2015).

The menu has been considered as the primary tool for sales and communication in a restaurant operation, as it drives the production and purchasing decisions for both the customers and the restaurant owners. As tablets with touch input have become widely disseminated over the last few years, more and more industries make use of these devices. Upscale restaurants started to introduce tablets like the iPad as digital menus in order to replace traditional printed menus. By being able to introduce more media featuring the quality of available dishes and ideas behind them, and by designing the decision-making process more interactive, those digital menus aim at improving the customer experience.

Tabletop tablets are quickly appearing in certain restaurants within the casual-dining table service category. By using tabletop tablets, customers can browse through the menu, place orders, and make payments from their sitting tables directly. By implementing tabletop tablet ordering system, the restaurants may experience increased employee productivity, higher seat turnover rates, and increased menu item sales. It also provides a richer description of the dishes, eliminates order errors by servers, and quickens services. In addition to that, customer satisfaction can also be improved because they feel more involved with the dining process and they can see readily what would be on their plates via the interactive pictorial depiction of the dishes in tabletop tablet ordering system. Each feature adds to the cost effectivness.

Kitchen Production Screen

Learning Objective 6

Describe the purpose of a kitchen production screen and explain how it works.

When kitchen orders are placed by the server in the POS system or by guests using a tabletop tablet, the menu items requested are displayed on a kitchen production screen, as shown in Figure 8.8, for the cook responsible for preparing that item. Simultaneously, the system tracks the speed of service for the table that the order is for and initiates a timer when the order is entered into the system. As each cook who is preparing an item for the table completes the item, they confirm completion by "bumping" the item from their order production screen. When all items for the table have been "bumped," the table number begins to flash on the

FIGURE 8.8
Kitchen Production Display Screen. Courtesy of NCR Corporation.

POS service screen notifying the server and dining room manager. Additionally, a paper ticket may print at this time, to be used by the server or food runner to tray the items and deliver to the table. When the food order leaves the kitchen, the server or food runner bumps the item from the speed-of-service screen. The system alerts the server and the manager of orders that are taking too long to be prepared so that corrective action can be taken and the guest appropriately communicated with. The speed-of-service screen displays the number of orders in the kitchen, how long each order has been in the kitchen, and which orders are prepared and awaiting deliveries to the guest.

Handheld Pay-at-the-Table Devices

Learning Objective 7

Know how a handheld pay-at-the-table device functions.

Handheld pay-at-the-table devices can be integrated into the restaurants' POS system. These devices can be presented to the guests in addition or as opposed to a paper check. The guest can then review their bill on the handheld screen, pay their bill, and add a gratuity by swiping their credit or debit card on the device. These devices protect the guest from credit card fraud, prevent mistakes when multiple credit cards are used as tenders for a single check, and facilitate PIN (Personal Identification Number) debit transactions as the guests can enter a PIN on the device. These devices speed up the payment process and are also useful for transactions such as curbside to go, or located at long distances, such as poolside and banquet rooms.

Alert Manager Application

Learning Objective 8

Describe the benefits of an alert manager application.

This application allows for certain POS events to trigger an alert to managers via an RF (radio frequency) pager, text, or e-mail. Certain events concern loss prevention and security such as an extraordinarily large void or discount. Other notifications involve events that may detract from the guest experience, such as a long ticket time in the kitchen or a long waiting time to be seated. Alerts can also be configured to notify of events requiring recognition, such as the ordering of a bottle of wine from the reserve list, or a single guest check that exceeds $1,000. This technology facilitates communication among the restaurant staff and insures that guests receive prompt and appropriate attention.

CRM (Customer Relationship Management) Application

Learning Objective 9

Understand the value of a customer relationship management application.

This is an application that is integrated into the restaurants' POS system, which allows the restaurant to collect, store, and query data about each customer. Typically, guest loyalty, VIP cards, and opt-in newsletters are examples of CRM programs. The restaurant makes an effort to collect information from guests, such as name, address, phone, e-mail, birthday, and dining preferences, which can then be used to communicate with the guest. These applications are most effective when they are integrated with customer loyalty programs. This allows for the tracking of each customer's purchase history, frequency, and total spending. This information is made available to hosts and servers during a guest's visit and can be used to personalize and enhance the dining experience. Importantly, the information can be stored and queried to customize communication with guests. For example, the restaurant is hosting a wine dinner featuring Italian red wines. The restaurant can query its CRM database to discover the e-mail address of all guests who have purchased any bottle or glass of any red wine during past visits.

Employee Scheduling and Communication

Learning Objective 10

Know the functions of employee scheduling and communication.

The cost of labor is one of the key determinants of restaurant profitability. Restaurateurs are constantly challenged by the necessity to have enough employees to adequately serve guests while avoiding the costs of overstaffing. The effective scheduling of employees is paramount to the restaurant's success, the satisfaction of guests, and the welfare of employees. Several hosted scheduling solutions (available to restaurants via a subscription) exist today to meet these needs. Schedules can be written online and then broadcast to individual employees via text message or e-mail. Additionally, critical employee communications can be delivered via the same format. Employees can receive important memos delivered directly to their mobile devices or e-mail accounts. Employees can make schedule requests, offer shifts for pickup, or trade shifts via these hosted solutions. Managers and owners can approve schedule requests or make schedule changes from anywhere they access the Internet. These applications greatly improve management's effectiveness and productivity and offer employees the utmost in convenience.

Training with Technology

Learning Objective 11

Recognize the effectiveness of training with technology.

Online content has largely replaced paper training manuals or training CDs. Providers host the restaurant's content on centralized servers and control access via username/password. This insures that content is current, accurate, and also allows for the learner to access the materials anywhere they have Internet access and on any device. Training can be accomplished in the restaurant via the POS screens. Employees can access these materials on the job as they perform the job. For example, a bartender can view a drink recipe on the POS screen, and a cook might review the plating of an item by viewing a short video on the kitchen display screen.

Online Table Reservation Applications

Learning Objective 12

Understand online table reservation applications.

Restaurants need to be able to take reservations in real time 24 hours a day every day with an online table reservation application that goes directly to the restaurant's website. The best way to facilitate this is through a cloud-based reservation system that allows customers to book a reservation at any time from any device; and also allows third-party reservations such as Open Table to go directly to the restaurant's website. The availability of time slots and number and sizes of tables are configured by the restaurant. The manager may decide to limit the number of reservations available during peak periods, which can increase business during the slower periods as customers are shown openings at other available times.

After the reservation has been booked, the customer instantly receives a reservation confirmation. This is followed by an e-mail/text reminder before the scheduled reservation time. Then after the dining experience, an e-mail/text (thank you note) from the manager promptly follows that may also allow the customer the opportunity to comment about the dining experience in a return e-mail/text message.

Customers can provide specific information and make specific requests in conjunction with their reservation. For example, the guest might indicate that the reservation is for a birthday dinner, may request a table on the patio, or may note a personal food allergy or dietary restriction. This information is not only used by the restaurant to meet the guest's needs for the reserved dining experience, but is also stored in their CRM database for use in the future. If the restaurant has a customer loyalty program, the customer will enter their member loyalty account number when booking the reservation. This allows the dining room staff to know in advance when a loyalty member will be arriving.

When the dining room staff has information about the guests from the moment they arrive, it further enhances the dining experience. For example, when the maître d' or host greets Mr. and Mrs. Smith and knows that they prefer Sally as their server, she can then individualize her greeting to Mr. and Mrs. Smith upon their arrival. Therefore, the service begins prior to the guests arriving at the restaurant.

Table Management Applications

Learning Objective 13

Describe how table service management applications function.

A table management application integrates the duties of the maître d' or host into the restaurant's POS system and facilitates better communication among the dining room staff, speeds up table turns, and manages the waitlist. Reservation details go directly to the table management application so that the maître d' or host can be better informed on wait-times for guests arriving without reservations. The table management application consists of a restaurant floor plan with an at-a-glance status of every table from an iPad or smartphone. The application suggests a table for the maître d' or host to seat the next guest on the waitlist based on programmed variables such as table size and server availability. The maître d' or host then "seats" the guests within the application, which pages or may send a text message to the guest, opens a check for the appropriate server within the POS system, and assigns the guest's name to the check, allowing the server to greet the guest by name when approaching the table.

When a table is cleaned and available to seat, the server or the server's assistant (busser) confirms this on any POS screen within the restaurant and the available status is displayed at the host stand on the table management application screen. The maître d' or host uses an iPad to *check-in* reservations as guests arrive at the restaurant and to add walk-in guests to the waitlist. The table management application suggests the waiting time to the maître d' or host based on the number of parties waiting to be seated, and the historical turn time of the current meal period. The maître d' or host enters the number of guests into the table management application. Waiting guests can view their position on the waitlist by viewing a flat screen that may be located in the lounge, foyer, or other waiting areas. These screens, referred to as marketing clients, can display the waitlist as a crawl over TV programs, or as a list or crawl over in-house content such as promotional videos merchandising menu items, specials, or upcoming events. The use of marketing clients eliminates the inconvenience of guests having to inquire "how much longer" of the maître d' or host.

Web Presence

Learning Objective 14

Describe the functions of a restaurant website.

Many restaurants have created websites to promote their establishments. Websites are a way to communicate vital information such as the menu item descriptions and prices, location, directions, and hours of operation to potential customers. A restaurant's website is also an important e-commerce opportunity that facilitates the sale of gift cards and branded merchandise. The website also serves as the central portal to the various hosted solutions that the restaurant employs. For example, guests can click through to Open Table or other reservation software, or guests can "opt-in" to the restaurant's CRM (Customer Relationship Management) program by providing requested data and agreeing to terms and conditions. Employees can sign in to secure areas of the website to access training videos and materials or click through to the restaurant's hosted scheduling solution such as Schedulefly or HotSchedules (applications that can be accessed via a subscription by the restaurant). The website can also be used to accept online employment applications. Finally, guests can provide feedback to the restaurant via the website. A restaurant's Web presence also includes its website link being placed on other websites. These include various travel and dining sites that potential customers and leisure and business travelers might visit to decide where to dine. Other sites to consider in establishing Web presence are general information sites that have replaced traditional telephone directory yellow page advertising. Care must be taken to insure that the restaurant's website responds favorably to common search terms entered into search engines.

RESTAURANT REALITY: WE HAVE ONLY 30 MINUTES FOR LUNCH

The host was escorting Jacquie and Marsha to their table when Jacquie said to the host, "We only have 30 minutes for lunch." The host replied, "We have a great selection of lunch specials that can be quickly served." Jacquie and Marsha were seated and the host pointed to the tabletop tablet while saying, "Our menu is at your fingertips," as the server's assistant placed their water glasses.

Jacquie quickly ordered a bowl of Three Lentil Chili, described as a classic Vegetarian Chili made with French red and brown lentils; among the bread choices she selected the freshly baked corn bread. Marsha ordered a cup of Tomato Basil with Rice Soup, described as an Italian style Tomato Soup loaded with rice and fresh basil; she also ordered a Tuna and Cucumber half sandwich on a freshly baked baguette. Jacquie ordered a cup of Dark Roast Brewed Coffee with Half & Half and Marsha ordered Iced Coffee.

Jacquie and Marsha were discussing their busy workweek and within a few minutes they were served their beverages by the server's assistant. Their food order promptly arrived a few minutes later and was served by Juan as he introduced himself with a smile. Juan briefly described the items as he was placing the dishes in front of his guests, followed by his asking if they would need anything else. Just then, they were joined at their table by Susan, a coworker from their office. Susan did not think that she would have time to join them for lunch, but a meeting was postponed so she was able to slip out of the office. Susan quickly scanned the menu and then ordered a Hazelnut Latte and an Orange Scone. Within a few minutes, Juan returned to the table with the latte and scone, while saying, "I'm also your barista." He also brought additional honey butter in anticipation of

Jacquie needing it for her corn bread, and then offered to refill the coffee beverages.

Jacquie, Marsha, and Susan enjoyed their lunch together and were each able to pay and tip separately with their credit cards, opting to have their receipts sent to their e-mail addresses. They were finished with lunch in less than 30 minutes, and as they were leaving, Marsha said, "We need to let everyone at the office know that this is a great place for lunch." Jacquie added, "Once I read the description of the Three Lentil Chili and saw the picture of the warm corn bread with honey butter, it became easy to decide." And Susan commented, "Yes, and the service staff were polite and very accommodating."

Note: The system allows management to track guest orders, kitchen production time once the orders are received, and service time.

Summary

Restaurant technology continues to grow and expand in fulfilling the requirements and application needs of the rapidly growing restaurant and hospitality industry. Employees, managers, and owners of restaurants are quickly gaining technology competence in order to succeed and remain competitive.

A POS system is fast and easy to use, and designed to accomplish the following:

- Seat guests more quickly and accommodate any requests.
- Increase the speed of guest service by reducing order turnaround time.
- Increase the accuracy of food and beverage preparation and pricing.
- Accommodate guests who need separate checks, particularly when seated in large parties.
- Eliminate common mathematical errors.
- Provide prompt, accurate guest check presentation when guests are ready to leave.
- Reduce cash-handling problems and/or errors.
- Provide fast and efficient credit card authorization.

Additional technology applications include online reservations, table manage-ment, CRM applications, product management applications, handheld touch-screen tablets, kitchen display screens, and pay-at-the-table devices. Technology can man-age and control all aspects of a restaurant operation if properly used. A POS can be designed to simplify the difficult task of maintaining tight financial control, eliminate costly errors, save time, and be the vehicle that allows servers to provide the best customer service.

Restaurant websites have the capability of promoting a restaurant's business, and serving as the central hub of communications between a restaurant and its guests, employees, and business partners.

Discussion Questions and Exercises

1. Define five benefits of technology for the restaurant industry.
2. Identify eight areas of improved guest service that result when technology is properly implemented.
3. Describe the functions of handheld touch-screen tablets.
4. What are the advantages to servers using a product management application?
5. List three advantages tabletop tablets provide to restaurant guests.
6. List three advantages tabletop tablets provide to restaurants.
7. Visit a restaurant where tabletop tablets are being used and report your experience with menu selections, ease of ordering, and service.
8. Explain how a kitchen production screen works.
9. List three advantages of a handheld pay-at-the-table device.
10. What would be the value of having an alert manager application?
11. Search out restaurants in your community that are using a CRM application to communicate with their customers. Pick one such restaurant and describe your reaction to its e-mail messages.
12. View a training session through an online training service and discuss your judgment of the competence and professionalism of the training presentation.
13. Define the advantages of online table reservations.
14. Explain how table management functions.
15. Schedule an appointment with the owner or manager of a restaurant in your community that may be using some or all of the technology presented in this chapter. Inquire how their information requirements and application needs are being met. Then write a one-page report describing your findings.
16. Visit several restaurant websites and compare the various options that those websites may offer to their current and potential customers.

CHAPTER 9

Dining Room Management

INTRODUCTION

There are different styles of restaurants and restaurant services in the United States and throughout the world. Each of them will require a certain number of employees to serve their guests so that they are able to meet and ultimately exceed the guests' expectations. There are counter-style restaurants in which the guests place an order and the server delivers the food. There are full-service, casual restaurants in which guests order through a tabletop tablet or a server, who will also deliver the food and take payment from the guests. Finally, there are full-service, fine-dining restaurants in which the restaurant focuses on high-end food and a luxurious experience.

The dining room of a full-service restaurant, either casual or fine-dining, is typically managed by a dining room manager, maître d', or host. Depending on the size of the dining room, the management responsibilities may range from supervising, training, and scheduling dining room employees to greeting and seating guests. Therefore, the position can function in many different ways—according to the type and size of the restaurant, its organizational structure, and the needs of the individual operation.

Many guests are aware of the importance of the whole dining room experience, which begins as soon as they enter the restaurant. It is the first impression that a guest has, and it is very important that the guest feel comfortable. This is the beginning of meeting or exceeding the guests' expectations and can ultimately establish or lose repeat business. A maître d' or host must have specific skills to be successful in their job. Their success affects everyone in the restaurant, including the servers in the dining room and the chef in the kitchen.

CHAPTER 9 LEARNING OBJECTIVES

As a result of successfully completing this chapter, readers will be able to:

1. Understand the duties, functions, and responsibilities of a maître d' or host.

2. Identify the role of the chef during a menu meeting.

3. Understand the functions of managing reservations.

4. Describe the procedure that the maître d' or host should follow when taking a guest's telephone reservation or "take-out" order.

5. Understand the appropriate way to greet and welcome guests to the restaurant.

6. Explain how a table service management system functions and why table selection makes a difference.

7. Describe the professional courtesies that a maître d' or host would extend to guests.

8. Understand how the maître d' or host should respond to guest complaints.

9. Explain the training procedure for a new server.

CHAPTER 9 OUTLINE

Responsibilities of the Maître d' or Host

Menu Meetings

Managing Reservations

Taking Telephone Reservations and "Take-Out" Orders

Greeting Guests

Responsibilities of the Maître d' or Host

Learning Objective 1

Understand the duties, functions, and responsibilities of a maître d' or host.

The maître d' or host may be responsible for many front-of-the-restaurant details, all of which are assigned by the restaurant manager. These include but are not limited to the following essential areas of responsibility:

- Check the work schedules for servers and server's assistants (bussers) to ensure proper staffing. Also, inquire if anyone on the schedule has called in sick or unable to come to work for any other reason.
- Check the reservation list and compare the number of reservations with the normal amount of open business to verify that there are adequate number of servers and server's assistants (bussers).
- Assign servers to their stations and reservations to stations, if needed. For example, to accommodate a party of 12, three tables may need to be moved together and set.
- Check restrooms to ensure that they are sparkling clean and adequately supplied.
- Check foyer (entrance area) for cleanliness.
- Check menus and remove any that are soiled or damaged.
- If appropriate, check lighting and music.

Menu Meetings

Learning Objective 2

Identify the role of the chef during a menu meeting.

As discussed in Chapter 4, Service Readiness, a restaurant may have menu meetings just before the shift begins, depending upon the needs of the restaurant operation. The meetings should be short and focused, include the maître d' or host, and feature specific information to help the service staff. The menu meeting should generate enthusiasm, develop teamwork, and build morale within the restaurant. Items that could be discussed during these meetings include the following:

- New menu items or daily specials. The chef could explain the ingredients along with the cooking methods and serving procedures. The servers could also be allowed to taste a sample, preparing them to discuss these items when suggesting to guests.
- Recognition for accomplishments and specific praise for strong performance by servers and staff.
- Openness to feedback from servers and staff.
- Announcement for upcoming special events or other items pertaining to the restaurant.
- Review of restaurant policies, if needed.
- Review of side-work schedules.
- Finally, an inspection of personal appearance and uniforms.

Managing Reservations

Learning Objective 3

Understand the functions of managing reservations.

Restaurant guests appreciate the ease and convenience of being able to make online reservations on the restaurant's website at any time of the day from any device and use third-party reservation services such as Open Table (see Chapter 8, The Technology of Service). The availability of time slots and number and sizes of tables are determined by the restaurant management. The manager may decide to limit (block-out) the number of reservations available during peak periods or holidays such as Mother's Day, allowing the increased business to be moved to slower periods as guests are shown reservation openings at other available times.

The maître d' or host is responsible for effectively managing all reservations and attentively note and accommodate guest requests. Guest requests include a request for a table near a window that offers a panoramic view, a request for a favorite server, a request for a special menu due to a food allergy or dietary restriction, or a special request to observe a special occasion such as a birthday or an anniversary. If the restaurant has a customer loyalty program, a reservation by a loyalty member must be given the proper recognition upon the guest's arrival.

Taking Telephone Reservations and "Take-Out" Orders

Learning Objective 4

Describe the procedure that the maître d' or host should follow when taking a guest's telephone reservation or "take-out" order.

The telephone should always be answered according to restaurant policy, typically in no more than three rings using the appropriate salutation; for example, "Good evening, (name of the restaurant), May I help you please?"

When the maître d' or host is recording the reservation on the reservation page in the POS system, they should repeat the guest's name: "That is Ms. Giannasio" (ask for the spelling of a name that may be difficult to pronounce). Repeat the number in the party: "A party of four"; and the time, "6:00 P.M." Specify the day and date (Friday, month, and day); also note any special occasion such as a birthday or an anniversary. Some restaurants request the guest's telephone number and/or e-mail address. The reservation page in the POS system will show the seating availability for that day and time and confirm the reservation or suggest an alternate time if the requested time slot is not available.

When taking a reservation for a special occasion such as a birthday or an anniversary, take the opportunity to presell specialty items such as a birthday cake or a bottle of champagne. This can also be an opportunity to point out signature items that the restaurant may be known for. When reservations are requested for larger-than-normal parties, they should be referred to the manager according to the policy of the restaurant. Many times, the restaurant will have a banquet menu to accommodate large groups.

The maître d' or host may also be responsible for "take-out" orders. The specifics of those orders should be just as detailed as when taking a reservation. The maître d' or host should know the restaurant menu well and upsell using the appropriate suggestions. Repeat the guest's name, telephone number, menu order, and the time that the guest will be picking up the order. Then state the cost of the order.

Occasionally, people may call to request directions for getting to the restaurant. This is particularly the case for out-of-town visitors who may be staying in town for a few days or just traveling through. The maître d' or host should be familiar enough with the community to be able to accurately give directions, and then say, "We look forward to welcoming you to (name of the restaurant); shall we make a reservation for you?" Often, when paying their guest check, guests will ask for directions to a certain theater, museum, shopping area, or other place of interest. The maître d' or host should always be able to provide accurate directions.

People may also call the restaurant to inquire about the menu. The maître d' or host should use the server skills of suggestive selling (see Chapter 7, Guest Communication). The key is to ask the right questions and attentively listen to the answers in order to be in a position to intelligently inform the person about the menu offerings and then make appropriate suggestions. Then follow up by asking, "Can I make a reservation for you?"

Greeting Guests

One of the most effective business practices is to make a good first impression. It is that first impression that a guest will often remember when they are making a future dining decision. The service that guests receive the moment they walk in the door sets the stage for the service that they anticipate receiving once they are seated. Therefore, the maître d' or host should have a professional appearance and the appropriate uniform. This should include meticulous personal grooming and in most cases a conservative appearance. The maître d' or host must practice excellent interpersonal skills to make the guest feel welcome; this includes the following: smiling, good posture, open body language, positive attitude, attentiveness, courtesy, and confidence. The essential skills—do's and don'ts—are listed in Table 9.1.

The maître d' or host position in most restaurants is one of an official greeter, as this is the person who in some cases actually opens the door and welcomes guests into the restaurant. Therefore, the personality of the maître d' or host requires the ability to take pressures such as handling a mealtime rush, accommodating various sizes of parties, effectively taking care of guests in a hurry, and assisting families with unruly children. The effective maître d' or host will never allow this type of pressure to affect their performance with guests.

Whenever possible, guests should be greeted as soon as they enter the restaurant. Restaurants with a large seating capacity will schedule more than one maître d' or host during a busy shift. One would remain at the door at all times managing reservations and greeting guests when they enter the restaurant, while the other would be responsible for escorting guests to their table.

The things that a guest would expect upon their arrival include a smile with eye-to-eye contact, good posture, uncrossed arms, and a positive greeting in a clear voice.

Skills	Do's	Don'ts
Smiling	Genuine smile Eye contact Fresh breath	Insincere or fake smile No eye contact Unfresh breath
Good Posture	Stand up straight	Leaning on tables, podium, etc.
Body Language	Arms to sides Shoulders back	Crossed arms Slouching
Positive Attitude	Happy to be at work Use time productively Willing to go above and beyond	Unhappy or dreading work Unable to use time wisely Only do what is asked of you
Attentiveness	At the door listening Nodding in agreement Focused on guest	Unavailable at the door Distracted or on the phone Distracted

Courtesy	Use proper language—
	    "please" and "thank you"
		Inappropriate and casual
		    language

Confidence	Full understanding of the job Helping wherever needed	Not sure what to do Watching not doing

TABLE 9.1
Skills—Do's and Don'ts

Guests expect the maître d' or host to speak first, and then they will reply. The maître d' or host who projects sincerity, maintains eye contact, and conveys a genuine attentiveness for guests will inspire a positive answer to the greeting, "Good evening, how are you tonight?" An appropriate casual conversation between the maître d' or host and guests helps to eliminate any uncomfortable feelings when a guest enters the restaurant.

Some restaurants take reservations while others do not. If a reservation is expected, ask if they have a reservation when applicable; if not, that is fine as well. A reservation system is an excellent way to get to know guests by name. Therefore, every effort should be made to remember guests' names to add value to their visit. Guests without reservations may be asked their name so that the host could then record it and remember it in the future. Some reservation systems can accommodate additional information such as the name of the guest's workplace or affiliation, which can be helpful for the host as a reminder of the guest's name and professional affiliation. An example would be, "Dr. Smith—Community Medical Clinic." All guests appreciate when they are recognized from a previous visit, which allows them to feel pampered and special.

After the initial greeting and check-in at the door, the maître d' or host identifies the number of guests and then selects an appropriate table size and location according to the size of the party. There are different restaurant policies for seating guests; some seat the guests as they arrive, while others like to wait until all the guests in a party arrive before seating them. Waiting until all guests arrive allows the server to work more efficiently making fewer trips to the table.

The maître d' or host should be particularly attentive and courteous to single diners who may be more likely to welcome casual conversation. Whether there is one guest or a large party of guests, all guests should be made to feel important and treated as individuals.

During certain peak periods, there may be a waiting period for guests even if they have a reservation. When this occurs, along with asking the guest's name for a waiting list, the maître d' or host should communicate the waiting time to the guest in a sincere and courteous manner. If the exact waiting time is uncertain, it is better to slightly overestimate the expected waiting time and be able to seat the guests sooner, rather than underestimating the time and having disappointed guests. Hungry guests can be difficult, so the maître d' or host must be masterful in communication and keeping guests at ease. If the restaurant has a lounge or bar area, offer to immediately seat the guests in the lounge where they can order drinks and appetizers. Then let the guests know that they will be seated as soon as their table is available. Check on the guests as often as possible to give them confidence in the establishment's operations. When the guests' table is ready, offer to help carry the unfinished drinks to their table, if applicable. Some restaurants may use a guest page or send a text message to the guest (see Chapter 8, The Technology of Service) or may have a waitlist display as a crawl over TV programs if a flat screen is in use.

Table Selection

Learning Objective 6

Explain how a table service management system functions and why table selection makes a difference.

Most restaurants assign servers a section of tables that the maître d' or host is responsible for seating. The number of tables in a station may vary with the style of the restaurant. Regardless, proper seating is one of the most important aspects of the maître d' or host's job. The maître d' or host must keep track of the number of guests seated in each station so that the servers can carry an equal workload. If the maître d' or host does not accurately seat the guests, it can affect all the positions in the establishment. Therefore, if too many guests are seated in one station that server could be overworked and will not provide the best possible service. The server may feel rushed and then could make mistakes that may then affect the kitchen staff. To facilitate the speed and accuracy of table selection, some restaurants use table service management systems (see Chapter 8, The Technology of Service). These systems help the maître d' or host seat guests accurately. They typically provide a graphical table display on the POS screen that shows available tables for immediate guest seating, as well as tables already in use. Controlling the seating flow is essential to maintaining a smooth tempo for the entire restaurant, as guests are alternately seated in servers' stations allowing for a smooth flow of service that avoids overloading any one station.

It is important to select tables that will provide the maximum comfort for guests. Therefore, guests should never be tightly seated at a table. Guests should always have plenty of "personal space" in order to be able to enjoy their meal. Since all guests' needs are not the same, the maître d' or host should always personalize table selection. If regular guests request the same table, make it a point of remembering it, and tell them that "their special table" is ready. These are the personal touches that can distinguish a restaurant's service from others in the community.

Strategic seating is an effective tool during slow periods in a restaurant, such as at the beginning of a meal period or in the afternoon when the dining room may be empty. A host should consider the placement of guests during these times. Guests should be seated in the center of the room where they can be seen from the door, near a window, or near other guests, giving the impression that the dining room is somewhat busy. Large parties may tend to be noisy; if possible, they should be seated near the back of the restaurant so that they will not disturb other guests. A guest with special needs should be seated in a convenient location away from traffic flow.

Professional Courtesies

Learning Objective 7

Describe the professional courtesies that a maître d' or host would extend to guests.

The maître d' or host should be prepared and ready to help remove guest coats, if appropriate, and if the guest acknowledges wanting the help. When this occurs, the procedure is to stand behind the guest and lift the shoulder of the coat while carefully slipping the coat off the arms. If the restaurant has a coat checkroom, this should take place there; otherwise, it should take place at the table. Coats then should be taken to a coat rack unless the guest wants to keep it and hang it on the chair. If that is the case, be careful that the coat does not drag on the floor where it could be soiled or tripped over.

When showing a table to the guests, the maître d' or host should always walk a step or two ahead of them at a comfortable pace, perhaps sharing a conversation that will allow them to feel comfortable and at ease. As you arrive at the table, pull out the chairs for guests to be seated. If a woman is being seated, you may want to lightly push the chair back as she sits down, unless her escort advances to do that for her. A high chair for infants or booster seat for small children may need to be furnished. Offer to help seat the child if the guests desire the service.

Open and present a menu directly in front of each guest, suggesting a specific appetizer, chef's specialty, or menu items that have made the restaurant famous. Make sure the guests are comfortable and tell them that their server will be right over. If you know their names, personalize it by saying, "Mr. and Mrs. _____, your server Mary will be right with you." If it is extremely busy and the server cannot immediately bring the water to the table, the maître d' or host should do so, while assuring the guests that any delay in service is only temporary. Also, the maître d' or host should inform the server of guests' special occasion such as a birthday, anniversary, or school graduation. Guests will often indicate this when making an online reservation or mention it to the maître d' or host while being seated at their table.

The maître d' or host is usually expected to help whenever possible. When it is extremely busy, they may be required to buss tables, pour coffee, fill waters, and help with orders. This means that the maître d' or host has to be flexible by nature, having the capacity to perform multiple tasks in order to help make the operation run smoothly. Therefore, a maître d' or host should be able to set an effective and efficient pace for the service staff to follow. Then teamwork allows the guest to receive the best possible service.

The maître d' or host, at times, may also act as the cashier. In this case, they should always promptly process guests' payment. The maître d' or host must juggle seating and payment. This can be difficult. The maître d' or host should always immediately acknowledge an incoming guest while processing the guest's payment. Guests who have finished dining and wish to leave should not be inconvenienced by having to wait to pay for their meal. Also, many guests do not put down a tip until after they have paid and acquired change. Therefore, the process should be made quick and easy for the guest.

As guests are leaving the restaurant, the maître d' or host may have the opportunity to open the door for the guests and bid them good-bye, along with an appreciative thanks and sincere invitation to return again soon.

Responding to Complaints

Learning Objective 8

Understand how the maître d' or host should respond to guest complaints.

The maître d' or host may get the bulk of any guest complaints. Guests who have a complaint about their visit to a restaurant sometimes wait until they have paid their check before they complain. The way the maître d' or host handles a complaint could mean saving or losing this guest's future business. If the complaint is a serious one, the manager should be called immediately to discuss the problem with the guest. It might be a valid complaint that requires the manager's immediate attention. At any rate, the presence of the manager indicates to the guest that management is concerned and wants to correct problems that cause guest dissatisfaction. If the problem does not seem serious enough to call the manager and the guest does not request the manager, the maître d' or host should write the complaint down on a notepad or enter it into the POS for the manager's attention; by doing this in the presence of the guest, it assures them that the issue will receive the manager's attention. Further, ask the guest if they would like to leave a name and telephone number for the manager to call. Then thank the guest, sincerely apologize for the problem, and extend a warm invitation to return again soon. The note should be quickly given to the manager, with any further explanation, if necessary, at the close of the shift.

Server Training

Learning Objective 9

Explain the training procedure for a new server.

The dining room manager or maître d' often supervises server training. New employees are first introduced to the restaurant operation through an orientation session that typically includes the policies and procedures of the restaurant that employees are expected to follow. The server training may include online training in addition to hands-on training directed by an experienced server who is competent in training new servers. The hands-on training may begin with the new server following and observing the experienced server working in their assigned station; a procedure that is often referred to as "shadowing." This begins with the experienced server demonstrating the correct method of taking guests' orders, followed by the correct method of serving the food and beverages. At a predetermined point, often half-way through the shift, the new server will begin taking guests' orders and serving their food and beverages. The training server then shadows the new server for the remainder of the shift. Then the dining room manager or maître d' will observe and verify if the new server has met and demonstrated the standards of service established by the restaurant or may need to have additional training time. In addition, the dining room manager or maître d' continually observes if all of the servers and servers' assistants are maintaining the standards of service established by the restaurant.

RESTAURANT REALITY: HOW TO RECOVER FROM DISAPPOINTING CIRCUMSTANCES

Herbert is the maître d' for a fine-dining restaurant in an upscale suburban community near a major city. The restaurant has a loyal following of customers who can afford to dine at the restaurant on a regular basis, and their dining preferences are consistently accommodated. There are also customers who come to the restaurant only for special occasions, and Herbert makes every effort to assure that their dining experience is both memorable and satisfying.

Saturday morning when Herbert checked the online reservations, he noted that a couple had made a reservation for 7 P.M., and were celebrating their first wedding anniversary. The reservation also indicated that the couple requested to have a small, gluten-free white cake served for dessert, and to have it served with one candle. They also requested a window table with a view of the nearby park. Herbert checked the table management application and was able to enter the couple's name for a center table for two with a widow view. He also placed the order for the gluten-free white cake with the kitchen and was looking forward to welcoming the couple to the restaurant when they arrived.

A rain and hail storm occurred Saturday afternoon that cracked the large center window, which needed to be replaced. The restaurant manager immediately called to have the window replacement work done. The procedure was to secure the cracked window by covering it with flat wooden boards until the following Monday morning when the window could be completely replaced. Surely, customers would understand this unforeseen circumstance as the storm caused damage throughout the community.

When the young couple arrived for their dinner reservation, Herbert greeted and welcomed them to the restaurant. He apologized for the covered window and explained what had occurred. The couple were disappointed but understood the situation. Herbert seated the couple at their reserved table; although the view they hoped for was blocked by the wooden boards, they were still happy to be dining at the restaurant. As the couple finished dinner and were anticipating their anniversary cake for dessert, the server sadly informed them that in preparing to light the candle, the server was accidently bumped by another server and the cake fell to the floor. The server was so sorry for the accident, but as a consequence they could choose from any of the items on the dessert menu at no charge. The couple were again disappointed, declined the offer, and just asked to have their dinner check. This was not the fine-dining experience that the couple had planned for their first anniversary.

Herbert observed their disappointed facial expressions, personally apologized for the unfortunate situations, and inquired if there was anything else he might offer them. They just said, "Thanks" and then left. Herbert immediately explained the situation to the restaurant manager. The couple were promptly sent an e-mail message to expect a delivery to their home from the restaurant the following day by noon. They were sent a fruit and cheese basket with a bottle of champagne along with a white gluten-free cake, compliments of the restaurant. The couple were overwhelmed and planned to return to the restaurant as often as possible, plus told of their experience many times over with their family and friends.

Summary

The dining room manager, maître d', or host position can function in many different ways, according to the type and size of restaurant along with the restaurant's organizational structure. The maître d' or host must be able to manage reservations and take pressures such as handling a mealtime rush, accommodating various party sizes, effectively taking care of guests in a hurry, and assisting families with unruly children; they must never allow those pressures to affect their performance with the guests.

The maître d' or host should be competent in tactfully handling table delays by offering to seat guests in the lounge, when possible, where they can order drinks and appetizers until their table is ready. It is important to keep communication going by giving realistic waiting times and keeping guests informed of the situation. The selection of tables that will provide maximum comfort for guests to fully enjoy their meal is also important. The maître d' or host has the responsibility to control the seating flow in order to maintain a smooth tempo for the entire restaurant, as guests are alternately seated in servers' stations allowing for a smooth flow of service.

Among the many professional courtesies that the maître d' or host should perform are helping guests with their coats, pulling out chairs for guests to be seated, and opening and presenting a menu in front of each guest. Also, they should be flexible during the busy times and assist with bussing tables, pouring coffee, filling waters, and helping with orders. The maître d' or host, when also acting as the cashier, should be attentive in handling any guest complaints, and be sincere when inquiring about the guest's dining experience.

When taking telephone reservations and/or "take-out" orders, a specific procedure should be followed to ensure accuracy at all times. The maître d' or host should also be familiar with the community in order to provide guests with directions and points of interest within the community.

The maître d' or host will often have additional duties and therefore must be able to control the front-of-the-restaurant operations, including proper planning and assignments.

Discussion Questions and Exercises

1. What will determine the duties and responsibilities of a maître d' or host?
2. Explain four important duties and responsibilities of a maître d' or host.
3. List five topics that could be discussed at a menu meeting.
4. Describe the procedure a maître d' or host should follow when managing online reservations.
5. What procedure should the maître d' or host follow when taking a guest's telephone reservation?
6. What procedure should the maître d' or host follow when taking a guest's "take-out" order?
7. The maître d' or host must practice excellent interpersonal skills to make the guest feel welcome. List six of those skills.
8. When a guest's name is known, why should it always be used?
9. What should the maître d' or host tell guests when they will have to wait for a table?
10. Explain how a table management system operates.
11. When should guests be seated in the center of the dining room and why?
12. What is the proper procedure when a maître d' or host helps a guest remove her coat?
13. When the restaurant is extremely busy, what other duties is the maître d' or host often expected to perform?
14. Why would the maître d'-cashier or host-cashier process the payment of a guest check before seating arriving guests?
15. How should the maître d' or host, when acting as cashier, respond to any guest complaints?
16. What is the role of the dining room manager or maître d' in server training?

CHAPTER 10

Banquet, Catering, and Buffet Management

INTRODUCTION

Banquet, catering, and buffet service can accommodate any size group ranging from a dozen to any large number of guests. The capacity of the room will dictate the number of people who can be served. A banquet, catering, or buffet menu can be limited and served quickly, or it may consist of several courses, elaborately presented and served. It may be a traditional breakfast, lunch, or dinner menu.

A *banquet* is a dining event that may honor a special guest(s) or be a celebration for a special occasion, such as an awards banquet. Many restaurants have fixed banquet menus, which are limited to the choices offered on the menu. This is a very important feature of banquet-style service because it helps the restaurant accommodate various occasions. A distinguishing feature of banquet-style service, which sets it apart from restaurant service, is that all elements of the event are predetermined: the date and time, the number of guests, the arrangement of tables, and the style of service. This enables the business to purchase the correct amounts and types of food and to schedule staff as appropriate.

An on- or off-premise *catered event* is created for the specific occasion and has a predetermined menu, with options for those with dietary restrictions. The event being celebrated typically influences that menu, including a wedding reception, birthday party, anniversary party, holiday party, bar or bat mitzvah, communion, or any other special occasion. An on-premise catered event takes place at a restaurant or hotel. An off-premise catered event can take place away from a restaurant or hotel, in a natural environment such as a botanical garden, near a scenic waterway, or at a historical landmark.

A formal or informal *buffet* allows guests to select the food and serve themselves, from a simple or an elaborate menu. A buffet has a built-in advantage: a restaurant can service a large group of guests in a short amount of time and can provide a wide variety of food to accommodate a range of menu preferences and can appeal to a range of appetites.

Banquet, catering, and buffet services are each used to accommodate larger groups of guests. Restaurant operators use these service types because they allow for easy service and a limited number of employees to serve a large number of guests for all types of special occasions. Table 10.1 compares banquet, catering, and buffet services by location, advantages, and disadvantages for each.

CHAPTER 10 LEARNING OBJECTIVES

As a result of successfully completing this chapter, readers will be able to:

1. Understand the difference between a banquet, a catered event, and a buffet.

2. Recognize the value of using an event plan details work sheet.

3. Recognize the value of using an event management software program.

4. Identify the required customer information needed to initially begin the event plan.

5. Explain the different service presentation styles.

6. Recognize the importance of current menu pricing and customer preferences when creating the menu for a banquet, catered event, or buffet.

7. Explain the different types of bar service available to the customer hosting a cocktail service.

8. Understand banquet/catering room sizes and capacities by calculated measurements.

9. Know the many accessory details that are typically available to customers.

10. Understand event pricing and charges.

Learning Objective 1

Understand the difference between a banquet, a catered event, and a buffet.

Type of Service	Location of the Event	Advantages	Disadvantages
Banquet—food is plated and served to a large number of guests by a limited number of servers for a specific occasion.	Typically in a room that is on the property. The room can have special dividers to allow the establishment to increase or decrease the number of guests that can be accommodated.	All elements of the event are predetermined.	Food choices are limited.
		Can serve a large group of guests.	There can be lag time between the first and last tables being served and food can get cold.
		Can be customized to fit the specific needs of the guests.	
Catering—foodservice where the food may or may not be plated but large numbers of guests are served in a limited amount of time by a limited number of servers for a specific occasion.	*On-premise catering.*	Same as above.	Same as above.
	Event takes place under the same circumstances as banquets.		
	Off-premise catering.	Same as above.	Can be difficult to move food, equipment, and staff to the desired location.

TABLE 10.1

Banquet, Catering, and Buffet Services Compared

Type of Service	Location of the Event	Advantages	Disadvantages
	Event can take place anywhere away from the property and can be customized to meet the guests' needs.		
Buffets—food is placed on tables and chafing dishes. Guests help themselves to food items from the buffet line. Servers will serve beverages to guests and clear plates.	In a restaurant setting special room, or on location.	Same as above.	Need to purchase special equipment such as chafing dishes and service utensils. Buffet can get messy. Certain types of food do not hold well on buffets, so menus are limited.

TABLE 10.1

(*continued*)

The Event Plan

A banquet, catered event, or buffet always begins with a checklist of details as shown in Figure 10.1, followed by a level of professional service that enhances every detail of the event. The checklist should be thorough and complete in identifying everything that the restaurant (banquet/catering) operator is capable of providing. Furthermore, the customer may not be aware of all the options that can add to the success of the event. Therefore, the checklist serves to provide additional choices for the customer to consider. The typical checklist would include, but would not be limited to the items presented in Figure 10.1, Event Plan Details.

Event Management

An event management software program customized to meet the needs of the individual restaurant (banquet/catering) operation can efficiently manage all of the event details and special requests from start to finish, beginning with an event calendar for scheduling the date(s) and time(s) of a single event to multiple sub-events hosted by the same customer. A multiple sub-event may include lunch, seminar or conference meetings, and cocktails and hors d'oeuvres on a patio or poolside, followed by an elaborate dinner. The customer information and complete venue can all be efficiently managed, including the required scheduled deposits prior to the event.

The customized program would include up-to-date menu pricing when creating a menu along with a complete list of options that can be offered to enhance the event, as shown in Figure 10.1, Event Plan Details. The options range from custom printing for a price quotation to a final invoice that could include digital images, the restaurant (banquet/catering) operator's logo, menus, and pricing details printed and/or e-mailed to the customer. An example of this type of software program is Caterease (www.caterease.com).

EVENT PLAN DETAILS

CUSTOMER INFORMATION

Customer Name_____ Telephone # _____

Event Contact Name _____ Mobile # _____

Address _____ Fax # _____

Type of Event _____ E-mail _____

Date_____	Cocktails served (time)_____	Speaker(s) (start time)_____ (end time) _____
Day _____	Hors d'oeuvres (time) _____	Entertainment (start time)_____ (end time) _____
Arrival (time) _____	Bar service (time)_____	Dancing (start time)_____ (end time) _____
Departure (time) _____	Food served (time) _____	Photography (start time)_____ (end time) _____

Number of Guests: Approximate # _____   Guaranteed # _____   Confirmed # _____

SERVICE PRESENTATION   _____ Banquet   _____ Catered   _____ Buffet
MENU

Menu Items _____   Cake Order_____

_____   _____

_____   _____

Dietary/Special Menu _____   Special Desserts_____

Beverages _____   **BAR SERVICE** _____ Open _____ Cash _____ Combination

_____   Drink Choices _____

_____   Brands _____

ROOM LOCATION _____

Room Floor Plan *(see attached diagram)*   Table Setup: ___ Banquet _____ Round _____ Conference

Table Arrangement _____   Number of Chairs at Each Table _____

Table Numbers/Names _____   Head Table: _____ Banquet _____ Round

_____   Number of Chairs at Head Table _____

ACCESSORIES

Tablecloths (color) _____ Napkins (color) _____ Type of Napkin Fold _____

Chair Covers (color) _____ Bows (color) _____ Table Skirting (pleat/pattern style) _____

Candles (type) _____ Candelabras _____

Floral Arrangements (name specific flowers & details for each arrangement—real or artificial)

Centerpieces _____ Baskets _____ Sprays _____

Canopy _____ Plants _____ Trees _____

Room Decorations _____ Balloons (colors) _____ (size) _____ (wording) _____

Fountains: Beverage (type & mix)_____Chocolate (or) Cheese Fondue (list items for dipping) _____

Ice Carving(s) (name of design & size requested) _____

Coat Rack/Coat Checking (instructions) _____ Lectern _____ Speaker Podium _____

Portable Stage (height) _____ (size) _____ (skirting type & color) _____

Flags (placement location) _____ (name of flags and order of arrangement) _____

Tripod(s) (sizes) _____ (placement) _____ Easel(s) (sizes) _____ (placement) _____

Lighting Effects (list all areas requiring special lighting) _____

Sound System/Microphones: Cordless _____Standing ___ Lectern ___ Table

Background Music (start & end time) _____ (type of music/requested music) _____

Piano (date checked for tuning) _____ (placement location for the piano) _____

Registration Table(s) (size & number of tables) ___(number of chairs) ___(electrical requirements) ____

Miscellaneous Items: (big screen television **with DVD capability or smart television with web streaming,** costume rental, menu printing, large notepad & marker for meetings, etc.)

_____

Valet Parking (guests' arrival time) _____ (departure time) _____

Special Requests _____

ESTIMATED CHARGES

Guaranteed guest number of _____ at $ _____ per guest for a total of .... $ _____

(The final charge will be for the guaranteed guest number or confirmed guest number, whichever is greater)

Beverage Service (wine(s), espresso) $_____ Bar Service $_____ .... _____

Accessory Items _____ _____

_____ _____

Service Fee $ _____ _____

Estimated Total (not including tax)............ $ _____

Deposit Amount............................. $ _____

FIGURE 10.1

Event Plan Details

Customer Information

Customer information includes the name, address, telephone number, mobile number, fax number, and e-mail address of the person responsible for scheduling and paying for the event, and also the name of the event contact person if different from the customer name. It is essential for the restaurant (banquet/catering) manager to be able to conveniently contact the customer and/or the event contact person as the time for the event approaches. The type of function is also identified, such as, a community arts council lunch and meeting or a wedding reception.

Date and Time Schedule

The date, day, and arrival and departure times of the event must be identified and scheduled with enough advance notice to adequately prepare for and deliver first-rate service, which is often determined by the type and size of the event. Accommodating the customer's time schedule is a top priority for the restaurant (banquet/catering) operator. Therefore, it is important to establish an agreement that includes the time that the service begins and ends. When the menu is served on time, prepared and cooked to the highest quality, and perfectly presented, the customer and the guests will be satisfied. The experienced restaurant (banquet/catering) manager knows the amount of time required for preparation, cooking, and serving. When the food serving time is preceded by other activities occurring, beginning and ending time frames for those activities should be established, such as a set time for cocktails, hors d'oeuvres, bar service, speaker(s), entertainment, dancing, or photography. There are occasions when a specific time frame cannot be established, so an approximate time frame should be determined, such as during wedding reception photography. The restaurant (banquet/catering) manager must always be prepared with a contingency plan for delays. And when the unexpected happens, a logical alternative choice should be presented to the customer. For example, if half the guests attending an event are delayed for an hour due to a traffic backup, an alternative could be to hold the meal and offer appetizers to the guests who have already arrived.

The restaurant (banquet/catering) operator should also be prepared with names of bands, solo instrumentalists, singers, and professional photographers to answer a customer's request for possible choices. The customer would be responsible for determining the best choice for the occasion and event.

Number of Guests

An *approximate number of guests* attending the event must be determined in order to put an agreement in place, including the cost. Several days before the scheduled event, the customer will authorize a *guaranteed number of guests* attending, which is the minimum number that the customer is committed to pay for. If it is a large event that involves special ordered items, such as a wedding cake, then a week or more advance notice would be required. The *confirmed number of guests* served may be more or less than the guaranteed number, but the customer is responsible for paying for whichever is greater, the guaranteed number or the confirmed number of guests.

The kitchen prepares an additional amount over the guaranteed number of guests to be served. That amount will depend upon the size of the guaranteed number. For example, when the guaranteed number is 30, then it would be appropriate to prepare for 36, 20 percent more than the guaranteed number; if the guaranteed number is 100, then it would be appropriate to prepare for 110, a 10 percent amount over the guaranteed number. It is reasonable to anticipate that a smaller group might have up to an additional four to six guests, whereas the larger group may have up to an additional 8 to 10 guests; therefore, a larger percentage amount for smaller group versus the smaller percentage amount for larger group. The amount that is to be prepared over the guaranteed number should be discussed with the customer to find out if any unusual circumstances may exist that could influence a greater number of guests attending—for example, an important topic being presented at a business lunch meeting or a prominent speaker who may attract more guests than anticipated. The actual number of guests served is verified by the number of dinner plates used.

Service Presentation

Learning Objective 5

Explain the different service presentation styles.

If hors d'oeuvres or beverages are to be served on handheld trays during a social time prior to a banquet or catered event, *butler service* would be provided. This type of service is discussed in Chapter 3, Table Service, Table Settings, and Napkin Presentations.

A sit-down, individual plate service, commonly known as *American service,* is the typical method of service for most banquet or catered events. The food is plated in the kitchen and individually served to guests. The service is fast and efficient and equal portion sizes are maintained with each serving. This type of service is also discussed in Chapter 3.

Buffet service allows guests to choose among the food items being presented and serve themselves. The typical buffet is set up in the following order:

1. serving plates
2. salad selections
3. vegetables
4. potatoes/pasta/rice
5. rolls and butter
6. entrée(s)
7. dessert plates
8. desserts

The arrangement presents the food items in their natural order and allows the guests to fill their plates first with the items costing less, leaving enough space for an adequate portion of the entrée.

The average single-line buffet can comfortably accommodate 40–50 guests within 15 minutes, with an average of three guests per minute going through the line. The speed at which the line moves will be determined by the variety of foods and the complexity of the food presentation, with a greater variety requiring more time for guests to make selections. A double-line buffet, allowing guests to serve themselves from both sides of the table, will accommodate twice the number of guests within the same period of time. Several buffet tables could be set up to accommodate a large group with an elaborate presentation. An example would be a buffet table for appetizers, which may also include salads, salad dressings, fresh fruit, cheeses, breads, and crackers; a second buffet table for the entrée(s), sauces, vegetables, and potatoes/pasta/rice, and a carving station could also be placed at this table; and a third table for desserts.

When planning the menu for a buffet service, it is important to include food items that hold up well on a serving line along with being easy for guests to serve themselves. The visual presentation is enhanced by placing risers, trays, and chafing dishes at various angles to the table. A two-tier round buffet table is shown in Figure 10.2a and a white marble table cap in Figure 10.2b. Trays can be slightly elevated in order to slant toward guests, and they can be placed at different heights to add visual interest. When serving unusual food items or items not

(a)   (b)

FIGURE 10.2

(a) Two-Tier Buffet Table with Pleated Table Skirting; (b) Faux-Stone Heat Resistant Plastic Table Cap with Contour-Fitted Table Cover. Courtesy of SDI Brands.

easily recognized, the name of the item printed on a small card should be conveniently placed next to the item. When the food items become depleted with about one-quarter to one-third remaining in bowls or on trays, the server should replace or remove them and put the food items in smaller bowls or on trays to retain a fresh and full appearance.

The food items should at all times be kept at their recommended safe food temperatures: 135°F or above for hot foods and 41°F or below for cold foods. Chafing dishes are typically used for hot foods and large pans filled with crushed or small cubed ice can hold platters, trays, and bowls for cold foods. For certain events, the use of a hot or cold well buffet table (to insert trays and pans) provides additional safety and flexibility. The well for hot food would be similar to the heat maintained by burners on an electric range and the well for cold food similar to the chill maintained by a refrigeration unit.

Dinnerware

The choice of dinnerware should be banquet weight, which is lighter than the traditional dinnerware and more comfortable to handle. White-color dinnerware fits all decors and is traditionally used.

Menu

The menu will be identified according to the type of event and service required: banquet, catered, or buffet. The nature of the event and time of the year can affect the menu choices that the customer may consider. For example, a summer wedding reception might include a selection of fresh fruit appetizers or carved watermelons for a buffet table. The menu chosen and item portion sizes should be clearly identified—for example, prime rib 6 ounce cut, cooked medium or salmon 8 ounce,

FIGURE 10.3
Event Menu.
Photo by Gerald Lanuzza.

Learning Objective 6

Recognize the importance of current menu pricing and customer preferences when creating the menu for a banquet, catered event, or buffet.

grilled. This reduces the possibility of the customer being dissatisfied with a portion size or degree of cooking doneness. If children are attending the event, it is important to know the approximate ages and number attending to determine if a second menu selection should be considered. Furthermore if a guest has a dietary restriction, a special individual meal could be prepared. If a guest is being honored, perhaps a special dessert may be requested by the customer.

There are occasions when the customer may want to have copies of the event menu printed so that guests attending the event will know the food and beverage items that will be served. When this occurs, the menu is typically printed with the name of the host, the title of the menu, such as "Wedding Menu," and the food and beverage items printed in the order that those items will be served, as shown in Figure 10.3.

Cake Order

When a cake is requested for a wedding, anniversary, birthday, or special event dinner, it must be prepared and presented exactly to the customer's request. The restaurant (banquet/catering) operator may be able to prepare the cake or should have a choice of two or three specialty bakeries that could fulfill the order. The operator should understand the capabilities and pricing for each bakery. The size and complexity of the cake will determine the amount of advance order time required.

Beverages

The banquet/catering manager should always be able to recommend alcohol and nonalcohol beverages that complement the food being served. An understanding of wines (see Chapter 6, Beverages and Beverage Service) is an important part of the manager's function in helping the customer to make a selection that is paired with the menu when wine is to be served.

Nonalcohol beverage choices may include sparkling cider, plain or flavored mineral waters, flavored iced teas, specialty hot teas, and specialty coffees or espresso that may be paired with a dessert.

FIGURE 10.4

Portable Bar. Courtesy of Lakeside Manufacturing.

Bar Service

Learning Objective 7

Explain the different types of bar service available to the customer hosting a cocktail service.

There are occasions that may include bar service, such as prior to a dinner. The time allotted for the bar service is often a cocktail hour, an opportunity for guests to socialize from 7:00 P.M. to 8:00 P.M. before dinner is served at 8:00 P.M.

A number of drink choices (liquor, beer, wine) would be presented to the customer along with specific brands that the customer's guests may request. When the customer determines the number of drink choices and identifies the specific brands to be served, the restaurant (banquet/catering) manager can calculate the charge for the bar service.

The bar service can function as follows:

Open bar, paid for by the host.

Cash bar, also referred to as a no-host bar, in which guests pay for their drinks.

Open bar–cash bar combination, for which the host agrees to pay for the first one or two drinks with drink tickets and any subsequent drinks would require payment by the guest.

The restaurant operator typically has a portable, full functional bar that can be conveniently set up and in place to serve guests as shown in Figure 10.4.

Room Location

Learning Objective 8

Understand banquet/catering room sizes and capacities by calculated measurements.

A restaurant, hotel, resort, or club may have several rooms that can accommodate small to large groups. The rooms may adjoin and be configured to fit the needs of a particular function—for example, a room to serve cocktails and hors d'oeuvres as guests arrive next to the room in which guests will be served their dinner. The choices should be presented to the customer so that the room(s) location can be reserved in advance. The *room temperature* will rise when the room becomes fully occupied. Therefore, the room temperature should be 5 to 10 degrees cooler prior to guests' arrival. The restaurant (banquet or catering) manager should be familiar with the cooling and heating conditions of each room. It is important to be able to establish temperature settings that will accommodate the guests' comfort

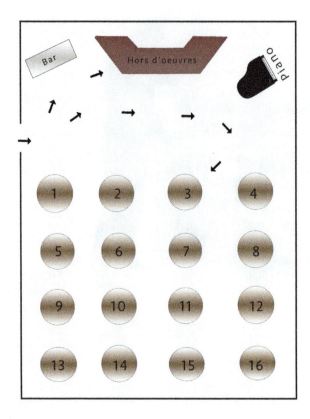

FIGURE 10.5

Floor Plan Diagram. Graphic by Dwayne Philibert.

(typically 68°F to 72°F) during any season of the year. If a room temperature is either too hot or too cold, the guests will be uncomfortable, which can result in them not enjoying the event.

Room Floor Plan

A room floor plan is presented in a printed diagram, which accompanies the event plan details for the customer's approval. Figure 10.5 is a diagram that shows a portable bar, hors d'oeuvre table, piano, and 16 round tables set according to the customer's preference. This is of the utmost importance for certain events that require specific room settings such as a head table or conference table seating for meetings or seminars, a stage, podium placement, buffet tables, and room decorations.

The size of the room determines the seating capacity for banquet, round, and conference size tables. If banquet table seating (long tables lined up in a row) is planned then the total square footage of the room is divided by 12. For example, if a room is 60 by 80, the total square footage is 4,800 (60 × 80 = 4,800) divided by 12 (4,800 ÷ 12 = 400), seating for 400. If traditional seating (individual or round tables) is planned then the total square footage of the room is divided by 15 (4,800 ÷ 15 = 320), seating for 320. Figure 10.6 shows a room setup for round table seating.

If the room has an unusual layout such as long and narrow or has floor to ceiling columns, then an allowance should be made for adequate spacing. The seating arrangements should allow for the comfort of the guests and provide easy traffic flow for safe and efficient service. Also, additional space will have to be allowed for if a portable bar, hors d'oeuvre buffet table, or piano are to be set in the room. For example, if a portable bar as shown in Figure 10.7 and hors d'oeuvre table as shown in Figure 10.8 are set up for a cocktail hour prior to a full-service menu being served with traditional seating, then the following calculations would be appropriate: 3,600 square feet room; 1,200 square feet allowed for the bar, hors d'oeuvre

FIGURE 10.6
Round Table Seating ("Gala" Liberty Science Center; Jersey City, NJ).
Courtesy of Restaurant Associates.

table, and stand-up socializing prior to the dinner being served; and 2,400 square feet allowed for tables (2,400 ÷ 15 = 160), seating for 160.

When setting up the tables, it is critical to remember to set up for the total number that the customer requested. For example, if the customer has guaranteed the guest count number to be 150, and had requested the restaurant operator to be prepared to accommodate 10 more over the guarantee, then seating for 160 would be adequate. If 6-feet round tables with seating for 10 at each table were being used then 160 divided by 10 (160 ÷ 10 = 16) would equal 16, which would be arranged and set up for service as shown in Figure 10.5.

FIGURE 10.7
Portable Bar for Cocktail Reception (10 on the Park, Time Warner Building, NYC). Courtesy of Restaurant Associates.

FIGURE 10.8
Hors d'oeuvre Table.
Photo by Gerald Lanuzza.

Table Setup

The tables should be set up well in advance of the event, allowing enough time to be thorough and complete. Tablecloths should be draped approximately 1 inch above each chair. The tables should be set with the appropriate plates, beverage glasses, coffee cups, saucers, and flatware to accommodate the menu being served. Each table setting should be approximately 24 inches wide and 15 inches deep. This will allow a comfortable space for guest seating and dining, as well as adequate serving room. Tables and chairs should be arranged so that guests can be conveniently seated and served. Chairs, when in use, will normally extend 18–20 inches from the table edge and 18 inches in width. Allow 24–30 inches from back to back (when in occupied position) for comfortable service between tables. When a head table is being used, the other tables should be arranged so that the majority of the guests will be able to view the head table. The server is typically assigned 12–18 guests to serve, depending upon the menu and the method of service.

Table Sizes

The typical table sizes with seating capacity are as follows:

Length	Width	Seating
Banquet Table Sizes (as shown in Figure 10.9)		
4 feet	30 inches	4 (5 or 6 if chairs are added to the opposite ends of the table)
6 feet	30 inches	6 (7 or 8 if chairs are added to the opposite ends of the table)
8 feet	30 inches	8 (9 or 10 if chairs are added to the opposite ends of the table)
Round Table Sizes (as shown in Figure 10.10)		
4 feet	round	6 or 7
5.5 feet	round	8 or 9
6 feet	round	10 or 11
Conference Table Sizes (as shown in Figure 10.11)		
6 feet	18 inches	3
8 feet	18 inches	4

Conference tables are used for groups holding meetings as shown in Figure 10.12, but they can also be used for buffet or display tables. If they are needed for meal service, the tables can be placed together side by side forming a 36-inch-wide dining table, which would be covered with a tablecloth.

Table Arrangements

Banquet tables can be arranged in several different configurations for dining, buffets, and elaborate food presentations as shown in Figure 10.13. Some examples are as follows:

- *U-Shape — where several banquet tables are set to form the shape of the letter "U," with chairs around the outside*. The inside of the "U" is covered with *table skirting* or *draped tablecloth* reaching approximately 2 inches above the floor.

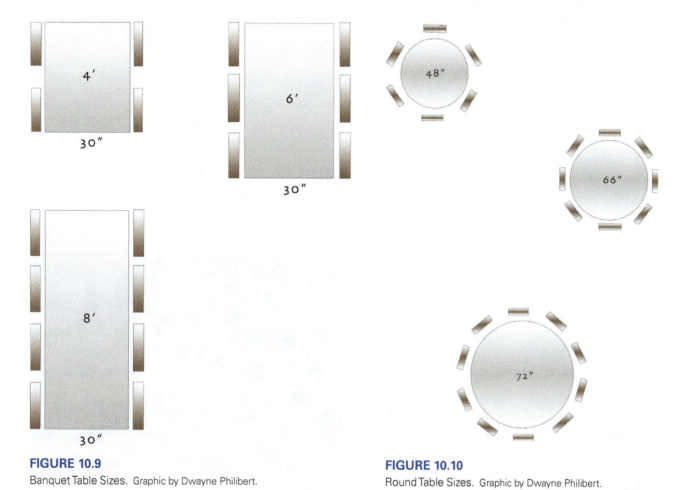

FIGURE 10.9
Banquet Table Sizes. Graphic by Dwayne Philibert.

FIGURE 10.10
Round Table Sizes. Graphic by Dwayne Philibert.

This layout is often used for business meetings or discussions that immediately follow the meal service.

Table Skirting is easy to install and is secured and held in place with clips, tape, or T-pins. The skirting is available in a variety of pleat styles and patterns. Valances that would attach along the top of the skirting can also be added for a bolder appearance as shown in Figure 10.14, and are available in a number of styles.

Draped tablecloth is held in place with masking tape. Head tables and buffet tables can easily be draped with tablecloths. For a head table, one tablecloth is draped over the front of the table reaching approximately 2 inches above the floor and secured with masking tape. A second tablecloth is draped in the usual manner. For a buffet table the front and back of the table would each be covered and secured with masking tape, and topped with a third tablecloth draped in the usual manner.

- *Hollow Shape — where banquet tables are set to form a square or rectangle, leaving the center open.* Both sides of the tables are covered with table skirting or draped tablecloth reaching approximately 2 inches above the floor. This layout is ideal for a formal buffet setting. The hollow center could accommodate a large ice carving. The carving would set in a pan on top of a skirted square table. A drain hose is connected to the pan and attached to a 5-gallon bucket placed under the table to control the flow of water as the ice slowly melts. The base of the pan would be covered with parsley or other greens.

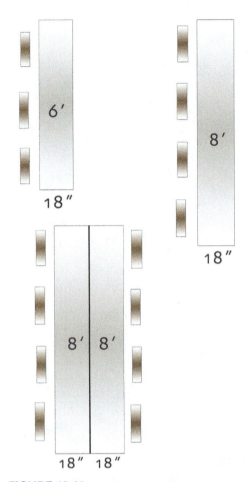

FIGURE 10.11

Conference Table Sizes. Graphic by Dwayne Philibert.

FIGURE 10.12

Conference Tables with Speaker Podium. Courtesy of SDI Brands.

- *T-Shape — where banquet tables are set to form the shape of the letter "T."* The top (horizontal part) of the "T" may serve as a head table with table skirting or draped tablecloth, with chairs facing the stem (vertical part) of the T formation, which would have chairs on both sides of the tables.
- *E-Shape — where banquet tables are set to form the shape of the letter "E."* The vertical part of the E formation may serve as a head table with table skirting or draped tablecloth, with chairs facing the horizontal parts of the E formation, which would have chairs on both sides of the tables.

Quarter-round and trapezoid tables can be arranged to create unique shapes as shown in Figure 10.15a and b, which are typically used for hors d'oeuvre tables, buffets, ice carvings (ice-carved serving bowls and vases shown in Figure 10.16), and decorative food displays.

Head Table

A head table is usually reserved for honored guests, speakers, or the bride and groom, parents (relatives), and the wedding party. When the room is set with a head table, it should be set apart from, and face, the other tables. The front of the head table should always be covered with table skirting or draped tablecloth reaching approximately 2 inches above the floor.

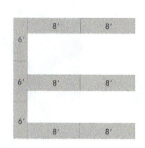

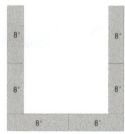

FIGURE 10.13

Banquet Table Arrangements. Graphic by Dwayne Philibert.

FIGURE 10.14

Valance Attached to the Top of Table Skirting. Courtesy of SDI Brands.

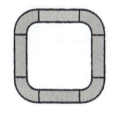
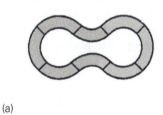
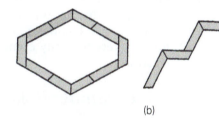

(a)

(b)

FIGURE 10.15

(a) Quarter-Round Table Arrangements; (b) Trapezoid Table Arrangements. Graphic by Dwayne Philibert.

FIGURE 10.16

Ice-Carved Serving Bowls and Vases. Courtesy of Ice Sculpture Designs and Apple Ice.

FIGURE 10.17

Stage with Head Table. Courtesy of SDI Brands.

FIGURE 10.18

Table Setting with "Best Wishes" Note for Honored Guest. Courtesy of SDI Brands.

If requested, a head table can be placed on a portable stage that is raised from 6 to 36 inches above the floor as shown in Figure 10.17, depending upon the nature and circumstances of the event.

There are occasions where the head table may be set apart from the other tables by an above-average-size centerpiece such as a tall floral arrangement, signifying the distinction of the table. This is often the case when a speaker podium is to be used. The table is set close to and off to one side of the podium allowing for speakers to easily come forward to the podium with the least amount of distraction.

Table Numbers/Names

Table numbers or names are used when the customer requests assigned seating for guests. This is often the case for functions that may have distinguished guests who would need to be seated near a head table or speaker podium, and also for events that sell tickets, whereby a group of individuals or a business may purchase tickets for a complete table. The table numbers or names are printed on cards and placed in the center of the table or clipped to a centerpiece. There may also be a request to place a note card next to gift for an honored guest, as shown in Figure 10.18.

Accessories

There are a number of additional items and services that the restaurant (banquet/catering) operator may be able to offer customers. These are items and services that can enhance the event and be an added source of revenue for the business. Each item is individually priced and added to the total cost of the event. The items and services may include the following:

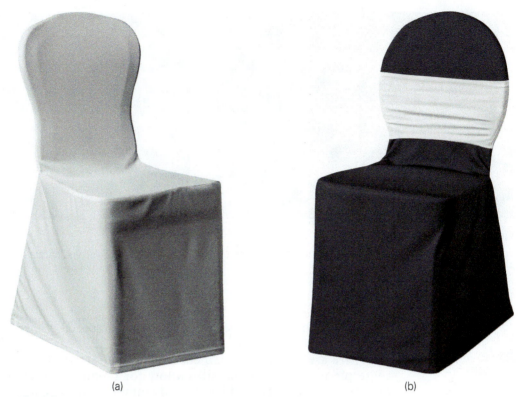

(a)   (b)

FIGURE 10.19

(a) White Chair Cover; (b) Black Chair Cover with Sash. Courtesy of SDI Brands.

Learning Objective 9

Know the many accessory details that are typically available to customers.

Choice of Linen Colors

Tablecloths, napkins, and chair covers and bows are available in different fabrics and a variety of colors. Table skirting comes in various pleat and pattern styles. All of these items are available from local rental stores and national linen rental companies. The national companies are able to fulfill size and quantity requirements within short notice and ship to any location.

There are many different types of napkin folds that add a distinctive look to the table (see Chapter 3, Table Service, Table Settings, and Napkin Presentations). The specific napkin fold selected for the event should be noted on the Event Plan Details form as shown in Figure 10.1, such as "Bird of Paradise" or "Rose."

Chair Covers

Chair covers as shown in Figure 10.19a and b are often used for distinguished guests, the bride and groom, or for a specific table. Chair covers with bows add a special touch of elegance and are available in a variety of colors.

Candles

Candles offer an added accent to each table and should be placed in the center of the table or evenly placed on banquet tables at a height that is not distracting to guests, as shown in Figure 10.20. If a formal event requires the use of candelabras, then it is important to remember to use dripless candles.

Floral Arrangements

The banquet/catering manager, at the request of the customer, often coordinates with a floral designer and local florist to provide the floral arrangements for an event.

FIGURE 10.20
Candelabras Placed on Banquet Tables. Courtesy of Restaurant Associates.

FIGURE 10.21
Floral Table Centerpieces (Corporate Dinner, Diker Pavilion, Natural Museum of The American Indian, NYC). Courtesy of Restaurant Associates.

This may be the case for wedding receptions or special dinners where fresh flowers are the preferred choice, as shown in Figure 10.21.

There are occasions when customers request artificial silk flowers for table centerpieces. The artificial silks allow for flexibility in choosing colorful and/ or exotic flowers. The additional advantage is the absence of any floral scents that could activate allergy conditions for some guests. The cost of artificial silks is relatively stable versus the cost of fresh flowers that will fluctuate according to seasons and general availability. The artificial silks can often be rented or, if purchased, can be offered by the host as gifts to guests to take upon leaving the event.

Baskets of fresh flowers or colorful sprays often add decorative accents to a room when appropriately placed by an entrance or near a head table. Plants and trees, real or artificial, are excellent choices to accent parts of a room or to create an aisle that will serve to guide guests' movement. A floral canopy can add an elegant touch to the entrance of a wedding reception or festive event.

Room Decorations

An atmosphere can easily be created with a few appropriately selected room decorations. Good judgment is the key factor in selecting items such as photographs, art, floral decorations, balloons, mobiles, and special effects lighting. The banquet/catering manager can work closely with a party-supply rental store in providing ideas and items that can meet the customer's expectations. The facility itself and the nature of the event may often dictate the appropriate decorations.

Balloons are a popular choice and come in numerous colors and sizes that can be decoratively placed on tables, chairs, arches, and throughout the room. Greetings and messages can also be printed on balloons, which add a personal touch. The balloons should not be prepared and put in place too far in advance of the event. Under normal temperature conditions, latex and Mylar balloons will retain helium for several hours.

Fountains

Beverage, chocolate, and cheese fountains have an excellent display effect in attracting the attention of guests. A beverage fountain allows guests to easily approach the fountain to fill or refill their cups or glasses. While in use, a service person would be assigned to maintain the necessary beverage quantity for the fountain to adequately function. Beverages should always be chilled before pouring into the fountain. If champagne or cider is to be used, it is important to not allow the beverage to remain in the fountain too long or it will become flat.

Chocolate fountains can fill a room with a delightful aroma as melted chocolate is pumped up the inside of the fountain and flows over the tiers. Items for dipping such as fresh strawberries, marshmallows, cookies, or biscuits are placed on nearby trays within easy reach for guests.

Cheese fountains, high temperature fountains that can hold cheese at 135°F or above at the base of the fountain, allow for guests to have a unique fondue experience. When chocolate and cheese fountains are in use, an attendant should be readily available to promptly wipe up any drips.

Fountains are typically positioned to the side of a room near an electrical outlet and the cord taped to the floor to avoid any possibility of a guest tripping. Depending upon the amount of use, many restaurant (banquet/catering) operators prefer to rent fountains from full-service rental stores.

Ice Carvings

Ice carvings are a work of art and can add an elegant touch to any event. Many creative designs in various sizes are carved by professionals skilled in the art of ice carving, as shown in Figure 10.22. The ice carving professionals will have photos of their work for prospective customers to review. Many of these talented people are also accomplished chefs working in prominent restaurants, hotels, resorts, and clubs within local communities. Once the design is decided upon, the amount of time needed to do the ice carving can be determined and scheduled.

Ice molds may be ideal when a smaller display would be appropriate. A sculpture mold is filled with water, placed in a freezer, and removed when ready to use. The mold is cut along a marked bead, peeled away, and discarded. The result is a decorative ice sculpture that is placed in an appropriate size pan. As it slowly melts, the water can be absorbed with dry bar towels that are covered with parsley or other greens.

FIGURE 10.22

Replica of Building Carved in Ice. Courtesy of Ice Sculpture Designs and Apple Ice.

Coat Rack/Coat Checking

As weather conditions prevail, a conveniently located coat rack for guests' coats, hats, raincoats, or umbrellas should be provided. But for events that take place during cold weather where most guests would be wearing coats, the restaurant (banquet/catering) operator may be asked to have one or more attendants assigned to coatroom checking. This is efficiently accomplished with the use of double theater tickets: One ticket is hung on the hanger with the coat and the other is given to the guest. The coats are hung on the rack in the order of the ticket numbers. When the event is over, the coatroom attendant(s) will be able to quickly return guests' coats.

Lectern or Speaker Podium

There are events that require the use of a lectern or speaker podium and the banquet/catering manager will need to be prepared to accommodate those requests. If a lectern is to be used, it is normally placed on top and at the center of a banquet table that has been prepared as a head table. Lecterns can be small and simple, with folding sides and top for easy portability, or large and equipped with a microphone, reading light, and perhaps the name and logo of the restaurant or hotel prominently displayed on the front. One or more glasses with a pitcher of ice water can be placed near the lectern or podium as per the customer's request.

If a speaker podium is to be used, it may need to be set up with a microphone, computer connection for PowerPoint, space in front for a floral display, or anything else relevant to a speaker's presentation. It is important to double-check that all technology is functioning properly prior to the event taking place.

Portable Stage

Stages are typically used to support a head table, speaker's stand, and band or orchestra. The height of the stage is determined by the size of the room: The larger the room, the higher the stage. Portable stages range in height from 6, 12, 24, to 36 inches with 4 by 4 or 4 by 8-foot adjoining sections. The front part of the stage that faces the guests should be covered with appropriate skirting from the edge of the stage to the floor as shown in Figure 10.23a and b.

Flags

There are certain event gatherings that request to have flags displayed, and the banquet/catering manager should be able to accommodate those requests. The rule in displaying flags is as follows: When the U.S. flag is displayed with the flags of other countries, states, schools, colleges, universities, clubs, and various organizations on a stage or as part of a room display, the U.S. flag should be placed to the right of any other flag and slightly higher than the flag of another country. When a speaker is addressing an audience, however, and flags are beside or behind the podium; the U.S. flag should be placed to the speaker's right as they face the audience. Other flags should be to the speaker's left.

Tripods and Easels

The customer may request to have a display area using skirted tables, tripods, and easels setup. There may be the need to display business products, company awards, family memorabilia, an individual's accomplishments, art objects, etc. Special lighting may also be necessary for the display. If the display request requires more than what the banquet/catering manager can accommodate, they should be able to suggest the names of companies that specialize in creating exhibit displays.

(a)   (b)

FIGURE 10.23
(a) Stage for Musicians; (b) Skirting Being Attached to the Stage. Courtesy of SDI Brands.

Lighting Effects

The restaurant (banquet/catering) operation should be able to accommodate the basic lighting needs of most events. For example, hors d'oeuvre or buffet table can be enhanced with the right degree of lighting; softening the lights to create a relaxed mood as food and beverages are served; or a stage or speaker podium may need spot lighting. Whatever the lighting requirements may be, all the lights must be tested and adjusted to the desired levels prior to the guests' arrival.

Sound System

The event may require the use of microphones for speakers and/or entertainers. The microphones could be either cordless, standing, attached to a lectern or podium, or placed on a table. The banquet/catering manager should be experienced and familiar with the types of sound systems that will provide the best-quality sound and functions for each specific use. The sound system should be tested, adjusted, and ready for use prior to the guests' arrival. A list with the names of reputable companies that specialize in sound systems as well as Disc Jockey service should be available for customers.

Background Music

A customer may request to have soft background music playing during a cocktail and hors d'oeuvres time and/or during dinner to add to the atmosphere. The specific times for the music to be played should be noted and followed. If the event is a Christmas party or has an Italian menu theme then the music selected could appropriately fit the event. Also to be included would be the music that the customer has specifically requested.

Piano

A piano is often available in many fine restaurants, hotels, resorts, and clubs for guests' entertainment. When a piano is to be used for an event, the banquet/catering manager should make certain well in advance that it will be in tune, and again check several days prior to the event. The piano should be placed in the most appropriate location in accordance with the customer's preference (refer to example in Figure 10.5).

Registration Table

A registration table is used at certain events that require guests to turn in or fill out a registration form, pick up a name tag, pay a fee, or simply to turn in their invitation to the event. The banquet/catering manager may be asked to set up one or more registration tables. Typically, banquet tables with table skirting along the front and sides of the tables are used, with chairs placed behind the tables. Electrical outlets and extension cords are conveniently placed for the customer to use their computer(s) and printer(s).

Miscellaneous Items

The restaurant (banquet/catering) operator may be asked to provide a big-screen smart television for web streaming and accessing that may be part of the event. A customer may request to have someone in costume stationed at the entrance of the room to greet guests, the costume being associated with the theme of the event, such as a ship's captain for a New England seafood menu. There are rental stores that can accommodate most of the reasonable requests.

Valet Parking

When valet parking for guests is provided, the time schedule for guests to arrive is an important factor in determining the number of attendants to schedule for the event. For example, if guests will be arriving within a short period of time, say between 7:30 and 8:00 P.M., more attendants would be needed. The same is true for departure time. The experienced manager will know exactly what it takes to keep traffic flowing smoothly in and out of the facility's parking areas according to weather conditions and in dealing with early or late arrivals and departures. Guests expect their vehicles to be carefully driven and parked in a safe and secure area. If there is the need for limousine service, the banquet/catering manager should be able to suggest the names of reputable companies that can professionally deliver the chauffeured service.

Special Requests

The customer may request a skirted table with a covered coffee dispenser and pastries for guests attending a morning seminar as shown in Figure 10.24; request for a decorative wedding gift table as shown in Figure 10.25; request to have a cocktail hour with an artisanal cheese buffet table as shown in Figure 10.26; request to have two different colors covering the round cocktail tables as shown in Figure 10.27; or perhaps have several servers join to sing Happy Birthday to a certain guest. Most of the special requests can be accommodated when properly planned and scheduled.

FIGURE 10.24
Covered Coffee Dispenser. Courtesy of SDI Brands.

FIGURE 10.25
Wedding Gift Table with Decorative Skirting and Valance.
Courtesy of SDI Brands.

FIGURE 10.26
Artisanal Cheese Station. Courtesy of Restaurant Associates.

FIGURE 10.27
Contour-Fitted Table Cover with Contour-Fitted Tabletop in a
Different Color. Courtesy of SDI Brands.

Estimated Charges

Learning Objective 10

Understand event pricing and charges.

The pricing for a banquet, catered event, or buffet is based upon several factors, which include the following:

- The type of foodservice operation (restaurant, hotel, resort, or club): *Upper Priced*—which is the finest food and beverage selections with superb service and elegant accessory details in a highly rated property. *Mid Priced*—represents most banquet, catered events, and buffets, where the food, beverage, service, and accessory details are carefully chosen and professionally presented. *Budget*

Priced—where the food, beverage, and service choices are limited to the dollar amount that the customer can afford to spend.

- The location such as a major city or vacation community and reputation of the restaurant, hotel, resort, or club. When a high level of quality and services are performed, which consistently meet customers' expectations, then the property's reputation commands a higher price.

Service Fee

A service or administrative fee of 20–25 percent of the total food and beverage charge is typically added to the final bill. The percentage assigned is often determined by the going rate within the local community restaurant industry. In lieu of the service fee, a restaurant operation may choose to include the fee in the price of the menu items being offered.

Deposit Amounts and Payment Schedules

A deposit amount can vary from 10 to 50 percent of the total estimated dollar amount of the event and is normally due at the time a contract agreement is signed. A payment schedule may require a 20 percent deposit followed by a second deposit (payment) of 40 percent 7 to 10 days before the scheduled event with the final payment due at the end of the event. Experienced restaurant operators have policies in place that set forth the terms and conditions for deposit amounts, payments, and cancellations.

Cancellations

A cancellation policy that clearly defines the terms, conditions, and charges if a customer cancels the contract should be reviewed with the customer before the contract agreement is signed. If something occurs that forces a customer to cancel the contract, all or part of the deposit may have to be forfeited. The determining factors would be to what extent food and beverage products had been ordered and prepared. Once the costs are identified, along with adding a service charge for the restaurant (banquet/catering) operator's professional services time, the balance of the deposit may be returned to the customer.

RESTAURANT REALITY: THE HELPFUL SERVICE AND DETAILS FROM A BANQUET/CATERING MANAGER

The Russell House is a fine-dining restaurant that is located in a college and agricultural community in central Iowa. The restaurant and banquet menus are affordably priced and the restaurant management and staff are known to go to great lengths in accommodating their customers. The 120-seat restaurant is busy every day of the week, and the 250-seat banquet room is often booked several months in advance for banquets and catered events.

In the first week in April, the banquet/catering manager received an e-mail from a gentleman in London, UK, requesting information for a catered event that he was planning for August 2nd. The e-mail stated that his parents would be celebrating their 50th wedding anniversary on that date, and that The Russell House has been one of their favorite restaurants for many years. He further mentioned that his dad had owned the local pharmacy and his mother was a professor at the college, now both retired.

The e-mail stated that there would be 200 invited guests with the possibility of several more attending. The evening would begin with hors d'oeuvres and cocktails from 6:45 P.M. to 7:30 P.M. immediately followed by dinner paired with two wine selections. The menu

details would be determined by June 15th when he would return from his business assignment in London and could meet with the banquet/catering manager. He furthered inquired if the banquet/catering manager could help with the following:

1. A person to play the harp from 6:45 p.m. to 8:15 p.m. (90 minutes)
2. A magician to perform a few entertaining tricks for about 15 minutes following dinner and just before the cutting of the anniversary cake
3. A "Harry Connick Jr." type singer accompanied by DJ music ranging

from old favorites to contemporary songs from 9:00 P.M. to 10:00 P.M.

4. An open space in the banquet room for dancing from 9:00 P.M. to 10:00 P.M.

The banquet/catering manager promptly replied to the e-mail by confirming a reservation for the August 2nd event date. She also noted that the request for dancing from 9:00 P.M. to 10:00 P.M. could easily be accommodated, and that she would do her best to help with the first three requests. The banquet/catering manager knew that the anniversary party would be attended by many people from the community who were long-time restaurant customers, and that the menu and entertainment for the event needed to be memorable. She began by contacting the music department at the college and asked if they could suggest some possible names and contact information

for a harpsichordist along with a "Harry Connick Jr." type singer; finding a magician might be a more difficult task. She did a quick Internet search and discovered the website of a local fifth-grade teacher who also performed magic tricks for children and adult gatherings and parties.

When the banquet/catering manager met with the host of the anniversary party, she was able to present a list that included the following:

1. The name and contact information of a harpsichordist, an elderly lady who regularly played the harp for holiday services at her church and would be delighted to play the appropriate music for the anniversary party.
2. The names and contact information of two singers: one who would need to be accompanied by a pianist and the other who could bring a portable

sound system with DJ music to accompany his singing.
3. The name, contact information, and a video link to a recent stage performance by the magician.

The host was pleased for the help and planned to make the contacts by the end of the day. He and the banquet/catering manager completed the menu and beverage details for his parents' anniversary party. She also suggested some additional items that further pleased the host, knowing that the event would definitely be enjoyable and very memorable for his family and invited guests. But just before leaving, the host had one more request—if she could suggest the name of a bus or shuttle service to pick up about 14 guests from the nearby town that was 30 miles away and then after the party drive the out-of-town guests back home. She responded. "I'll do my best!"

Summary

The functions and many details that can be involved in a banquet, catered event, or buffet are presented and explained. Through the use of an event plan details work sheet, as shown in Figure 10.1, the restaurant (banquet/catering) operator can review important details with a customer. The event plan ensures that the customer and establishment agree and understand the expectations of the event. It is a valuable tool that is the foundation of a successful event. There are accessory details that the customer may not be familiar with but will often appreciate being made aware of in order to choose additional services that can further enhance the event.

Three types of bar service—open, cash, and combination open–cash bars—are explained. The guidelines for setting up and presenting different types of buffet lines are reviewed. Topics ranging from selecting the right dinnerware, being able to calculate a room's seating capacity, fountains, and ice carvings to the various conditions that affect pricing are presented and discussed.

Discussion Questions and Exercises

1. Outline the differences among banquet, catered event, and buffet.
2. Why is it important to have a complete list of event plan details available to review with a customer?
3. Explain why the time schedule is a critical factor in allowing for an event to function smoothly.
4. Define approximate guest count, guaranteed guest count, and confirmed guest count.
5. Name two or more menu details that are important to discuss with the customer.
6. Contrast the difference between an open bar, cash bar, and combination open–cash bar.

7. List five key factors for a successful buffet including food safety.
8. What should be considered when selecting dinnerware?
9. Calculate the banquet seating for a room that is 50 feet by 30 feet.
10. What are the most popular table sizes used for banquet and catered events?
11. Explain the guidelines for seating arrangements.
12. Explain the purpose of a head table and the way it is set up.
13. Why would table numbers be used?
14. Approximately how many degrees cooler than normal should a room be set for prior to an event?
15. What are the different choices available when choosing tablecloths, napkins, table skirting, and chair covers and bows?
16. Explain the benefits of silk floral arrangements.
17. List several food items that could be placed on trays next to a chocolate fountain.
18. What should be considered when deciding on an ice carving?
19. Describe the procedure for coatroom checking when double theater tickets are used.
20. What are the typical sizes and heights of a portable stage?
21. Explain how to position the U.S. flag when displayed with another flag, and explain the one exception to that rule.
22. When a piano is requested by a customer, what should be checked well in advance?
23. How does the event's time schedule for valet parking affect the number of attendants working?
24. What is the average service fee range and how is it determined?
25. When pricing a banquet, catered event, or buffet, what are the factors considered?

GLOSSARY

Common Menu Terms

À la (ah-la)   After the style or fashion.

À la broche (ah-lah-brosh)   Cooked on a skewer.

À la carte (ah-lah-cart)   A separate price for each item on the menu.

À la king (ah-lah-king)   Served in a cream sauce with mushrooms, green peppers, and pimentos.

À la mode (ah-lah-mode)   Usually a dessert (pie) served with ice cream.

Al dente (ahl-den-ta)   Cooked firm to the bite—pasta.

Aioli (all-i-oli)   A sauce made of garlic and olive oil.

Amandine (ah-mahn-deen)   Almonds added.

Ambrosia (am-broh-zha)   Fruit mixture of oranges, grapefruit, bananas, cherries, and shredded coconut.

Antipasto (ahn-tee-pahs-toh)   An appetizer that can have a variety of Italian meats, cheeses, olives, and vegetables.

Aspic (ass-pik)   A clear jelly made from meat, fish, poultry, or vegetables.

Au gratin (oh-grah-tin)   Foods with bread crumbs, cheese, or sauce topping usually made by browning top.

Au jus (oh-ju)   Meat served in natural juices.

Basted   Cooking juices (drippings) spooned over meat while cooking.

Battered   Covered with flour or other starch mixture.

Béarnaise (bear-naz)   A sauce usually containing butter, egg yolks, tarragon, shallots, and white wine or vinegar.

Béchamel (bay-shah-mehl)   A white sauce usually containing butter, flour, milk, and seasonings.

Bill of fare   List of foods on the menu.

Bisque (bisk)   Cream soup usually made with seafood (shellfish).

Blanquette (blang-ket)   White stew usually made with veal or poultry.

Bombe glacé (bongh-glaz-ay)   Frozen dessert usually made with cake, ice cream, or a combination of several dessert items, and molded in a round ball.

Bon Appétit (bone-ah-pet-tee)   "A good appetite to you," "May you enjoy your meal."

Bordelaise (bohr-dih-layz)   A brown sauce usually made with meat stock, beef marrow, butter, carrots, onions, red wine, bay leaf, and a variety of seasonings.

Borscht (borsht)   A beet soup, may also include cabbage.

Bouillabaisse (boo-yah-bays)   A fish stew usually made with several types of fish and vegetables.

Breaded   Rolled in bread crumbs (plain or seasoned), cracker crumbs, cornmeal, or other dry meal, generally used prior to pan- or deep-frying.

Brioche (bre-ohsh)   A sweetened, soft bread with eggs and butter.

Brochette (bro-shet)   Meat chunks broiled, grilled, or baked on a skewer, often with onion, green or red pepper, and tomato.

Cacciatore (kah-che-ah-toh-reh)   An Italian sauce usually made with tomatoes, garlic, onions, peppers, sausage, and spices.

Calamari (kah-lah-mah-re)   Squid.

Canapé (kah-nah-pay)   Small bread, toast, or cracker spread (topped) with tasty food mixtures and served as an appetizer.

Cannelloni (kan-a-lo-ne)   A pasta stuffed with cheese and/or spicy meat and served with Italian tomato or meat sauce.

Capers   Small flower buds from the caper plant that have been pickled.

Carbonara (car-boh-nah-rah)   A sauce usually made with cream, butter, onion, peas, bacon, Parmesan cheese, and various seasonings.

Carte du jour (kahrt-du-joor)   Menu of the day.

Chanterelle (shahn-the-rehl)   A funnel-shaped mushroom mild in taste.

Chantilly cream (shahn-tee-lee)   Vanilla whipped cream.

Chantilly sauce (shahn-tee-yee)   A mixture of thick sauce supreme and whipped cream.

Chatêaubriand (shah-toh-bree-ahn)   A roasted tenderloin of beef, center cut.

Chiffonade (sher-fon-ad)   Shredded vegetables used as a topping for salads or soups, or as a garnish or bedding.

Chive (ch-eye-vuh)   Slender, green, dried onion tops.

Chorizo (choh-re-soh)   A mild or spicy Mexican pork sausage.

Chowchow   A spicy hot relish usually made with pickles and pickled vegetables.

Chutney (chuht-ne)   A sweet-and-sour condiment that is usually made of fruits or vegetables.

Cobbler   A deep-dish fruit dessert.

Compote (kahm-pote)   A stewed fruit mixture.

Consomme (kon-so-may)   A clear broth.

Couscous (koos-koos)   Crushed wheat grain often cooked by steaming and served as an alternative to potatoes or rice.

Crème brûlée (krehm broo-lay)   Cream custard with a caramelized sugar glaze top.

Creole (kree-ol)   Style of cooking common in Louisiana; prepared with tomatoes, peppers, onion, and unique seasoning blends.

Crêpe (krehp)   A thin pancake.

Crêpes suzette (krehp-soo-zeht)   Crêpes cooked in a sweet orange sauce consisting of sugar, lemon juice, butter, and oil from the skins of Mandarin oranges.

Croquettes (crow-kets)   A mixture of chopped cooked foods, shaped into small balls, rolled in egg and bread crumbs, and deep-fried.

Croutons (crew-tahns)   Bread cubes sautéed and seasoned.

Currants   Small, red or black dried fruit from a shrub related to gooseberries.

Drawn butter   Melted butter.

Duchess potatoes   Mashed potatoes usually made with egg yolks, butter, milk, salt, ground white pepper, and nutmeg.

Duxelles (ducks-elz)   Finely chopped mushrooms, shallots, and garlic sautéed in butter and then simmered in a stock and made into a coarse paste.

En casserole (ahn-kahs-eroll)   Baked or served in an individual dish.

Endive (ahn-dev)   A leafy salad vegetable with a bitter taste.

Escargot (es-kar-go)   Snails served as an appetizer.

Escarole (ehs-kah-rohl)   A curly leaf salad vegetable similar in taste to endive.

Feta (feh-tah)   A Greek white cheese that has been pickled.

Filet (fih-lay)   A boneless loin of meat or a boneless strip of fish.

Filet mignon (fih-lay-meen-yoon)   Tenderloin of beef.

Flambé (flahm-bay)   Flamed.

Flan (flahn)   A caramel custard.

Florentine (floor-ahn-teen)   Prepared and/or served with spinach.

Foie Gras (fwah-grah)   Goose or duck liver, of a pâté.

Fondue (fon-du)   Melted or blended for dipping bread, meat, etc.; most common is cheese fondue; dessert fondues often feature chocolate or caramel for dipping fruit.

Frappé (frap-pay)   A frozen drink served over crushed ice.

Fricassée (frick-ah-see)   Stewed meat or chicken served with thickened white sauce.

Gazpacho (gahs-pah-choh)   A cold tomato and vegetable soup.

Glacé (glaz-ay)   A glazed coating made by reducing fish, meat, or poultry stock.

Gnocchi (nyoh-ke)   A small Italian dumpling usually made from potato.

Gouda (goo-dah)   A smooth mild Dutch cheese.

Granita (grah-ne-tah)   A flavored frozen beverage.

Gratinée (grah-tan-ay)   A food that is sprinkled with bread crumbs and/or cheese, and baked until browned.

Gruyère (grue-yair)   A sharp dry cheese with a nut-like flavor.

Guava (gwah-vah)   A tropical fruit with a sweet flavor.

Gumbo   A soup usually made with seafood or chicken, tomatoes, peppers, and various ingredients and spices.

Hollandaise (haw-lawn-dez)   A sauce made with egg yolk, butter, and lemon juice.

Hors d'oeuvres (ohr-durv)   Savory foods served before meal as appetizers, to stimulate the appetite.

Hush puppies   A popular southern dish of deep-fried cornmeal.

Indian pudding   A baked pudding made with cornmeal, milk, eggs, brown sugar, and raisins.

Jardinière (jar-duhn-air)   A mixture of vegetables.

Jarlsberg (yahrls-berg)   A Norwegian cheese with large holes, like Swiss cheese, and a smooth nut-like flavor.

Julienne (julie-en)   Thin strips of food about 2 or 3 inches long.

Kabob (keh-bahb)   Cubes of meat and other foods, such as peppers, onion, and tomato, grilled or broiled on a skewer.

Kimchi (kihm-che)   A Korean relish usually made from spicy, pickled vegetables.

Kipper (kih-per)   A cold, smoked herring.

Kiwi (ke-we)   A fruit with brown skin, green flesh, and tart taste.

Knockwurst   A large smoked German sausage.

Kosher   A method of cooking that strictly follows Jewish dietary laws.

Kumquat (kuhm-kwaht)   A mildly bittersweet citrus fruit.

Langostino (lang-goh-ste-noh)   A large prawn that has the appearance and taste of a small lobster tail.

Leek   A very sweet type of onion.

Lox   Smoked salmon.

Mango   A fruit with a juicy, light orange flesh and a pineapple and peach taste.

Marengo   A chicken or veal sautéed in olive oil with tomatoes, mushrooms, and olives.

Marinara (mah-re-nah-rah)   An Italian tomato sauce with various spices.

Medallions   Small round cuts of food, often round cuts of meat.

Meringue (mar-rang)   Baked dessert of beaten egg whites and sugar.

Meunière (moon-yair)   A lightly floured piece of fish, sautéed in butter, seasonings, parsley, and lemon juice.

Milanaise (me-lan-ayz)   A food item that is breaded, sautéed, and topped with Parmesan cheese.

Mornay (mor-nay)   A white cheese sauce.

Mortadella (mohr-tah-dehl-lah)   A spicy Italian pork and beef sausage.

Mousse (moos)   A chilled, light, whipped dessert made with cream, egg white, gelatin, and flavoring; or a cold molded purée of meat, fish, or poultry.

Mozzarella (moth-sah-rehl-lah)   A soft, white mild Italian cheese.

Münster (moon-ster)   A semisoft German cheese with a light pungent flavor and aroma.

Napoleon   A layered pastry with custard or cream filling.

Neapolitan (ne-oh-pah-le-than)   A layered ice cream and cake dessert, layered in different colors of ice cream and cake.

Newberg   A creamed seafood dish made with egg yolks, sherry, and various spices.

Panettone (pa-neh-toh-neh)   A bread with candied fruit.

Parboiled   Boiled until partially cooked.

Parfait (par-fay)   A chilled dessert of layered ice cream, fruit, whipped cream, and/or other confections served in a parfait glass.

Parisienne potatoes   Small, round potatoes that can be cooked by boiling, steaming, or baking.

Parmesan (pahr-meh-jzahn)   A hard, sharp Italian cheese that is served grated and used as toppings for salads and soups.

Pastrami (pa-stra-mi)   Beef that has been slowly cured with spices.

Pâté (pah-tay)   A meat or fish mixture often baked in a small pastry shell.

Pâté de foie gras (pah-tay-de-fwah-grah)   A goose or duck-liver pâté.

Pesto (pehs-toh)   An Italian sauce made of olive oil, garlic, basil, and cheese.

Petite marmite (puh-teet-mahr-meet)   A consommé made with beef, chicken or turkey, and vegetables such as carrots, peas, and celery.

Petits fours (puh-tee-foor)   Small layered and frosted cakes or cookies, or small fruits glazed with sugar.

Pilaf (pee-lof)   Rice that has been cooked slowly with onions and stock.

Piquant (pee-kahnt)   Heavily seasoned.

Polenta   Boiled cornmeal.

Prâline   Almonds or pecans caramelized in boiling sugar.

Primavera (pre-mah-veh-rah)   Fresh spring vegetables served as part of a main dish.

Prosciutto (proh-she-oo-toh)   Dry-cured smoked ham.

Provençale (pro-vahn-sahl)   An item usually cooked with tomatoes, garlic, and spices.

Provolone (proh-voh-loh-neh)   A hard, sweet-tasting Italian white cheese.

Purée (pu-ray)   Fruits or vegetables that have been sieved or blended into a thick liquid; also a thick soup.

Quiche   A mixture of cream, eggs, Swiss cheese, and various other ingredients baked in a pie shell.

Radicchio (rah-de-ke-oh)   A small, red leaf lettuce.

Ragoût (rah-goo)   A stew of highly seasoned meat and vegetables.

Ramekin (ram-kin)   A small oven-proof baking dish used for individual food portions.

Ricotta (re-kah-tah)   A soft, bland Italian cheese.

Risotto (re-soh-toh)   Sautéed grains or rice that is boiled in stock and seasoned with cheese.

Rissole (ree-soh-lay)   Browned.

Romano (roh-mah-noh)   A hard Italian cheese with a strong flavor and aroma.

Roquefort (roke-furt)   A French white cheese made only in Roquefort, France.

Roulade (rue-lad)   Thin meat that can be braised or sautéed and rolled around stuffing.

Scalappine (skah-loh-pe-na)   Small pieces of veal.

Scampi   Shrimp in butter sauce.

Shallot   An onion variety.

Shiitake (she-e-tah-keh)   A Japanese mushroom.

Sorbet (sore-bay) (or sherbet)   A frozen mixture made with fruit juice or fruit purée.

Soufflé (soo-flay)   A baked, fluffy, light egg mixture combined with ingredients such as cheese, spinach, or chocolate.

Spumoni (spoo-moh-ne)   An Italian ice cream made with chocolate, vanilla, and cherry flavors along with candied fruit.

Stir-fry   To cook vegetables alone or with meat or poultry in oil over high heat in a wok, frequently stirring to retain the crispness of the vegetables.

Sweetbreads   The thymus glands of young animals such as calves and lambs.

Tortoni (tore-toh-ne)   An Italian vanilla ice cream topped with crushed almonds or macaroons.

Tournedos (toor-nuh-doe)   Small-size tenderloin steaks.

Trifle   A decorative dessert made with several layers of sponge cake and fresh fruit, soaked with brandy or rum, and topped with custard or whipped cream.

Truffles   A fungi-like tuber similar to a mushroom but with a strong aroma; or can be ganache-filled rich chocolate candies.

Velouté (vel-oot-eh)   A thick cream sauce made from fish, veal, or chicken stock.

Vichyssoise (vee-shee-swaz)   Potato and leek soup served cold.

Vinaigrette (vee-neh-gret)   A dressing made with oil, vinegar, salt, and pepper.

Watercress   Green type of small crisp salad leaves used on sandwiches, in salads, and as garnishes.

Wiener schnitzel (vee-ner-schnit-zl)   Breaded veal sautéed and served with lemon wedge.

Wonton   Noodle stuffed with ground pork or chicken served in Oriental soup.

GLOSSARY

Wine, Beer, Spirits, and Beverage Terms

Wine General Terminology

Acetic   Vinegar smell and taste. Spoiled wine.

Aeration   Letting a wine "breathe" before drinking it, preferably in the glass, in order to soften the tannins and improve the overall quality. Red wines benefit most from aeration.

Alcoholic   Used to describe a wine that has too much alcohol for its body and weight, making it unbalanced. A wine with too much alcohol will taste uncharacteristically heavy or hot as a result. This quality is noticeable in aroma and aftertaste.

Awkward   Poor structure, clumsy, or out of balance.

Backbone   Full bodied, well structured, and balanced by a desirable level of acidity.

Backward   Used to describe a young wine that is less developed than others of its type and class from the same vintage.

Balance   A wine has balance when its elements are harmonious and no single element dominates.

Character   Describes distinct attributes of a wine.

Clean   Wine without disagreeable aromas, taste, or flaw.

Closed   Wines that are concentrated and have character yet are shy in aroma or flavor.

Complexity   Displays subtle, layered aromas, flavors, and texture.

Cooked   Wine that has been exposed to excessively high temperature; flawed.

Delicate   Light, soft, fresh—usually describes a white wine.

Dense   Describes a wine that has concentrated aromas on the nose and palate. A good sign in young wines.

Dumb   Describes a phase young wine undergoes when the flavors and aromas are undeveloped. The same as "closed."

Earthy   Used to describe both positive and negative attributes in wine. At its best, a pleasant, clean quality that adds complexity to aroma and flavors. The flip side is a funky, barnyard character that borders on or crosses into dirtiness.

Elegance   Well-balanced and full wine with a pleasant distinct character.

Fading   Describes a wine that is losing color, fruit, or flavor, usually as a result of age.

Flawed   Wine that is poorly made and shows faults.

Flinty   Extremely dry white wines such as Sauvignon Blanc. More often an aroma than flavor. Smell of flint struck against steel; a mineral tone.

Floral   Tasting and smelling of flowers. Mostly associated with white wines.

Fresh   Having a lively, clean, and fruity character. An essential for young wines.

Fruity   Having obvious aroma and taste of fruit(s).

Graceful   Describes a wine that is harmonious and pleasing in a subtle way.

Grapey   Characterized by simple flavors and aromas associated with fresh table grapes; distinct from the more complex fruit flavors (currant, black cherry, fig, or apricot) found in fine wines.

Grassy   Aromas and flavors of fresh-cut grass or herbs. A signature descriptor for Sauvignon Blanc.

Harmonious   Well balanced, with no component obtrusive or lacking.

Hearty   Used to describe the full, warm, sometimes-rustic qualities found in red wines with high alcohol.

Heady   High in alcohol.

Herbaceous   Herbal or vegetal in flavor and aroma.

Length   The time the sensations of taste and aroma persist after swallowing; the longer the better.

Light   Soft, delicate wine; pleasant but light in aroma, flavor, and texture.

Maderized   The brownish color and slightly sweet, somewhat caramelized, and often nutty character found in mature dessert wines.

Mature   Ready to drink.

Meaty   Describes red wines that show plenty of concentration and a chewy quality; they may even have an aroma of cooked meat.

Medium-Bodied   Good weight and texture but softer than "full-bodied."

Nouveau   A light, fruity red wine bottled and sold as soon as possible. Applies mostly to Beaujolais.

Oaky   Describes the aroma or taste quality imparted to a wine by the oak barrels or casks in which it was aged. Can be either positive or negative. The terms *toasty, vanilla, dill, cedary,* and *smoky* indicate the desirable qualities of oak. *Charred, burnt, green cedar, lumber,* and *plywood* describe its unpleasant side.

Peak   The time when a wine tastes its best—very subjective.

Potent   Intense and powerful.

Raw   Young and undeveloped. A good descriptor of barrel samples of red wine. Raw wines are often tannic and high in alcohol or acidity.

Robust   Means full-bodied, intense, and vigorous, perhaps a little too much so.

Rustic   Describes wines made by old-fashioned methods or tasting like wines made in an earlier era. Can be a positive quality in distinctive wines that require aging. Can also be a negative quality when used to describe a young, earthy wine that should be fresh and fruity.

Simple   Light wine with limited aromas, flavors, and texture; similar to "thin."

Stale   Wines that have lost their fresh, youthful qualities are called stale. Opposite of "fresh."

Stalky   Smells and tastes of grape stems or has leaf- or hay-like aromas.

Stemmy   Wines fermented too long with the grape stems may develop an unpleasant and often dominant stemmy aroma and green astringency.

Vegetal   When wines taste or smell like plants or vegetables.

Vinous   Literally means "wine-like" and is usually applied to dull wines lacking in distinct varietal character.

Yeasty   Fresh dough, biscuit-like aroma and/or flavor.

Sight

Appearance   Refers to a wine's clarity.

Brilliant   Absolutely clear appearance of a wine.

Browning   Describes a wine's color, and is a sign that a wine is mature and may be faded. A bad sign in young red (or white) wines, but less significant in older wines. Wines 20–30 years old may have a brownish edge yet still be enjoyable.

Cloudiness   Lack of clarity to the eye. Fine for old wines with sediment, but it can be a warning signal of protein instability, yeast spoilage, or re-fermentation in the bottle in younger wines.

Hazy   Used to describe a wine that has small amounts of visible matter. A good quality if a wine is unrefined and unfiltered.

Legs   The drops of wine that slide down the sides of the glass when it is swirled.

Murky   More than deeply colored, lacking brightness, turbid, and sometimes a bit swampy, mainly a fault of red wines.

Smell

Acetic   Vinegar smell. Spoiled wine.

Acrid   Describes a harsh or pungent smell that is due to excess sulfur.

Aroma   Traditionally defined as the smell that wine acquires from the grapes and from fermentation. Now it more commonly means the wine's total smell, including changes that resulted from oak aging or that occurred in the bottle—good or bad. "Bouquet" has a similar meaning.

Bouquet   Wine's aroma from post fermentation and through aging.

Cigar Box   Another descriptor for a cedary aroma.

Cedary   Denotes the smell of cedar wood associated with mature Cabernet Sauvignon and Cabernet blends aged in French or American oak.

Esters   The aromatic compounds of wine.

Mercaptans   An unpleasant sulfur smell found in some very old white wines.

Musty   Having a moldy or mildew smell. The result of a wine being made from moldy grapes, stored in improperly cleaned tanks and barrels, or contaminated by a poor cork.

Nose   The smell, aroma, or bouquet of wine.

Nutty   Aroma found in sherry, Madeira, port, and "cooked" wine.

Perfumed   Describes the strong, usually sweet, and floral aromas of some white wines.

Pungent   Having a powerful, assertive smell linked to a high level of volatile acidity.

Smoky   Aromas caused by low acid, tannin, or both. Imparted from the oak barrel.

Toasty   Wine aroma derived from the fire bending of the oak barrels staves.

Unclean   Covers any and all foul, rank, off-putting smells that can occur in a wine, including those caused by bad barrels or corks. A sign of poor winemaking.

Taste

Acidic   Used to describe wines that taste tart or sour and have a sharp edge on the palate.

Acrid   Describes a harsh or bitter taste that is due to excess sulfur.

Aeration   Letting a wine "breathe" before drinking it, preferably in the glass, in order to soften the tannins and improve the overall quality. Red wines benefit most from aeration.

Aftertaste   The taste or flavors that linger in the mouth after the wine is tasted, spit, or swallowed. The aftertaste or "finish" is the most important factor in judging a wine's character and quality. Great wines have rich, long, complex aftertastes.

Aggressive   Unpleasantly harsh in taste or texture, usually due to a high level of tannin or acid.

Astringent   Extremely dry acidity, bitter; gives a dehydrated sensation in the mouth.

Austere   Used to describe relatively hard, high-acid wines that lack depth and roundness. Usually said of young wines that need time to soften, or wines that lack richness and body.

Bite   A noticeable level of tannin or acidity. Desirable in rich, full-bodied wines.

Bitter   Along with salty, sweet, and sour, this is one of the four basic tastes. Not a desirable trait in wine, it often signifies too much tannin.

Blunt   Strong in flavor and high in alcohol.

Body   Tactile impression of weight or fullness on the palate. Commonly expressed as full-bodied, medium-bodied, or medium-weight, or light-bodied.

Brawny   Used to describe wines that are hard, intense, and tannic and that have raw, woody flavors. The opposite of elegant.

Briary   Describes young wines with an earthy or stemmy wild-berry character.

Bright   Used for fresh, ripe, zesty, lively young wines with vivid, focused flavors.

Brut   A general term used to designate a relatively dry-finished Champagne or sparkling wine, often the driest wine made by the producer.

Burnt   Describes wines that have an overdone, smoky, toasty, or singed edge. Also used to describe overripe grapes.

Buttery   Rich, creamy aroma and flavor associated with barrel fermentation, often referring to Chardonnay.

Chewy   Deep, heavy, tannic wines that are full-bodied with mouth filling texture.

Cloying   Describes ultra-sweet or sugary wines that lack the balance provided by acid, alcohol, bitterness, or intense flavor.

Coarse   Usually refers to excessive tannin or oak. Also used to describe harsh bubbles in sparkling wines. The opposite of smooth.

Corked   A wine that has been tainted with moldy smell from a bad cork.

Depth   Describes the complexity and concentration of flavors in a wine. The opposite of shallow.

Dry   No sugar or sweetness remaining. A fruity wine can be dry.

Empty   Similar to hollow or devoid of flavor and interest.

Extra-Dry   A common Champagne term not to be taken literally. Most Champagne so labeled is sweet.

Extract   Richness and depth of concentration of fruit in a wine. Usually, a positive quality, although high-extract wine can also be highly tannic.

Fat   Full-bodied, high-alcohol wines low in acidity give a "fat" impression on the palate.

Finesse   Delicate and refined texture and structure.

Finish   The lasting impression, or aftertaste, of a wine on the palate. Can be long or short.

Firm   High in acidity or tannins, usually describes young red wines.

Flabby   Soft, feeble, lacking acidity and mouth feel.

Flat   Having low acidity; the next stage after "flabby." Can also refer to a sparkling wine that has lost its bubbles.

Fleshy   Soft and smooth in texture with deep flavor.

Full-Bodied   Rich, mouth-filling texture and weight on the palate; opposite of "thin."

Green   Taste of unripe fruit, tart, and sometimes-harsh flavors and texture.

Grip   A welcome firmness of texture, usually from tannin, which helps give definition to wines such as Cabernet and Port.

Hard   High in acidity or tannins that do not allow flavor perception.

Harsh   Astringent or burns the palate. Wines that are tannic or high in alcohol.

Hollow   Lacking in flavor.

Hot   High-alcohol content that tends to burn. Acceptable in Port wines.

Jammy   Sweet concentrated fruit character.

Leafy   Describes the slightly herbaceous, vegetal quality reminiscent of leaves. Can be a positive or a negative, depending on whether it adds to or detracts from a wine's flavor.

Lean   Lacking in fruit.

Lingering   Used to describe the flavor and persistence of flavor in a wine after tasting. When the aftertaste remains on the palate for several seconds, it is said to be lingering.

Lively   Young wines that are fresh and fruity with bright vivacious flavors.

Lush   Wines that are high in residual sugar.

Malic   The green apple-like flavor found in young grapes that diminish as they mature.

Off Dry   A slightly sweet wine.

Pruney   Having the flavor of overripe, dried-out grapes. Can add complexity in the right dose.

Puckery   Describes highly tannic and very dry wines.

Raisiny   Having the taste of raisins from ultra-ripe or overripe grapes. Can be pleasant in small doses in some wines.

Rich   Intense, generous, full flavors, and texture.

Round   Smooth flavors and texture; well balanced, not coarse or tannic.

Soft   Describes wines low in acid or tannin (sometimes both), making for easy drinking. Opposite of "hard."

Spicy   Spice flavors such as anise, cinnamon, cloves, mint, nutmeg, or pepper.

Structure   A wine's texture and mouth feel—a result of a particular combination of acid, tannin, alcohol, and body.

Subtle   Describes delicate wines with finesse, or flavors that are understated rather than full-blown and overt, a positive characteristic.

Supple   Describes a smooth soft texture, mostly with red wines.

Tanky   Describes dull, dank qualities that show up in wines aged too long in tanks.

Tannin   The mouth-puckering substance, mostly in red wines, that is derived primarily from grape skins, seeds, and stems, but also from oak barrels. Tannin acts as a natural preservative that helps wine age and develop.

Tart   Sharp tasting because of acidity. Occasionally used as a synonym for "acidic."

Thin   Lacking body and depth; unpleasantly watery.

Tight   Describes a wine's structure, concentration, and body, as in a "tightly wound" wine. *Closed* or *compact* are similar terms.

Tinny   Metallic tasting.

Tired   Limp, feeble, or lackluster.

Velvety   Having rich flavor and smooth texture.

Volatile (or Volatile Acidity)   Describes an excessive and undesirable amount of acidity, which gives a wine a slightly sour, vinegary edge. At very low levels (0.1 percent), it is largely undetectable; at higher levels, it is considered a major defect.

Ales, Lagers, and Nonalcohol Beers

Types of Ales

Altbier   "Alt" in German means "old." This style of top-fermenting light ale is cold conditioned, making them more in taste like lagers than ales.

Barley Wines   A high-alcohol ale (7.5–14 percent) with a dark brown hue, usually bittersweet, it is matured for a long time in casks.

Bitters   Style of English ale that is dry and usually served draft. Should not be served too cold.

Brown Ale   A strong, dark-colored ale that is somewhat sweet, from the stewing of barley. Brown ale is stronger than pale ale and lightly carbonated.

Cream Ale   Mild and sweet ale made in the United States.

Golden Ale   Light to medium body with some hop aroma and clean finish.

India Pale Ale   Fruity, super-premium ale that has a strong flavor of hops. India Pale Ale sometimes has a touch of oak.

Lambic   A spontaneously fermented style of wheat beer unique to Belgium. Usually full bodied with an acidic, yeasty palate.

Pale Ale   Dry, delicate flavored, English-style ale.

Porter   Deep brown ale, lighter in body than a stout, originating in London in 1722.

Scotch Ale   Strong, malt-style ale, which is often served as a nightcap. Can be served in winter with hearty food.

Stout   Descended from Porter, stout is a thick, sweet, and relatively low-alcohol content.

Trappist   There are six breweries operated by monks of the Trappist order, typically producing strong, fruity, sedimented ale, bottle conditioned, undergird fermentations in the bottle.

Weisse   German word meaning "wheat." Top fermented, most are light and tart in taste with bread or yeast aroma.

Common Ale Brands

Alaska Amber—U.S.	Rolling Rock—U.S.
Bridgeport Blue Heron—U.S.	Thomas Kemper—U.S.
Full Sail—U.S.	Widmer Hefeweizen—U.S.
MacTarnahan's—U.S.	Widmer Hop Jack—U.S.
Napa Ale Works – U.S.	Widmer Wildberry—U.S.

Common Stout Brands

Anderson Valley—U.S.	Napa Ale Works—U.S.
Guinness—Ireland	Red Hook—U.S.
McAuslan—Canada	Youngs & Co.—UK
Murphy's Irish Stout—Ireland	

Types of Lagers

American Lager   Largest selling beer in the USA with broad categories. Derived from European Pilsners, clean and crisp with more carbonation and less hop character.

Bock   A strong lager that is served very cold, usually bottom fermented. It is full bodied, sweet, and sometimes syrupy.

Dortmunder   From the German city with the same name. Their export style of beer is pale and medium dry, with more body and alcohol content than pale lagers from Munich to Pilsen.

Dry   Styled in Germany with thorough fermentation creating high-alcohol content. Popularized by Japanese brewers. The American version has no "beery" aftertaste with conventional alcohol content.

Ice   Developed by Labatt of Canada.

Marzen   Originally brewed in the month of March for consumption in the summer months. Eventually became a malty, medium-strong version of the Vienna-style beer.

Munchener   Dark brown lager with a sweet malt and slight hop flavor that is more creamy and aromatic than light lagers. The dark color and malty flavor come from roasted barley.

Pilsner   A very dry, pale lager. Lots of hop aroma. A true Pilsner can only come from the town of Pilsen, Czechoslovakia. Most light lagers are styled after Pilsner beer but have less body and character.

Vienna   Amber-red kilned malt producing style beer. Originally produced in Vienna.

Common Lager Brands

Amstel Light—Holland
Asahi—Japan
Budweiser—U.S.
Bud Light—U.S.
Coors—U.S.
Corona—Mexico
Dos Equis XX—Mexico
Fosters—Australia
Grolsch—Holland
Harps—Ireland
Heineken—Holland
Henry Weinhard's—U.S.
Henry Weinhard's Dark—U.S.
Lowenbrau—Germany
Michelob—U.S.
Miller Genuine Draft—U.S.
Miller Lite—U.S.

Moosehead—Canada
Samuel Adams—U.S.
Sapporo—Japan
Saxer Lemon—U.S.
St. Pauli Girl—Germany
Steinlager—New Zealand
Thomas Kemper—U.S.
Tsingtao—China

Common Nonalcohol Beers

Bavaria Malt Bier—Germany
Bitburger Drive—Germany
Buckler—Holland
Dortmunder Union—Germany
Gerstel Brau—Germany

Grolsch—Special Malt, Holland
Haake Beck—Germany
Kaliber—England
O'Doul's—U.S.
Sharps—U.S.

Spirit Brands, Related Cocktails, and Beverage Terms

American Bourbon Whiskey

Straight Bourbon

Ancient Age	Jim Beam	Old Grand Dad
Beams Choice	Jim Beam Black	Makers Mark
Ezra Brooks 90	Knob Creek	Bookers
Evan Williams	Mattingly & More (M&M)	Wild Turkey
Gentleman Jack	Old Crow	Wild Turkey 101
Jack Daniels	Old Forrester	

Blended Bourbon

Beams Blend 8 Star	McCormick	Brokers Reserve
Kessler	Seagram's 7 Crown	Monarch

Straight Rye Whiskey

Old Overholt	Wild Turkey Rye

Canadian Whiskey

Bottled In Canada

Black Velvet Sipping	Crown Royal Sp. Resv.	Seagram's V.O.
Canadian Club	MacNaughton	V.O. Bold
Canadian Mist 1885	Northern Light	
Canadian R&R	Seagram's Crown Royal	

Bottled in the United States

Black Velvet	Lord Calvert	Monarch Canadian
Canadian Mist	MacNaughton Lt. Wt.	Potters Crown Canadian

Common Bourbon Whiskey Cocktails

CC—7	Old Fashioned
Manhattan	7&7
Mint Julep	Whiskey Sour

Irish Whiskey

Black Bush Irish	Jameson	Tullamore Dew
Bushmills Irish	Jameson 1780	
Bushmills Single Malt	Tyrconnell	

Scotch Whiskey

Blended Scotch

Ballantine	Grants	Pinch
Black & White Grant's	J&B	Scoresby
Chivas Regal	Johnnie Walker Blue	Sheep Dip

Clan MacGregor	Johnnie Walker Red	Teachers
Cutty Sark	Old Smuggler	
Dewars (White Horse)	Passport	

Blended Scotch—12 Years

| Buchanan's Deluxe | Chivas Regal | Johnnie Walker Black |

Blended Scotch—15 Years

| Haig & Haig Pinch | Glenfiddich Solera | |

Single Malt Scotch

Balvenie	Glenlivet	Lagavulin
Cardhu Highland Malt	Glenmorangie 10 Years	Laphroaig
Cragganmore	Glenmorangie 18 Years	Macallan 12 Years
Dalmore	Glenmorey 12 Years	Macallan 18 Years
Dalwhinnie	Glenmoray Tin	Oban
Glenfarclas 12 Years	Glendronach	Talisker
Glenfiddich Ancient	Highland Park	Tambowie
Glenkinchie	Knockando	Tamnavulin

Common Scotch Cocktails

| Rob Roy | Rusty Nail | Scotch Mist |

Cognac and Brandy

Terms

V.S.—Very Superior

V.S.O.P.—Very Superior Old Pale

X.O. Extra Reserve—Usually denotes the oldest cognac from a particular producer.

Brandy

American Brandy

Christian Brothers	Korbel	Paul Masson
Clear Creek	Lejon	Potters
Domain Charbay	Martel	
E&J	Monarch	

Imported Brandy

Asbach Uralt	Funador	Presidente
Boulard Calvados	Maraska Sliovitz	St. Remy VSOP
Don Pedro	Metaxa	Viejo Vergel

Cognac

Courvoisier VS	Hennessey VSOP	Remy Martin Louis XIII
Courvoisier VSOP	Hennessey XO	Remy Martin VSOP
Hennessey VS	Martel VS	Remy Martin XO

Grappa

Acqua Di Amore	Clear Creek	Peak

Liqueurs

(Liqueurs listed with identifiable flavors)

Liqueurs—Flavors

Amaretto Di Saronno—almond
Bailey's Irish Cream—chocolate
Benedictine—herb spice
B & B—cognac
Carolans Irish Cream—chocolate
Chambord—cognac/raspberry
Cointreau—orange
Crème de Bananas—bananas
Crème de Cocoa—chocolate/ vanilla
Crème de Cassis—currants
Crème de Menthe—mint
Crème de Noyaux—almond
Curacao—orange
Drambuie—scotch/honey
Frangelico—hazelnut
Godiva—chocolate
Galliano—anise-vanilla/licorice

Goldschlager—cinnamon (100 proof)
Grand Marnier—cognac/orange
Irish Mist—honey
Kahlua—coffee
Kamora—coffee
Midori—honeydew
Ouzo—licorice
Peppermint Schnapps—mint
Sambuca—licorice
Sloe Gin—plum
Southern Comfort— bourbon/peach
Tia Maria—Jamaican coffee
Triple Sec—orange
Tuaca—cocoa
Yukon Jack—Lt whiskey

Gin

American Gin

Gilbey's	McCormick	Seagram's Extra Dry
Boords	Monarch	Seagram's Lime Twisted
Gordon's	Potters	

Imported Gin

Beefeater	Bombay
Boodles	Tanqueray

Common Gin Cocktails

Gibson	Gimlet	Tom Collins
Gin Tonic	Martini	

Rum

Jamaican

Bacardi Anejo	Bacardi Solera

Puerto Rico

Bacardi 8	Bacardi 151 (proof)	Lemon Hart
Bacardi Dark	Captain Morgan	Malibu
Bacardi Light	Captain Morgan Spiced	Mt. Gay
Bacardi Limon	Castillo	Ronrico

Virgin Islands

Cruzan Clipper	Montego	Redrum
Monarch	Potters	

Common Rum Cocktails

Cuba Libra
Piña Colada
Mai Tai
Daiquiri

Tequila

Aguila Blue Agave	Monarch	Sauza Commerativo
Arandas Oro	Monte Alban	Sauza Hornitos
Baja	Montezuma	Tarantula Azul
Cuervo 1800	Pancho Villa	Torada
Cuervo Anejo	Patron Anejo	Tres Generationes
Don Julio	Patron Reposado	Two Fingers
Giro	Patron Silver	Rio Grande
Herradura	Pepe Lopez	Sauza
Hussongs	Potters	Matador
Jose Cuervo Gold	Puerto Vallarta 100%	
Jose Cuervo White	Agave	

Common Tequila Cocktails

Bloody Maria	Tequila Shot
Margarita	Tequila Sunrise

Vodka

Absolut—Sweden	Gordon's—United States	Smirnoff—U.S.
Absolut Citron—Sweden	Kamchatka—U.S.	Stolichnaya—
Belvedere—Poland	Lukweska—Poland	Russia
Finlandia—Finland	Popov—U.S.	Tanqueray
Gibley's—U.S.	Skyy—U.S.	Sterling—UK

Common Vodka Cocktails

Bloody Mary	Kamikazi	Vodka Collins
Chi Chi	Lemon Drop	Vodka Martini
Cosmopolitan	Martini	Vodka Rocks
Gibson	Salty Dog	Vodka Tonic
Gimlet	Sea Breeze	
Greyhound	Screwdriver	

Common Mixed Drinks

B-52	Boiler Maker	Café Royal
Black Russian	Brave Bull	Cape Codder
Champagne Cocktail	Godmother	Mud Slide
Collins	Golden Cadillac	Pink Lady
Colorado Bull Dog	Grasshopper	Pink Squirrel
Creamsicle	Harvey Wallbanger	Presbyterian
Dr. Pepper	Long Island Iced Tea	Whiskey Sour
Eggnog	Melon Ball	White Russian
Fuzzy Navel	Midori Sour	
Godfather	Mimosa	

Alcohol Coffee/Tea Drinks

B-52	Café Royal	Mexican Coffee
BFK	Hot Apple Toddy	Nudge
Blueberry Tea	Hot Toddy	Royal Street Coffee
Café Diablo	Irish Coffee	Spanish Coffee
Café Jitz	Jamaican Coffee	
Café Pucci	Kioke Coffee	

Beverage Terms

Aperitif: A drink before the meal to stimulate the appetite. Appetizer wine or spirit.

Bitters: Bitters are usually used to flavor mixed drinks.

Blended: Mixed in a blender until creamy. *Flash Blended:* A flash (quick) mix in a blender.

Brown Goods: A term often used to describe distilled spirits brown in color (whiskey and brandy).

Call Brand: When a guest requests a drink by brand name.

Coke: Any cola soft drink.

Diet: Usually diet cola.

Dirty: A beverage that includes green olive juice.

Dry: Usually refers to martinis, meaning a touch of vermouth. *Extra Dry:* no vermouth

Easy: Smaller portion.

Frappé: Iced. A liqueur served with finely crushed ice.

Garnishes: Products accompanying a cocktail used to enhance or alter the flavor. Also used to provide a decorative presentation. These could include olives, cherries, cocktail onions, pineapple, orange, grapefruit, celery, limes, lemons, and fruits in general.

High: A term indicating the beverage is to be served in a highball glass over ice.

Mary: Bloody Mary cocktail or spirits served with Bloody Mary mix.

Neat: Not mixed. Liquor never touches ice. Brandy-based spirits are served in a snifter glass and heated on request. Liqueurs are served in a cordial glass. Brown spirits are served in a rocks glass.

Proof: This is the alcohol content in a given spirit. Note that in America alcohol is doubled to equal proof. Therefore, 50 percent alcohol is 100 proof. This is how a 151 proof rum consists of 75.5 percent alcohol.

Rocks: Served over cubed ice.

7-up: Seven-up, or lemon-lime soft drink.

Shot: Can range from 7/8 ounce to 1½ ounces depending upon the policy of the house.

Shaken: Shaken by hand, usually in a bar mixing tin.

Smokey: A beverage that includes a splash of Scotch.

Soda: Club soda.

Tall: Tall glass.

Tonic: Tonic water.

Twist: A slice or sliver of lemon or lime rind.

Up: Usually refers to martinis and served in the classic martini glass. Spirits are chilled and strained.

Virgin: No alcohol.

Well Brands: Brands that the house has identified as a standard.

White Goods: A term often used to describe clear spirits (vodka, gin, rum, and tequila).

WEBSITE REFERENCE

Aprons, Chefs Apparel, and Uniforms

www.uncommonthreadschefappare.com
www.waitstuff.com

Beverages

www.bjcp.org   Beer Judge Certification Program
www.coffeeschool.org   The American Barista and Coffee School
www.worldteaacademy.com   Certified Tea Sommelier Training Program

Dinnerware, Drinkware, Flatware, and Holloware

www.steelite.com

Employee Scheduling

www.hotschedules.com
www.schedulefly.com

Event Planning and Management, and Supply/Linen Rental

www.bbjlinen.com
www.fabulousevents.com

Food and Wine Pairing Guide

www.foodandwinepairing.org

Foodservice Utility Carts

www.elakesidefoodservice.com

Glassware

www.riedel.com   Wine glass guide

Guest Checks

www.nationalchecking.com

Ice Carvings

www.icesculpturedesigns.com

Linen Rental

www.tabletoppersinc.com
www.linennstuff.com

Minimum Wage Laws (Federal and State)

www.dol.gov/whd/state/tipped.htm   Minimum wage for tipped employees

Napkin Folding

www.millikentablelines.com/en-us/support/napkin-folding

National Restaurant Association

www.restaurant.org

POS Systems, Software, and Tablets

www.alohancr.com	NCR/Aloha POS Systems
www.caterease.com	Catering Management Software
www.micros.com	ORACLE/Micros—POS Systems for Hospitality
www.rmpos.com	ASI-Restaurant Manager POS Systems
www.ziosk.com	ZIOSK Restaurant Tablets

Responsible Alcohol Server Training

www.nraef.org —*ServSafe Alcohol*®   Manager and server training

Restaurant Table Reservations

www.opentable.com

Safe Food Handling

www.ServSafe.com   Manager and employee food safety training

Safety Slip Resistant Shoes

www.info@warsonbrands.com   Official Licensee of Reebok International Ltd

Table Linens, Skirting, Clips, and Contour Covers

www.sdibrands.com   Snap Drape Brands

Table Service Products

www.serviceideas.com

Table Top News and Events

www.tabletopjournal.com

INDEX

Note: Page numbers followed by f or t represent figures or tables, respectively.